BECOMING FIRE

An Introduction to the Spiritual Life

Fr Ken Barker MGL

Connor Court Publishing

Copyright © Fr Kenneth Barker MGL 2023

ALL RIGHTS RESERVED. This book contains material protected under International and Federal Copyright Laws and Treaties. Any unauthorised reprint or use of this material is prohibited. No part of this book may be reproduced or transmitted in any form or by any means, electronic or mechanical, including photocopying, recording, or by any information storage and retrieval system without express written permission from the publisher.

ISBN: 9781922815798

Cover design by Br Lawrence Yuen MGL

Printed in Australia

Nihil Obstat: Joseph Rheinberger. D.D., M.A, Censor Deputatus

Imprimatur: Most Rev. Francis Carroll D.D., DCL. Archbishop of Canberra and Goulburn

Acknowledgements

I wish to thank Selina Hasham for her work on editing the text and preparing the revised book for publication.

Thanks also to Br Lawrence Yuen MGL for providing the new cover design.

I also want to thank Archbishop Francis Carroll, Emeritus Archbishop of Canberra-Goulburn, who provided the foreword for the original book, and was an inspiration to me when I was a young priest.

I am also grateful to the members of the Disciples of Jesus Community for their strong commitment to growth in holiness, and to my brothers and sisters in the Missionaries of God's Love who inspire me to live religious life as a radical way of love.

CONTENTS

INTRODUCTION		viii
CHAPTER 1	THE FIRE OF GOD'S LOVE	1
	The Fire of the Cross	9
	The Flame of the Spirit	13
	Finding our Identity in Christ	16
	Entrustment to Mary our Mother	20
CHAPTER 2	BEING PURIFIED BY FIRE	
	Freedom from Slavery	22
	Breaking with the World	23
	Dealing with Sin	27
	Dealing with the Flesh	36
	Self-denial and Fasting	43
	Dealing with Temptation	47
	The Activity of the Enemy	49
	Strategy for Preventing Temptation	51
	Handling the Moment of Temptation	55
CHAPTER 3	BECOMING FIRE	
	Freedom for Christ	58
	Growing in Virtue	58
	Theological and Moral Virtues	65
	Practical Love	67
	Humility	82
	Humility as Service	86
	Obedience	89
	Prayer of Petition	95

CHAPTER 4	**YIELDING TO THE FIRE**	
	Conditions for Growth in Christ	100
	Desire to be Holy	100
	Detachment	106
	Trust in the Providence of God	115
	Suffering and Holiness	119
CHAPTER 5	**STOKING THE FIRE**	
	Context for Growth in Christ	126
	Plan of Life	128
	The Call to Solitude	129
	Relationships in Community	133
	Listening to the Word of God	136
	Spiritual Reading	141
	Nourished by the Eucharist	143
	Sacrament of Reconciliation	149
	Intercession, Evangelisation and Compassion	154
CHAPTER 6	**ABIDING IN THE FIRE**	
	Towards Contemplation	161
	Gift of Desire	162
	Friendship with God	163
	Prayer as Reality	164
	Modes of Prayer	167
	Prayer and Conversion of Life	169
	Practical Ways towards Contemplation	171
	Ignatian Approach	173
	Lectio Divina	175
	Growth in Prayer	177

CONTENTS vii

	Difficulties in Prayer	180
	Prayer as Self-Emptying Love	185
CHAPTER 7	FANNING THE FIRE	
	A New Life in the Spirit	189
	Supplication	189
	Docility to the Inspirations of the Spirit	192
	Thanksgiving, Praise and Adoration	195
	Living in the Gaze of God	201
	The Practice of the Presence of God	203
CHAPTER 8	GUARDING THE FIRE	
	Developing a Discerning Heart	206
	Some Rules for Discernment	208
	Examen of Consciousness	215
	Particular Examen	217
	Making Decisions	218
	Spiritual Direction	221
CONCLUSION		227
ENDNOTES		231
APPENDIX I	PRAYERS OF POWER	238
APPENDIX II	GIFTS AND FRUITS OF THE SPIRIT	243

INTRODUCTION

We live in an ecclesial climate which is conducive for the making of saints. This book was first published at the turn of the century when Pope John Paul II had prophesied a new springtime for the Church. He proposed the new millennium would be a time for deeper repentance and sincere commitment to holiness. I believe this prophecy is being fulfilled, but maybe not exactly as John Paul II had expected. The unfolding social, cultural and political dynamics of the 21st century lend a new sense of urgency for the heroic witness of saints. The book remains as relevant as it was twenty years ago. It offers a primer in the spiritual life, insight into how we can cooperate with the grace of God to grow in genuine holiness. Nothing could be more relevant and important for followers of Jesus today.

This century has ushered in a time of great confusion and uncertainty in the world at large. It has become almost a cliche to declare we live in "trouble times". The dominant Western culture is in a moral melt-down under the pressures of aggressive secularisation. The Church has in the eyes of many lost its moral authority due to the sexual abuse crisis and is regarded in the popular mind as an antiquated institution, almost dangerous to the modern secular experiment.

We preach the gospel in a cultural situation not unlike the challenges facing the first Christians after Pentecost. The same Holy Spirit who birthed the Church is being poured out upon us in a new way. With the fire of the Spirit from this new Pentecost we can, like the first apostles, give clear and powerful witness to our contemporaries that Jesus is Lord. At this critical time for the Church and the world, the Lord is again raising up ordinary men and women to make an extraordinary response to the message of the Gospel. He wants to immerse us in his love so we can bring the gospel to the impoverished hearts of many. This will only be possible if we allow the Spirit to change us to become truly holy, genuine witnesses of God's love and ready to sacrifice all for him.

It would be easy in today's Church to lose sight of this evangelical goal through anxiety about internal problems that assail us, and the influence of the secular mind-set on many Catholics. We need to be listening to the Spirit. The Spirit of God is inspiring us to respond in this time of crisis by living the gospel wholeheartedly; so we can carry forward in the 21st century the flame of love that burst into the world through the Incarnation, death and resurrection of Jesus Christ, and is now burning in all the baptised through the indwelling of the Holy Spirit. The work of the "new evangelisation", which is incumbent on every baptised person, will only be effective if we deepen in holiness. These are the days of a new Pentecost, when we can reclaim the best of the Catholic spiritual tradition and allow the Spirit to set us on fire again with the love of God and zeal for his kingdom.

This book aims to give the beginner in the spiritual life a vision and framework for an on-going life in the Spirit, and to give some insights into the dynamics of spiritual growth, as well as some practical means for moving ahead. I have attempted to present a vision which is biblical, practical, personal, evangelical, God-centred and faithful to the spiritual tradition of the Church. The vision is centred on the transforming power of the fire of God's love for us, revealed in the death and resurrection of Jesus, and now recreating us by the indwelling of the Holy Spirit. This radical and personal transformation takes place within the Christian community. I have tried to describe some of the most important dynamics for our individual spiritual growth, through conversion, a life of virtue, and prayer.

This book will hopefully be useful for anyone beginning a committed spiritual journey. It should be particularly helpful for those who have begun to experience the activity of God in their lives and find within themselves a thirst for a deeper life with him. Often when people have been touched by God through a weekend retreat or through contact with one of the fresh spiritual movements in the Church today, they flounder in doubt and confusion in the aftermath of their experience. They feel unsure about what God is doing and lack support and direction, and the practical tools, to be able to develop a rich spiritual life. Unfortunately, some wander off into spiritualities foreign to Christianity, such as the New Age, Eastern religions and transcendental meditation. Others fall back into the old ways after a while, writing off what had been a genuine experience of God as an illusion, derived from psychological need, which they believe they have now shaken off. Some, in the search for growth, turn to self-help books in pop psychology to fill the void. This book is written to meet the need of those who are spiritually hungry and looking for a way ahead. It is intended to offer a spiritual vision for genuine disciples in the Catholic tradition.

Chapter One sets the theme by showing how the fire of God's love changes us through experience of the cross and the indwelling of the Spirit. Chapter Two focusses on the purifying quality of the fire of God's love. We look at the challenge of breaking the power of sin, the world, the flesh, and the devil. This is conversion from the power of darkness. Chapter Three, entitled "Becoming Fire", looks at the more positive side of conversion, which is embracing Jesus Christ fully, so that his virtues become evident in our lives. There is particular attention given to the virtues of practical love, humility, and obedience. Chapter Four on "Yielding to the Fire of God's Love" outlines some critical graces that we need, in order to advance towards union with God. They are desire and determination; detachment and surrender; and trust in the providence of God. Chapter Five sets forth the basic elements of the environment necessary for spiritual growth to occur. It is called "Stoking the Fire", because these elements are primary means for growth in the love of God. They are solitude, community, reading the word of God, Eucharist, the sacrament of Reconciliation, and evangelisation. Chapter Six gives special attention to growth in contemplation, which is "Abiding in the Fire". Some of the difficulties we face in prayer are discussed here. Chapter Seven turns towards the challenge of praying always through supplication, praise, and the practice of the presence of God. These are ways of "Fanning the Flame". It remains then for Chapter Eight to teach about "Guarding the Fire" which is within us, through developing a discerning heart.

In organising the material, I have decided not to use the traditional scholastic approach of first stating the ends, and then giving the means to attain these ends. I have opted for a more integral approach. Nevertheless, the ends, or purposes, of the spiritual life are primarily presented in the earlier Chapters 1-4. The means towards these ends are primarily in Chapters 5-8. There are two notable exceptions to this. The treatment of petitionary prayer, a primary means towards holiness, appears in Chapter Three with the section on growth in virtue. And the discussion of self-denial, also another important means, is found in Chapter Two when dealing with overcoming the flesh.

I wish to acknowledge a debt of gratitude to the many people who have contributed to the development of this work. I am thankful for the inspiration I have received from the Carmelites at Varroville, from the Jesuits at Pymble, and from the Benedictines at Arcadia and New Norcia. I am particularly grateful for the monks at New Norcia, who provided hospitality and the use of their library while I wrote the initial version. I am grateful especially for my brothers and sisters of the Disciples of Jesus Covenant Community, who have inspired me by their commitment to the Lord and have encouraged me to seek the path of holiness. Among these I am most grateful to the young men and women of the Missionaries of God's Love, who are so dear to me, and who challenge me to live the gospel radically in imitation of Jesus.

I have written this book from what I believe was a leading of the Holy Spirit. I trust that anyone who reads this book will be inspired by the Spirit to love Jesus more and to give glory to the Father Almighty now and always.

Fr. Ken Barker MGL

1
THE FIRE OF GOD'S LOVE

"I have come to bring fire to the earth…" (Lk 12:49)

The starting point for the spiritual life and the means to all growth is the experience of God's love. It is totally unmerited gift from God. His love for us is completely unconditional and has no limits. The single most important thing in anyone's life is to encounter this love. To become holy involves many steps, but underneath it all is simply letting God love you and responding wholeheartedly and unconditionally to this love. St. Paul says: "The love of God has been poured into our hearts by the Holy Spirit, which has been given us" (Rom 5:5). We cannot make ourselves love God. Often very earnest people get this wrong. They try to earn his love by striving to be good. They make themselves a spiritual treadmill of all sorts of religious practices. They assert much effort to climb the ladder of perfection. But this is starting the journey the wrong way around. John, the beloved apostle, sets us right when he says, "This is the love I mean: not our love for God, but God's love for us when he sent his Son to be the sacrifice that takes our sins away" (1John 4:10). What matters is that God has first loved us. "What proves that God loves us is that Christ died for us while we were still sinners" (Rom 5:8). We only have to spend time dwelling on the wounds of Jesus, and the Holy Spirit will convict us of the truth of his saving love. Paul says: "The love of Christ overwhelms us when we reflect that if one man died for all, then all should be dead" (2Cor 5:14).

We become persuaded by his love, we become won by it, and we find ourselves surrendering to it with a whole-hearted response.

St. Francis de Sales begins his *Introduction to the Devout Life* assuring us that it is not fasting, long hours of prayer, penitential disciplines, heroic almsgiving, or other ascetical practices which are the essence of the spiritual life.[1] These activities may be helpful means to an end. But the essence of the spiritual life is the love of God.

When the Pharisees asked Jesus what is the greatest commandment, Jesus answered: "You must love the Lord your God with all your heart, with all your soul, and with all your mind…" and "You must love your neighbour as yourself" (Mt 22:37-40). But Jesus was not giving us a commandment without the infusion of grace to be able to live it. He intended to give us his own power of loving. He came to make it possible for us to have the same fire of love within us which burnt in his own heart. He cried out in Luke's gospel: "I have come to bring fire to the earth, and how I wish it was blazing already…" (Lk 12:49). He was speaking of the fire of his own love, which would be demonstrated so profoundly on the cross. He says: "There is a baptism I must still receive, and how great is my distress till it is over". He is referring to the baptism of his suffering and death, which in itself was to be the fire of his love cast to the earth. This fire that Jesus longed for was also the fire of the Spirit to be poured out at Pentecost after he had risen.

Growth in the spiritual life, then, is letting this fire of God's love penetrate us, change us, and empower us. There is a story of a young monk in the desert who had been working hard on his spiritual life. Eager to gain perfection he approached a revered spiritual Father and said: "Father, I have been reciting the psalms, and doing long fasts. I have forgiven my neighbour and have kept guard over my thoughts. What more can I do?" The old man raised his hands to heaven, and cried out, "Why not *become* fire!" This is the aim—to be so penetrated by God, who is "a consuming fire", that we are changed into his likeness.

St. John of the Cross has a helpful image to explain what it is like to come into contact with the fire of God's love.[2] I am using it in a more general way than John intended, and adapting it for our purposes. When you pick up a damp log from the wood heap, take it inside, and throw it on the fire, you may notice that some spiders come scurrying out because of the heat. In the same way, when we first make contact with the fire of God's love, we are delivered of the evil spirits that may have had some access to us. Next you may notice that the log on the fire begins to ooze some dark fluid as it is being dried out. This could speak to us of the necessity of repentance, as the fire of the Spirit shows us areas in our lives where we need to break with sin in all its ugliness. Then, you may see that the log actually ignites! This is the time of growing commitment to the ways of God, and a growing personal, loving relationship with the Lord. We are actually on fire with God's love. We can say: "Zeal for your house consumes me!" We are responding with committed prayer, genuine love for others, and a zeal for the salvation of all.

Yet there is still a further stage. Returning to the log, after a long time of being penetrated by the fire, you notice that it is no longer easy to differentiate between the log and the fire. They are one. This is when you have *become* fire! This is the aim of the spiritual life, and it is not attained quickly, nor easily, because it is union with God. Notice from the image that the spiritual life is all God's work. The fire of his love is active within us, winning us to himself, purifying us of sin, inspiring us to greatness, empowering us for holiness, overwhelming us, and consuming us. Unlike a piece of log, though, we need to be actively cooperating with his action in our lives, and doing all we can to allow him to have his way with us.

A more relational image of the transforming power of God's love can be taken from the musical *Man of La Mancha*, based on the story of Don Quixote. Again, I will adapt the story to our needs.

A young woman, named Aldonza, was a barmaid in a tavern in a small Spanish village. She had little self-respect, offering her body to be used by the men at night, and verbally abused by them in the day as she served the drinks. She hated herself, and maintained a hard, impenetrable face before her regular patrons. There was no joy in her life; only bitterness and contempt for others, even for life itself. Then, one day, into the village came a young man with a song on his lips, sunshine in his eyes and a spring in his step. He came to the inn. Beholding Aldonza, he saw through the hard exterior. He looked upon her inner beauty. He addressed her by a new name, "Dulcinea", in Spanish, "the beautiful one". She spat at him and spurned his approaches. Each day he would return with gifts, and each day he would address her by her new name, "Dulcinea", the beautiful one. She cursed him to his face, refused to listen, and hit out at him with all her strength. But he persisted, each time calling her by her new name.

Gradually something began to happen in Aldonza. She began to think "Maybe it is true!" Despite herself she began to let the gift of love penetrate the barriers she had built for her self-protection; she became vulnerable to love. And a miracle began to happen! People could see Aldonza was changing. Now there was a smile on _her_ lips, and sunshine in _her_ eyes, and a spring in _her_ step. She was loved, and was allowing its mysterious power to change her, and set her free from her self-imposed prison, and to heal her wounds inflicted by others.

This is a story that speaks of the reality of grace, the free gift of God, who comes to us in our broken, sinful condition, and redeems us by his love. The Lord speaks to each one of us personally, "Do not be afraid, for I have redeemed you; I have called you by your name, you are mine" (Is 43:1). Notice that Aldonza had to cooperate with the gift given to her, to take the risk to trust in the offer of love and to say "yes". Much of our growth in the spiritual life is simply this. It is painful, and we shrink back from the Lord. We don't listen to his approaches, we spurn his advances, and we avoid him if he comes too close. It takes courage to let oneself be possessed by the Lord, to let him have his way with us, to take the steps necessary to avail ourselves of the infusion of his Spirit and the power of his love. As John, who rested on the breast of Jesus at the Last Supper, says, "We ourselves have known and put our faith in God's love towards us" (1Jn 4:16).

In the Song of Songs, the bride sings a beautiful song, which becomes our song too: "My Beloved is mine and I am his" and "the banner he raises over me is love" (Sgs 2:16, 4). It is a nuptial image; we allow the bridegroom to "conquer" us with his love. There is a further image suggested by the raising of the banner. When a conquering general took a territory, he had the standard of the King raised over that territory as a sign of victory. When the King of love has been allowed to "conquer" us in the depth of the heart and has won the territory for himself, then he raises his standard of love within us. The territory has fallen to him; all that was at enmity with Christ has been expelled. As Paul says: "You are not your own property; you have been bought and paid for" (1Cor 6:19). And the price that was paid to win us from the slavery of sin was very high indeed; not silver or gold, but the precious blood of Jesus (1Pet 1:19). Now we are his, we joyfully belong to him in love.

The fire of the Spirit which dwells within us and changes us is not like the type of wild bushfire that burns rapidly and is over like a flash. It is a quiet burning fire, deep within, that is constant and lasting. It has its effect through years of transforming action. It is what Jeremiah in all his suffering experienced, when he exclaimed, "You have seduced me…you have overpowered me: you were the stronger…I used to say, 'I will not think about him, I will not speak in his name any more'. Then there seemed to be a fire burning in my heart, imprisoned in my bones. The effort to resist it wearied me" (Jer 20:7-9). Even though, in the flesh, Jeremiah resisted the call of the Lord on his life, there was a power at work within him that kept winning him to the Lord's purposes. Even his sufferings at the hands of others became a source of grace for him.

Another image that can help us understand the mysterious working of God's grace within us is offered by Francis de Sales. He invites us to consider God's love toward us to be like a magnet attracting iron filings: "As soon as iron feels the magnet's power, it is attracted towards it, quivers with satisfaction, begins to move, and strives at all costs for contact, for union"[3]. God is constantly seeking to attract us to himself, to draw us by his love. Jesus said: "No one can come to me unless he is drawn by the Father who sent me" (Jn 6:44).

God is madly in love with us, and he has an infinite longing for us to love him so that we may be in union with him forever. He allures us, attracts us, inspires us, awakens us and enchants us. Unlike the iron filings we have precious free will. He never pressures us. But he seeks to win us to himself. His grace within precedes anything we do. He attracts us by awakening desire in us for union with him, by giving us inspirations of his Spirit, by bringing light to the mind and fervour to the heart, by stirring us to love him in return for the way he has loved us. It happens through the grace of repentance, in which "God often hides the fire of his love in the depths of our hearts".[4] Francis de Sales expresses it thus: "Grace lays hold of the heart so graciously that it in no way impairs the will's freedom. It pulls the strings of the soul powerfully; yet so delicately that free will suffers no compulsion from it. Grace is powerful - not to compel the heart, but to allure it...".[5]

God loves us so that we will return his love. His love for us is infinite and unconditional, and, because it is love, it seeks union with the beloved. He seeks to captivate us with his love. He has firstly given us the beauty of his creation, and surrounded us with countless gifts. A beautiful sunset, or the crashing of waves on the shore, or the grandeur of mountain ranges, all creation's beauty speaks of God's immense love for us. It awakens in us gratitude for the Creator, and a desire to return his love. Secondly, when we were separated from him, in his great love he chose to become one of us in order to redeem us. Love seeks union. His love for us led him to take on our frail human flesh, and he did so in a way that would attract our stubborn wills to respond to his love.

Christmas day, says Alphonsus Liguori, is "a day of fire", as we are stirred by the self-emptying love of our redeemer, who chose not to be born in a place fit for human beings, but amongst the animals. Coming as a vulnerable, defenseless child, born like all others, the Son of God seeks to win us to himself. What could be less threatening than a child in a manger? Jesus came with none of the trappings of worldly power, none of the usual finery we associate with royalty. The simplicity and humility of his coming disarms us and appeals even to the hardest heart. He wins us with love.

Yet there is a third movement to this symphony of love. His excessive love for us took him to the cross for our sake. He was put to death as a criminal. During his life on earth, he longed with all his heart to be able to give himself completely for us. The cross was his "hour"; the appointed time to show "how perfect his love was" (Jn 13:1). During his preaching he had said, "I have come to bring fire to the earth, and how I wish it were blazing already..." (Lk 12:49). He was speaking of the fire of love for us already burning in his heart, which he would demonstrate outwardly in his passion. He suffered so that he could win us to himself. Our hard and obstinate hearts melt and become inflamed with love for him when we consider his passion, the proof of his love for us. We are won by love.

The Incarnation broke down the natural barrier between us and God. The cross broke down the barrier caused by sin. Yet God's love which seeks union was still not satisfied. He wanted to find a way of union with us here on earth that surpasses all other ways. The fourth great act of love was the master stroke, designed to achieve this end. He emptied himself even further, giving himself to us as food in the Eucharist. At the Last Supper he said, "I have longed to eat this passover with you…" (Lk 22:15).

The heart of Jesus yearns for union with us, and in the Eucharist this union is effected powerfully for those who are receptive. "He who eats my flesh and drinks my blood abides in me and I in him" (Jn 6:56). This whole story is the initiative of God who has come to us in self-emptying love. It calls forth within us a response of self-emptying love in return. We are to allow him to capture us with his love. Lovers desire that where there was formerly two, there now be one. We allow the bridegroom to take hold of the bride. The whole Christ is given to us in Holy Communion. The divine fire that is in the human heart of Christ sets our hearts burning with love for him; once this fire is alight within us nothing less than complete union will satisfy.

The Fire of the Cross

We become inflamed with the love of God in a powerful way when we meditate on the wounds of Jesus crucified, and now risen. Alphonsus Liguori says: "the one who loves Jesus Christ and wants to grow in his holy love has nothing that he can think about with greater profit than the passion of our most holy redeemer."[6]

In John's Gospel, after relating Jesus' death, and his side being opened with the lance, John, who was an eyewitness, tells us this happened to fulfill the words of Scripture, "They will look upon the one whom they have pierced" (Jn 19:37). As we gaze upon the crucified Jesus, and allow the Spirit to pierce our minds with the truth, we find our hearts break open in gratitude and love for such a redeemer. We are persuaded, overwhelmed and consumed by his love. We know it was not the nails that held him to the cross, but his decision of love. And we know also that it was our own sins that were responsible for his piercing.

Roman crucifixion was originally a horrendous and horrible form of death. A cross was a symbol of condemnation and execution for criminals and slaves. It evoked terror in the hearts of all. When Jesus was laid on the cross, he changed a symbol of condemnation and slavery into a permanent sign of the enduring love of God, which burns in his heart for all men and women. When we meditate on the passion, our focus should not so much be on the awful physical agony and cruel insults that Jesus suffered, at least not for their own sake. Rather, we become persuaded by the madness of his love for us, which is only partly expressed by the excesses of his physical suffering.

The deepest suffering of Jesus, and, hence the most profound expression of love, was interior. On the cross Jesus cried out, "My

God, my God, why have you deserted me?" This is the beginning of Psalm 22, which we know is ultimately a prayer of trust. Yet this knowledge cannot detract from the harsh reality of this barren cry. Jesus is experiencing at that moment, in his human soul, the total lostness, desolation, estrangement and alienation of all the sin of the world. Paul says: "For our sake God made the sinless one into sin so that in him we might become the goodness of God" (2Cor 5:21).

In his self-emptying love, through total solidarity with our sinful condition, Jesus took upon himself the consequences of the sin of the world. When we consider all the pride, rebellion, hatred, injustice, violence, and every vile thing that speaks of hostility against God, and the separation from God which such rebellion brings, we get in touch with the reality of his cry of abandonment. It was not just a pious word to utter when close to death. Isaiah says: "he was pierced through for our faults, crushed for our sins. On him lies a punishment that brings us peace, and through his wounds we are healed" (Is 53:5-6). Jesus felt the full weight of the moral disfigurement of all of humanity past, present and future upon his soul. The darkness that came over the earth while Jesus hung on the cross was a cosmic sign of the darkness that he experienced in his soul.

It needed to be this way. It was not that the Father condemned him or deserted him. God is love. As Jesus suffered, the Father's heart was suffering with him. Just as we speak of the passion of Jesus, we can speak of the _com_-passion (suffering with) of the Father. The cross is a work of love achieved by both the Son *and* the Father. Jesus had said: "The Father loves me because I lay down my life in order to take it up again. No-one takes it from me; I lay it down of my own free will" (Jn 10:17-18). Jesus was not coerced by the Father. It was mutual love which was at work. It was a wonderful collaboration in love between the Father and the Son for our sake; the Father's heart broken as he gave up his Son for us all (Rom 8:31), and the Son's free decision in his humanity to comply with the Father's will.

Why did it need to be this way? Our redemption could have been won by another means. Nothing is beyond God. But we can see how wonderfully appropriate it was that it happened this way. And the more we deepen in this appreciation, we would not want to have had it any other way. Sin had entered the world through the disobedience of Adam, and we had all sinned in Adam (Rom 5:12). The only way to right the wrong was for a human being to make a perfect act of obedience to God on behalf of all humanity. But, more so, this act of perfect obedience, to be able to represent us all, needed to be made from a position of fallen humanity. It couldn't be fiction. It had to be real.

On the cross Jesus was in his soul at the bottom of the pit of the desperate condition that human sin and rebellion against God brings. He experienced the utter wretchedness of the lostness of sin, which brings the wages of eternal death. All of this even though he was the totally innocent one, without sin. From that position of the "hell" which sin reaps, he did not despair, but placed his trust fully in the Father, whom he loves. He died uttering the words of ultimate sacrifice, "Father, into your hands I commit my spirit"; the perfect act of obedience and trust. This is our redemption! Paul put it ever so succinctly, "As by one man's disobedience many were made sinners, so by one man's obedience many will be made righteous" (Rom 5:19).

Stories can help illustrate this wonderful mystery. There was a farmer whose property had been devastated by a bushfire. Afterwards, as he was walking around surveying the damage, his eyes fell on a strange black lump on the ground. Nonchalantly he kicked it. And out came six little chickens! When the fire had gone through, the mother hen had instinctively thrown herself over her chickens in an act of self-immolation. She died. They ran free. This is what Jesus has done for us; not by instinct, but by his own choice in love. He has allowed himself to be immolated that we may run free! Amazing love!

I also heard of a young man whose life was changed by an incident that happened while he was a soldier in the Second World War. He and his mate were occupying an underground dug-out, and the enemy were attacking. Suddenly a live hand-grenade landed between them. Both saw it. Both knew that in a matter of seconds they would be blown to pieces. His mate did not hesitate but threw his whole body over the grenade. When it exploded his mate was killed, but he was saved. His mate's action had sufficiently shielded him from the blast to come out of it with minor injury. Such an unselfish act of self-sacrificing love changed this young man's life. When the war was finished, he offered his life to the Lord as a missionary in gratitude. We can compare this sacrifice with what Jesus has done for us. Amazing love! As the significance of what Jesus has done for us sinks in, we too find ourselves changing; we too want to love.

This is the story of the tremendous love of our redeemer God, who became one of us to die for us. "A man can have no greater love than to lay down his life for his friends. You are my friends…" (Jn 15:13). As we meditate on these mysteries we are captured by his love. We find the folly of God's love irresistible. We yield to this jealous love, which has gone to such lengths for our sake. Some of those who have reflected on these mysteries would speak of the "excessive love" of God shown in the excessive *physical* sufferings of Jesus, as well as in his interior torment. Bernard of Clairvaux, referring to the shedding of Jesus' blood, would say: "Yes, what a drop might have done, he chose to do with a stream, in order to show us the excessive love he bore us". Alphonsus Liguori would say that in undergoing Roman crucifixion Jesus went well beyond what was necessary to atone for our sins. The madness of such love, he says, is designed to win over even the hardest heart, and to set on fire even the coldest heart with love for him. Well might the beginner on the spiritual journey follow the lead of Francis of Assisi, who simply said, "My book is Jesus crucified".

The Flame of the Spirit

The story of our redemption was not complete with the death of Jesus. We do not worship a dead figure on the cross, but we worship the resurrected Lord. Now all "should bend the knee at the name of Jesus" and "every tongue should acclaim Jesus Christ as Lord to the glory of God the Father" (Phil 2:10-16). The cross only finds its meaning in the light of the Resurrection. It proclaims hope, victory and power because the One who suffered has now entered his glory.

The same Spirit who hovered over the chaos at the first creation breathed upon the dead body of Jesus in the tomb beginning the new creation. Now his body is transformed into glory. When Jesus appeared to his apostles, he breathed on them the creative Spirit, and displayed his wounds to them, the permanent signs of his love for us until the end (Jn 20:19-29). His wounds are transfigured. As eternal flames of love they have power to change us into his likeness. The breath of the Spirit of the Risen Christ dwelling in us effects this power. Paul says: "Glory be to him whose power, working in us, can do infinitely more than we can ask or imagine" (Eph 3:20). He prays that the Father "give you the power through his Spirit for your hidden self to grow strong, so that Christ may live in your hearts through faith" (Eph 3:16). He testifies to the power for change that is given us through the indwelling Spirit, who brings to us the power of the resurrected Christ, "And if the Spirit of him who raised Jesus from the dead is living in you, then he who raised Jesus from the dead will give life to your own mortal bodies through his Spirit living in you" (Rom 8:11). This is why we can sing the ancient song:

> O, breath on me, O breath of God
> Fill me with life anew
> That I may love what thou dost love
> And do what thou wouldst do.
>
> O breath on me, O breath of God
> Till I am wholly thine
> Until this earthly part of me
> Glows with thy fire divine.

John the Baptist had prophesied that the one who was to come after him would baptise with the Holy Spirit and with fire (Lk 3:15). During his ministry Jesus identified himself as the bearer of "fire to the earth" (Lk 12:49). However, this new fire could not be unleashed until he underwent his own "baptism of fire" through his suffering and death. Then on Pentecost day the Spirit came upon the apostles and Mary as "tongues of fire", resting on each of them (Acts 2:4). This was the fulfilment of Jesus' promise, made before ascending to the Father , that "not many days from now, you will be baptised in the Holy Spirit" (Acts 1:5). The Holy Spirit is the fire of God within us. As our interior life develops, we are to "fan into a flame" the gift of the Spirit which God gave us when we were baptised and when we had hands laid upon us in Confirmation (2Tim 1:6). This is the source of life and power for spiritual growth and transformation.

The Holy Spirit is God's light, God's power, God's comfort within us. He is the sanctifier. Paul teaches that we are being changed into the likeness of Jesus from one degree of glory to the next by the work of the Spirit within us (2Cor 3:18). He is the Spirit of truth, who teaches us about Jesus, and guides us in God's ways. He is the Spirit of love, who inspires us in the love of God and neighbour. He is the Spirit who makes us holy by his purifying fire. He is the Spirit of sons and daughters enabling us to call God, "Abba, Father". He is the comforter, bringing healing to the soul. He is the one who enables us to say: "Jesus is Lord!" He is the Spirit of fiery zeal for the kingdom and boldness in preaching the gospel. He is the loving unity between the Father and Son from all eternity, and so he is the Spirit of unity, drawing us out of isolation into communion.

To be able to take the spiritual journey at all we need to invoke the Holy Spirit often. *"Veni sancte spiritus!"* Without the Holy Spirit our efforts towards sanctity are in vain. We live in what Pope Paul VI called a "privileged moment of the Holy Spirit"[7], when in the face of a highly secularised, rationalistic and humanistic world, the Holy Spirit is being poured out in the Church in fresh and surprisingly new ways. It is imperative for the spiritual life that we often call upon the fire of the Spirit. "Come Holy Spirit fill the hearts of your faithful, enkindle in them the fire of your love".

The power that we need to be able to change into the likeness of Jesus is found both at Calvary and at the Cenacle (the Upper Room). It is the transforming fire of God's love. This power flows from the wounds of the crucified and risen Christ. It changes us by the fire of his Spirit, who dwells within us. We need to often be at the foot of the cross, being won over by Jesus, and yielding our hearts to him as our Saviour and Lord. We need also to open our lives to the mystery of Pentecost each day. Paul says: "Do not drug yourselves with wine, this is simply dissipation; *be filled with the Spirit*" (Eph 5:17). The tense of the verb in the Greek suggests that we are to be filled each day, over and over again, at all times, with the Holy Spirit. Here is the source of power for our new life in Christ, the fire within the heart that will not be extinguished, the strength to persevere through whatever trials may come, and the means to live as a new creation.

Finding our Identity in Christ

We live in a society where there is a struggle for personal identity. Under the surface of many anxious and confused lives are fundamental questions: "Who am I?" "Do I have worth?" "Am I significant?" The deep search for personal worth and significance leads people to try and establish themselves through performance in grades and scores, or winning trophies; or to prove themselves through fashion, physical attractiveness, intelligence, success and social status. Many give up in a pit of loneliness, confusion or depression; or turn to disordered relationships and addictions to assuage the gnawing sense of emptiness in their hearts.

The Good News is that *we find our true selves in the love of God*, who has created us to belong to him. When we discover his infinite and unconditional love for each unique and unrepeatable person, we find that our value is in who we are, rather than in what we do. We become aware of being created in the image and likeness of God, and that we have inestimable worth because he has "carved us on the palm of his hand". Catherine of Siena, reflecting on the love of God the Creator makes a passionate prayer to the Trinity:

> Why did you so dignify us? With unimaginable love you looked upon your creatures within your very self, and you fell in love with us. So it was love that made you create

us and give us being just so that we might taste your supreme eternal good…O mad lover! And you have need of your creature? It seems so to me, for you act as if you could not live without her, in spite of the fact that you are Life itself, and everything has life from you and nothing can have life without you. Why then are you so mad? Because you have fallen in love with what you have made! You are pleased and delighted over her within yourself, as if you were drunk with desire for her salvation. She runs away from you and you go looking for her. She strays and you draw closer to her: You clothed yourself in our humanity, and nearer than that you could not have come.[8]

The search for identity is also a quest for meaning and purpose. Questions such as: Where have I come from? Why am I here? Where am I going? Consequently, people today latch onto one of the large arrays of worldviews or philosophies available to us in the modern world to provide self-definition and security. Some turn to the New Age movement, others to Eastern religions, others to ancient pagan cults, others to exotic sects, or the occult, or to one of the many social philosophies—all in the search of ultimate questions. The Good News is that I discover who I am through relationship with the great "I AM".

In John's gospel Jesus is revealed as the Son of God, identical with the God of the Old Testament, who was revealed to Moses as, "I Am who I Am" (Ex 3:14). Jesus says "*I am* the Way", "*I am* the good Shepherd", "*I am* the bread of life", "*I am* the light of the world". Through opening our hearts to the great "*I am*", we find the deepest security possible as human beings, and we are grounded in our true identity.

Paul did not have an identity crisis. He says: "I live in faith: faith in the Son of God who loved me and who sacrificed himself for my sake" (Gal 2:20). By opening his heart to Jesus as his Saviour, he is established in who he is. Elsewhere, he says: "I am no longer trying for perfection by my own efforts, the perfection that comes from the Law, but I want only the perfection that comes through faith in Christ…" (Phil 3:9). When we open our hearts to the saving love of Jesus Christ, our Redeemer, and receive the gift of his Spirit into us, we are established "in Christ". This is the gift of our baptism, which we need to appropriate more and more fully.

Paul never tired of reminding the early Christians that the Spirit of Jesus given to us in baptism has immersed us into the saving death and resurrection of Jesus and made us a new creation. "For anyone in Christ", he says, "is a new creation; the old is gone and the new is here" (2Cor 5:17). A baptised person needs to stand up in Christ and know who he or she is! Speaking to the Colossians, who were getting confused about their identity by the smorgasbord of philosophies and spiritual options put before them, Paul says, "You must live your whole life according to the Christ you have received—Jesus the Lord; you must be rooted in him and built on him…" (Col 2:6-7). Our fundamental security is built in Christ and nowhere else.

Through the gift of baptism, which has immersed us into the death and resurrection of Jesus, and given us new birth in the Holy Spirit, we can affirm certain truths about our identity:

- I am created in the image and likeness of God, and I have irreplaceable dignity and inestimable worth in his eyes.
- He has always loved me and finds me totally acceptable in who I am.
- Even though I sinned I am redeemed by the precious blood of Jesus, who "died for our sins and was raised for our justification".

- I am now a new creation in Christ.
- Through the Spirit of adoption who lives in me, I am a son or daughter of God, the eternal Father.
- Therefore, I am a co-heir in Christ, the Son, to all the blessings of the kingdom of God.
- I have an eternal destiny, which was determined by God when I was created. By the Spirit within me I have the promise and guarantee of the fulness of happiness in God forever.

I am emphasising this issue of identity because it is the bed-rock of the spiritual life. The self-help therapies of popular, humanistic psychology books would suggest that we can attain self-realisation and self-fulfilment through our own efforts. They present a false gospel. The truth is that we will find the fulfillment intended for us only by turning to Christ Jesus. Self-realisation will elude us if we try to attain it without Christ. We cannot make ourselves happy, no matter how hard we try. Our ultimate fulfillment is found in surrender of our hearts to the Lord Jesus. It happens through dying to the old self, which has been shaped by worldly thinking; and allowing the Spirit to bring forth the new self, fashioned in the image of Christ. Paul says: "I have been crucified with Christ, and I live now not with my own life but with the life of Christ who lives in me" (Gal 2:20). He has forsaken the egotistical "I". It has been put to death on the cross with Jesus.

The false self keeps us in illusion and lostness, unable to work out who we really are. In embracing Christ, we discover our real selves through the recreating work of the Spirit. This is the way the unique flowering of each one's person occurs. All of this is because of the immense love of God revealed to us in Jesus. He never ceases labouring in love for our happiness. He has given all for our sake to win us to himself, so he could make us new in his Spirit. As we surrender to the fire of his love, he changes us into the image of himself, which we were always meant to be before sin came into the world. As Paul says: "We are God's work of art, created in Christ Jesus to live the good life as from the beginning he had meant us to live it" (Eph 2:10).

Entrustment to Mary our Mother

To be able to experience the mystery of the cross and the cenacle, and be filled with God's love, we have no better guide than the Blessed Virgin Mary. John tells us that "Near the cross of Jesus stood his mother…" (Jn 19:25). She knows intimately the mystery of the cross. St. Bernard reflected that Mary experienced in her own heart the wounds that Jesus experienced in his body. Her heart was expanded in love through the journey of discipleship here on this earth. Now in resurrected glory she will take us into the heart of Jesus broken open in love for us on the cross.

We know also that before Pentecost, in the upper room, the apostles "joined in continuous prayer, together with… the mother of Jesus" (Acts 1:14). Mary not only had first-hand experience of the cross, but also of Pentecost. If we entrust ourselves to her, she will open the mystery of the fire of the Spirit to us. She is woman of the Spirit, having been overshadowed by the Spirit, when Jesus was conceived within her, and then anointed anew in the fire of the Spirit with the apostles in the Upper Room.

From the cross Jesus entrusted each disciple of his into the care of Mary our mother. Just before he breathed his last, Jesus said to John the Beloved, who was representing all of us, "This is your mother" (Jn 19:26). To be a disciple is to be entrusted to his mother. But she is not only Jesus' mother. By this action of Jesus she has become mother for each one of us in a personal way. He said to his mother, "Woman, this is your son". She now has maternal responsibility for each one of us in our walk with Jesus. In entrusting ourselves to her within our hearts, we will find the most grace-filled way to move towards deeper union with Jesus. She will nurture us in his love by sharing with us the mystery of his cross, and by drawing us into the fire of his Spirit.

2
BEING PURIFIED BY GOD'S FIRE
Freedom from Slavery

"God is light: there is no darkness in him at all." (1Jn 1:5)

The Holy Spirit comes to sanctify us and to make us holy. The Lord says: "Be holy, for I am holy" (1Pet 1:15). What does this mean? It does not mean becoming sanctimonious and excessively pious by multiplying devotional practices for their own sake. Nor does it mean necessarily becoming a monk or a professional religious. It simply means being formed into the likeness of Jesus, who is the Holy One of God (2Cor 3:18).

The word "holy" in the Scriptures means being "set apart". Through our baptism we are a "chosen race, a royal priesthood, a consecrated nation, a people set apart to sing the praises of God", who called us out of darkness into his wonderful light (1Pet 2:9). The Lord is a jealous lover, who wants us for himself and will not rest until we truly belong to him.

We need to ask the question: How much have we allowed ourselves to be converted by the Lord? To what depth has it happened? Unfortunately, people can sometimes have the language of a Christian, and even have many religious practices in place, while their conversion is still quite shallow. Their life is not showing the fruits of the Spirit of love, joy, peace, patience, kindness and self-control (Gal 5:22). Their ordinary life is not consistent with their spiritual devotions. They are compromised in their hearts. They are resistant to truly living the demands of the gospel of Jesus. They live with divided hearts.

Genuine conversion means putting the old self to death and putting on the new self in Christ (Eph 4:17-24). It can be likened to a process of transplanting a shrub from one part of the garden to another. It means pulling up the roots that have been feeding on the old environment which shaped the old self. Our roots must now be put down firmly into a new environment, which can provide nourishment for our lives, and can shape the new self, formed in the image of Christ. For this to happen, we must undergo a personal transformation, which involves four initial dimensions—breaking with the world, fighting against sin, overcoming the flesh, and dealing with temptation.

Breaking with the World

In the Scriptures "the world" has a number of meanings. It can mean the whole of creation, which God has made and found to be good. It can also mean humankind, whom God has loved so much that he gave his only Son to die for us (Jn 3:16). When we speak of "breaking with the world" we do not mean these senses of the word. It is rather "the world" spoken about in texts such as the following:

> You must not love this passing world or anything that is in the world. The love of the Father cannot be in any man who loves the world, because nothing the world has to offer—the sensual body, the lustful eye, pride in possessions—could ever come from the Father but only from the world; and world, with all it craves for, is coming to an end; but anyone who does the will of God remains forever (1Jn 2:15-17).

At the Last Supper, Jesus prayed to the Father, "They belong to the world no more than I belong to the world. I am not asking you to remove them from the world, but to protect them from the evil one" (Jn 17:14-15). And elsewhere John says that "the whole world lies in the power of the evil one" (1Jn 5:19).

From these texts it is clear that Christians are to be in the world, but not *of* the world. The "world" in this sense is the spirit of those who are excessively attracted to the things of this life for their own sake. These things become a barrier to union with God. There is a whole pattern of values, attitudes, ideals—a world-view or mind-set—that is commonly held by the prevailing culture of the "world". If you give the allegiance of your heart to this way of thinking, you cannot give your allegiance fully to the kingdom of God. We are like fish swimming in the "sea of the world". Fish do not reflect upon the water around them. Similarly, we are prone not to reflect on the beliefs and values that we are imbibing all the time. The "worldly" spirit is carried often by family and friends, and by significant others in our lives. It can have a profound influence upon us.

The question for each of us is whether we are going to live by the dictates of this world, or whether we are going to live by the values of the kingdom of God. The "world" is an ideal in the minds of people that suggests a heart captive to a whole way of life that shuts out the Good News of Jesus Christ—in the world money is very important, instant sexual gratification dominates the conversation, fashions and over-attention to clothes, the cult of "body beautiful", ambition, honour, and status. Jesus says: "No-one can be the slave of two masters: he will either hate the first and love the second, or treat the first with respect and the second with scorn" (Mt 6:24).

Sometimes people think that the easiest way to break with the "world" would be to get away from it all and join a monastery. Yet the old saying remains true: "It is easy to take the monk out of the world, but it is not so easy to get the world out of the monk!" In other words, it is a heart problem. If you are infected by the "world", then you have a serious spiritual "heart disease". We can liken it to the problem of physical heart disease. Many people walk around for years not realising that they have a developing heart problem, until the worst happens, and they are rushed to hospital. So also do many walk around with deeply embedded "worldly" attitudes, and do not realise the spiritual peril they are in.

It is like the case of the frog which felt very cosy when he jumped into some warm water in a saucepan on the stove. The frog did not realise that the temperature was rising. He was increasingly comfortable and cosy. Of course, he was eventually boiled alive without even knowing it. There are many Christians who are like the frog— cosy and comfortable, but slowly dying from being committed to the wrong environment.

Community is essential for the spiritual life to flourish in a young convert. No-one can go it alone. It is a question of culture. I either allow myself to be formed by the culture of the "world", or by the culture of the kingdom of God. Christian community provides an environment that nurtures and strengthens faith. It provides the encouragement and challenge we need from the word of God and the sacraments. The Christian community upholds a vision of life, a whole way of thinking and valuing that is different from the world. It is a counter-culture that speaks of the kingdom of God.

When the early Christians in a pagan environment were preparing adults for baptism, they required that the candidates break with any pagan practices, and adopt a whole new way of life in the Christian community. They even expected them to renounce certain occupations that were not consistent with the Christian life. In the early third century, for example, Hippolytus in Rome mandates that people seeking entry into the Christian community should desist from making idols for sale, from taking part in the games or being a gladiator, from the practice of magic and astrology, from acting in the theatre, which was notoriously immoral, and from many other professions which were not compatible with the Christian faith.[9]

When time came to celebrate baptism itself the candidates first faced the West—symbol of darkness, the kingdom of Satan—and renounced Satan and all his evil works. Then they faced the East, symbol of the rising Son of justice, and made a threefold profession of faith in the Father, Son and Holy Spirit. They took off their clothes and were plunged into the waters of baptism, symbolising immersion into the death and resurrection of Jesus. Then, coming out of the water, they were clothed in a white robe, symbol of the new creation, the rebirth that they had received by the Spirit. When they were stripped naked, they were aware that they were shedding the old self, which had been formed by the spirit of the age and wedded to the "world"; and when they were clothed with the white garment, they were consciously putting on the new self, formed in the mind of Christ, and wedded to him. They were then anointed by the bishop with the chrism oil and welcomed into the Christian community with the celebration of the Eucharist.

The whole celebration spoke of a decisive break with the world. To be a Christian is to be different; it is to be counter-cultural, to belong to a community of brothers and sisters who are seeking to live the Beatitudes as taught by Jesus. Non-Christians should be able to see these values incarnate in the community, so they can say, "See how these Christians love one another". This is the way the world is redeemed. As Paul says to the Ephesians, "This may be a wicked age, but your lives should redeem it" (Eph 5:16).

How important it is for us to keep realising the grace of our baptism, to live as a redeemed people of God, set apart for him; not still as friends of the "world". James says: "Anyone who chooses the world for his friend turns himself into God's enemy. Surely you don't think Scripture is wrong when it says, 'the Spirit which he sent to live in us wants us for himself alone?'" (Jm 4:4-5).

Each Easter we renew our baptismal promises and say that we "renounce the glamour of evil and refuse to be mastered by sin". Beginners in the spiritual life find they still have a strong attraction within them for worldly values, and are still fascinated with wealth, power, riches, honours, glamour and fashion. It takes years of feeding the mind with the word of God, daily partaking of the body and blood of Jesus, being challenged by spiritual companions on the journey, regular repentance through the sacrament of reconciliation and living an ordered life that has personal prayer at the centre to grow in the vision of the kingdom of God and deepen in the mind of Christ.

Dealing with Sin

The Holy Spirit dwells within us to sanctify us, to make us holy. He is to shape us into the image of Christ. He is making us perfect as our heavenly Father is perfect. It is God's work within us. We are to cooperate fully with his activity by making a total "yes" to his refining work within us.

In the first letter of John we are encouraged to "think of the love that the Father has lavished on us by letting us be called God's children; and that is what we are" (1Jn 3:1). However, in the light of the Father's love, and aware of our dignity as children of God, we find there is still sin within us. John goes on to point out that any sin within us is incompatible with being a child of God. It is God's intention to make us like him, and eventually to see him in heaven as he really is. "Surely everyone who entertains this hope", he says, "must purify himself, must try to be as pure as Christ" (1Jn 3:3). We cannot settle for a certain degree of conversion. Although we already belong to the Lord, we still do not belong to him fully. John says: "to live a holy life is to be holy just as he is holy; to lead a sinful life is to belong to the devil…" (1Jn 3:7-8). We must let God's work go more deeply into us, to purify us with his burning love. The Holy Spirit is a refining fire—he cannot abide with sin. He will always be convicting us of our sin and helping us renounce it.

We must aim to eliminate sin from our life. Mortal sin destroys the love of God in the soul and separates us from God. When committed with full knowledge and full consent it brings eternal death to the soul. Serious patterns of sin, such as fornication, adultery, drunkenness, violent assault, robbery, and the like render the spiritual life null and void. Our problem is more likely to be with persistent venial sin. It is less grave in matter but deflects us from the goal of union with God. It damages our relationship with God but does not break it totally. When we tell small lies, gossip a little, get angry with someone, or have envious thoughts, we weaken the love of God within us and grieve the Holy Spirit. Habit-patterns of venial sins predispose us to more serious sin. We need to work at eliminating them. As St. Augustine said:

> While he is in the flesh, man cannot help but have at least some light sins. But do not neglect these sins which we call "light"; if you take them for light when you weigh them, tremble when you count them. A number of light objects makes a great mass; a number of drops fills a river; a number of grains makes a heap. What then is our hope? Above all, confession.[10]

It is not enough to set about the battle against sinful actions. The Lord looks at the heart. Jesus taught that evil intentions come from the heart. He insisted: "if your virtue goes no deeper than the scribes and the Pharisees you will never enter the kingdom of heaven" (Mt 5:19-20). The Holy Spirit will show us how devious our hearts are. In Jeremiah, the word of God says, "The heart is more devious than any other thing, perverse too: who can pierce its secrets? I the Lord search to the heart…" (Jer 17:10). The spiritual tradition has identified for us eight "sicknesses of the heart", which are deeply ingrained in each human being because of our fallen condition. To grow in holiness, we need to call upon the precious blood of Jesus to be redeeming us of these basic disorders.

The classic "sicknesses of the heart" can be divided into three groups. The first group is related to our basic appetites, and includes gluttony, lust and greed. Gluttony is the drive to over-indulge in food and drink. Lust is the disordered drive for wrongful sexual pleasure. It involves thinking of the other person as an object of self-centred pleasure and failing to recognise his or her dignity. Greed is the inordinate attachment to material things for their own sake.

The second group is to do with disorder in our emotions. They are anger, envy and lethargy (*acedia*). Anger can be hot or cold. If it is hot, then the person has a heart that rages in response to others, and is full of wrath. If it is cold, then it is turned inwards in resentment and bitterness of heart, twisting the spirit and making a person altogether miserable. Envy is a sadness at others' gifts or blessings. It is the feeling that our own glory is being overshadowed by someone else. Consequently, we find it hard to rejoice in the triumphs or blessings of others and secretly delight in their failures and tragedies. Lethargy (or *acedia*, as it was called by the monks) is a slothfulness of spirit, a boredom and tepidity, which leads the person to be distracted from what is God's purpose for them and to ignore the work that he has for them at this moment. Some of the Fathers added an extra sickness of the heart in this group, called despondency or sadness. It is a loss of hope, a sadness of heart, a self-centred, self-pitying attitude, that becomes a dark and brooding spirit.

The third group is associated with the higher faculties, namely the intellect and the will. There are only two in this category, but these are the deepest of all disorders, and the hardest to detect and to root out of the heart. They are vainglory and pride. Vainglory is the subtle placing of yourself in the centre of all your imagining, plans and dreams. It is the subtle promotion of yourself with your own thoughts. It appears in prayer often, as we tend to put ourselves in the position of glory, and applause before others. Pride has many forms. It is the deepest problem in the human heart. It is a fundamental, primal disorder, and is based, as all these sicknesses are, in inordinate self-love. It is a form of self-exaltation, and a refusal to give due glory to God.

Sometimes these sicknesses are referred to as the "deadly sins". This is not accurate. They are not always manifest in mortal sin. A person can be living a very righteous life and still find these basic disorders in the heart. They are "thoughts of the heart", which have sometimes been called "capital sins".[11] This latter term has more accuracy about it, because it suggests that they are fonts (*capita*) from which spring all other sins. The spiritual person seeks to detect these "thoughts" and to guard the heart from them taking deep root within. Rather than just focus on our sinful actions, we need to become more aware of the sinful state in the depth of our hearts, and humbly call upon the precious blood of Jesus to have mercy on us and cleanse and purify us at the conscious, semi-conscious and unconscious levels of our being.

The sin in our lives can be represented by a tree in a garden with many roots. The roots would represent the deep sinfulness in the heart that needs to be cut out. Roots are the means by which the tree obtains nourishment and the way the tree stays firmly in place. We need to set the axe to the roots of the tree. As we do, however, we will find that there is a deep tap-root which is not at first obvious as we go about the task, but inevitably becomes the most difficult root of all to dislodge. This tap-root is pride. This is the sin which caused Lucifer to fall from heaven. It is the sin of Adam and Eve in the garden, when they were tempted to usurp God, through eating of the fruit of the tree of knowledge of good and evil.

In Romans, Paul describes this fundamental human disorder when he says, "The anger (wrath) of God is being revealed from heaven against all the impiety and depravity of men…they knew God and yet refused to honour him as God or to thank him…" (Rom 1:18-28). This sin of "impiety" is the refusal to give glory to God. It is a denial of our creaturehood, and a refusal to accept the fundamental purpose of our existence, which is to give praise, honour and glory to God here on earth and to be with him forever in heaven.

In facing up to the reality of our sinful condition we need to be careful not to become discouraged. The great friends of God in the spiritual tradition stress that we should first look to the love of God revealed in Jesus, especially in his merciful death on the cross. Only in the light of this knowledge can we have the courage to see the depth of our sinfulness and to do something about it. John of the Cross says it is like watching the sun shining through a glass window.[12] You notice the dirt on the window because of the sun's light. So you clean the window as best you can. Then later, when the sun is shining again even more brightly, you notice more smudges on the window. So, you clean again. This is the process of growth in holiness. The sunshine of God's love in the soul shows up the stains of sinfulness that are still there. In this light we have the confidence to continue the purifying work that is necessary to advance towards the Lord.

Once we have identified sinful patterns in our lives it is important to be decisive. We should not be happy to lie down in a comfortable bed with sinfulness, and say "that's me! That's how I am! I will never change!" The Lord's purpose is to bring change! We must be aggressive with sin. Jesus said: "If your right eye should cause you to sin, tear it out…" (Mt 5:29-30). This is strong language. He was using a deliberately exaggerated style of speech to make a point. Sin is like a cancer within us. If the doctor diagnosed that you had a cancer in your stomach, you would be very concerned to have quick surgery to get rid of it! Similarly with sin. It is an even more deadly disease. We must be intent on letting the Lord conduct deep surgery on the heart to get it all out. He does this through the grace of repentance.

The grace of repentance is a basic key for all spiritual growth. It is the way to joy and genuine peace of heart. Jesus told us the story of the prodigal son to show us the merciful heart of the Father. When we repent, we throw ourselves into the merciful arms of the Father who is so ready to forgive. Repentance does not mean feelings of remorse or self-condemnation. When confronted with the reality of our sin we do not have to become despairing. Psalm 103 tells us the Lord is "rich in mercy" and "as far as the East is from the West, so far does he cast our sins away".

The difference between Judas and Peter was not the gravity of their sin—both had seriously denied the Lord. Rather, it was that while Judas despaired of God's mercy, Peter trusted in God's mercy. Peter had gazed into the eyes of Jesus and seen there the mercy of God. Even though he went outside and wept bitterly, he still knew the love of God. This is what is most important to us (Lk 22:54-62).

Corrie Ten Boom, who, with her sister Betsie, endured the severe, dehumanising conditions of a Nazi prison camp in Ravensbruck, tells the touching story of her sister's death.[13] Betsie was dying of malnutrition and exhaustion from forced labour in a rock quarry. These two women of faith had learned in that hell-house to keep love and forgiveness in their hearts for their tormentors. Now, as she died, Betsie whispered to Corrie that she knew that Corrie would eventually be released from the prison, and that when this happens, she was to "go and tell the whole world that there is no pit so deep that the mercy of Jesus is not deeper!" This is the truth! Jesus entered into the pit of our sinful state so he could redeem us. There is now no human condition that is not redeemable. He rose out of the pit. This is our hope and our victory.

Repentance is a decision under grace to turn from sin and to turn fully to the Lord Jesus in love. The steps are simple. We will need to be doing this again and again. Firstly, identify the sin with honesty and courage. We can ask the Holy Spirit to show us the true state of our hearts, and for the grace to face the reality of our condition. Secondly, own the reality of the sin. That is, avoid making excuses and rationalisations, trying to explain it away. "I'm just a victim of circumstances" or "I just can't help myself" or "It's all their fault anyway!" Our blindness can sometimes be like David, who, after having arranged for Uriah the Hittite to be killed in order to satisfy his lust for Uriah's wife, was unable to see his own sin. Then Nathan, the prophet, came to David[14] to tell him a story about a rich man in the land who had forcibly taken a poor man's only lamb for himself in order to feed a guest. David was enflamed with anger at this injustice. "As the Lord lives" he said to Nathan "that man deserves to die". And Nathan said to David: "You are the man!" The Holy Spirit will convict us in this way, "You are the one!" While it is laudable to be able to see the sin of the world and deplore it, the Lord is always getting us to look at our own hearts.

There is a story of a little boy who was trying to put together a jigsaw puzzle of a map of the world. He was finding it too difficult. Then his Father mentioned to him that on the other side of the pieces there was a picture of a man. So he turned the pieces over and very quickly was able to put together the figure because of his familiarity with the individual features of a human being. Then he turned the whole thing over and there was the world together! His father then said to him: "You see son, if you put the person together, then the world will come together as well". Yes, we must attend first to our own hearts and their conversion, before we will be able to help in putting the world together again.

Once we have owned the responsibility for our sins and our sinfulness, the third step is to confess in the sacrament of Reconciliation. This sacrament should be used often to foster an attitude of on-going repentance, and an even greater appreciation of God's mercy. The fourth step is to firmly renounce the sin. In the sacrament this is called a firm purpose of amendment. We must be done with it. The power of the cross of Jesus can break the power of established patterns of sin in us. We will need to ask the Lord for the grace to be able to break the habit. When we go to the Eucharist, we can eat the body of the Lord and drink his blood into that particular area of our lives, having faith in his ultimate victory.

In dealing with sinfulness, we need to be in touch with our lingering affection for sin, and a perverse fascination with evil that can be deep within us. Even though our conscience would not allow us to commit again certain sins that we may have fallen into in the past, we can still find within us an affection for them. Our conniving with the sin of the world has built in us a liking for sin. We have to pray for the grace to hate sin, to be able to see it with God's eyes. We need to grow in a strong sense of the utter ugliness and contemptible nature of sin. "God is light; there is no darkness in him at all" (1Jn 1:5). The more we come into the light of the Lord the more we will see our desperate need for the precious of blood of Jesus to saturate us and break down these affections that hold us back from union with God.

In firmly renouncing sin we need to be thoroughly convinced of victory in Christ. Paul tells us that when we were baptised we were joined with Jesus in his death. It is as if we went into the tomb with him. Because Jesus rose from the tomb by the power of the Holy Spirit, so we share his resurrection life. Paul says: "When he died, he died once for all, to sin, so his life now is life with God; and in that way, you too must consider yourselves to be dead to sin but alive for God in Christ Jesus" (Rom 6:11). This is the Good News! Sin does not have to dominate our lives anymore. Bless God for his gracious mercy!

There is now a new power and new energy in the universe that scientists, New-Agers, and philosophers of this age know nothing about. It has come through the resurrection of Jesus. If the first creation began with a Big Bang, as some scientists would have us believe, the new creation began with an even greater explosion of power, when Jesus rose into glory. Because he is risen, we are no longer enslaved to our bodily passions, or to our disordered emotions and thoughts. We have been given new life through the waters of baptism. It is wonderful to realise that the same Holy Spirit who raised Jesus from the dead dwells in us. As Paul says: "if the Spirit of him who raised Jesus from the dead is living in you, then he who raised Jesus from the dead will give life to your own mortal bodies through his Spirit living in you" (Rom 8:11). We walk now in the confidence of being recreated by the power of the Holy Spirit. In the on-going battle with sin we are no longer losers. We are winners through the power of him who has loved us (Rom 8:37).

Dealing with the Flesh

If we belong to God, and want to be like Jesus, then we need to be led by the Spirit, not by the flesh. Paul says: "Everyone moved by the Spirit is a son (daughter) of God..." (Rom 8:14). To be a spiritual person is to be directed by the Spirit, not by the flesh. Within each of us there is a struggle for dominance of the Spirit over the power of the flesh. If we are alive in God then we will struggle with the flesh. Remember, dead people don't struggle! It is a sign that we are alive! Paul speaks of his own struggle in this regard, "I cannot understand my own behaviour. I fail to carry out the things I want to do, and I find myself doing the very things I hate... for though the will to do what is good is in me, the performance is not...". In the midst of the struggle, he cries out "What a wretched man I am! Who will rescue me from this body doomed to death?" And then the answer comes with a resounding voice that has echoed down through the centuries: "Thanks be to God through Jesus Christ our Lord!" (Rom 7:15-19).

By the "flesh" Paul means much more than lustful passions. The "flesh" is that powerful drive within us towards sin. Traditionally it has been called "concupiscence", the inclination towards sin, that remains after original sin is washed away in baptism. It is not our personal fault for having it, but if we allow it to grip us and to govern us, then we are guilty of sin. Some people think that the answer to life is "doing what comes naturally". More than often this means following one's flesh inclination! We are fallen human beings, and even though we are immersed into the redeeming mystery of Jesus in baptism, we retain this woundedness in our human condition, which means we are in a constant battle with the flesh.

To be holy is to be governed by the Spirit, not by the flesh. Paul once chided the Galatians that they were foolishly ending in the flesh what they had begun so well in the Spirit (Gal 3:3). Unfortunately, many Christians who start their spiritual journey well, slowly become more carnal in outlook and behaviour because they fail to engage in this battle. Paul warns that to set the mind on the flesh leads to death, but to set the mind on the Spirit brings life and peace (Rom 8:6).

The "flesh" can be described under four headings; self-gratification, self-glorification, self-preservation, and self-sufficiency. The focus is on self for its own sake. The Spirit, on the other hand, seeks to lead us to be given to God in love, obedience and humility.

Self-gratification is the attitude of the "me generation". "I want it, and I want it now". It is prevalent in the consumer society, where everything is geared for personal comfort, convenience, pleasure and ease. The message of the commercials is "you deserve it!", "you won't be happy without it!" This fosters an insatiable hunger for the satisfaction of all base desires, now. The Christian tradition has always considered pleasure to be good—a pleasant meal, good wine, beautiful music, enjoyment of friends, but all in moderation. Under the selfish drive of the flesh, pleasure becomes inordinate and damaging to the good of the person.

The Holy Spirit, on the other hand, fosters an attitude of healthy self-denial and self-mastery. When the Holy Spirit is governing, we are able to moderate our desires in a rational way, according to the plan and purpose of God. Paul says: "You cannot belong to Christ Jesus unless you crucify all self-indulgent passions and desires" (Gal 5:24). The Holy Spirit gives us the interior fortitude to order the passions in a godly way towards the ultimate goal of union with God. This will mean self-denial and renouncing often our immediate desires. Jesus said, "If anyone wants to be a follower of mine let him renounce himself, and take up his cross every day and follow me" (Lk 9:23).

Self-glorification, or self-promotion, is a deep tendency within us to avoid the inevitability of death. So, we will glory in our bodies, glory in our health, glory in our sport, glory in our intelligence, glory in our knowledge, glory in our social status, glory in our successes in the eyes of the world. Underneath it all is a deep fear of being diminished. So, we work at self-aggrandisement. We devise big plans for our lives without reference to God. Sometimes these plans can even be "spiritual" in appearance. However, at the centre of these plans is exaltation of self, not the glory of the Lord.

People can work hard at their career, but actually for selfish reasons, and to try and prove their significance. They can be high achievers in the academic, political, business or sporting world, but all is centred on the kudos it brings them. Underneath they are afraid of being a "nobody". Even within the Church people will seek to develop their spiritual guru status, or their sensational ministry of signs and wonders, or their position of power in the hierarchy. But, subtly at the centre is the big ego. It is not a bad thing to have big plans, as long as they are in the hands of the Lord, and according to his will; rather than subtly serving to massage our own egos and be motivated by fear. The attitude of self-glorification is "I will be Number One!"

The Holy Spirit acts in a totally different way. He seeks to develop humility in us. Paul said: "As for me, the only thing I can boast about is the cross of our Lord Jesus Christ…" (Gal 6:14). There's all the difference! To follow Jesus is to be nailed with him to the cross! So much for status and glory-seeking! This is a place of humiliation for the sake of his name. The flesh gets us to glory in ourselves; the Spirit gets us to glory in God. In the Spirit we see our true state as creatures, and that we are nothing without God. The Spirit also shows us how "all flesh is grass and its glory like the wildflower's. The grass withers, the flower falls, but the word of the Lord remains forever" (1Pet 1:24; cf Is. 40:6-7).

Once I was with an older priest, and we entered a room with many oil paintings of dignified prelates from an age gone past, many of them looking quite decorous in their robes and refinery. For my benefit, I am sure, the older priest exclaimed in Latin, "*Sic transit gloria mundi*", which means "Thus passes the glory of the world". I have never forgotten these words of wisdom. As the psalmist prays to the Lord, "Teach us to count how few days we have and so gain wisdom of heart" (Ps 90:12). One of the fundamental challenges in adult life is to know the fragility of our hold on this earthly life, and to place our trust fully in the Lord as to the time and manner of our death. Rather than glory in ourselves, we would better use the limited time we have serving others in humility.

Self-preservation, or self-absorption, is that drive within us to avoid suffering at all costs. It is fostered by the lie of our society which teaches that true happiness comes from the elimination of pain. So, we have become addicted to pain-killers, and can justify mercy-killing, and eugenic abortions. All is geared toward a "comfortable", easy existence, where there is no personal cost. The flesh does not want to make painful sacrifice. It screams "I will not serve!" Often people who have served for a while in a self-sacrificing way all of a sudden, for no accountable reason, dig in their heels and proclaim, "that's it, no more, I've done enough!" Self-preservation takes over. They will no longer make acts of self-sacrifice. It hurts too much!

The Holy Spirit, on the other hand, inspires us to a loving service. Jesus said: "Unless a grain of wheat falls on the ground and dies, it remains only a single grain; but if it dies, it yields a rich harvest" (Jn 12:24). The Holy Spirit invites us to pattern our lives on the death of Jesus, to enter more and more into sacrificial giving of ourselves for the sake of others.

As Mother Teresa urged her sisters: "Love until it hurts!" As we open our hearts to Jesus more, he expands our capacity for sacrificial love. We joyfully allow ourselves to be spent for the kingdom. The words attributed to Francis of Assisi become our way of life:

> *O Master, grant that I may seek not so much to be consoled as to console,*
>
> *not so much to be understood as to understand*
>
> *not so much to be loved as to love with all my heart.*
>
> *For it is in pardoning that we are pardoned*
>
> *In giving to all that we receive; and in dying that we are born to eternal life.*

Self-sufficiency, or self-reliance, is the attitude of the autonomous individual. The modern era has been shaped by the post-Enlightenment mentality of rugged individualism. It has been imaged on the popular screen by such figures as John Wayne or Clint Eastwood, riding high in the saddle, with six-guns blazing—me against the world. It is the attitude immortalised by Frank Sinatra in the song "I did it my way!" Those words would surely be an unfortunate epitaph to have on your tombstone! The attitude here is the obstinate spirit that professes "I will not obey!", "I am beholden to no authority, thank you very much!" This attitude ignores that human beings are fundamentally relational. We are meant to be in community, and, hence accountable to one another. The current cult of the autonomous individual makes the building of genuine community almost impossible.

The Holy Spirit, on the other hand, draws us into the obedience of Jesus, who was obedient unto death on the cross (Phil 2:8). Rather than wanting to do it our way, the Spirit prompts us to want to do it God's way. Rather than fighting battles by ourselves, in a spirit of independence, the Holy Spirit prompts us to enter into communion with others in relationships of *interdependence*. Rather than declaring ourselves autonomous, the Spirit prompts us to seek to do God's will and to live to please him. The Spirit teaches us to join with Jesus in saying: "My food is to do the will of the one who sent me" (Jn 4:34).

The Holy Spirit's way of helping us overcome the power of the flesh is to take us more deeply into the experience of the cross of Jesus. We will only learn self-mastery, humility, obedience, and love through the cross. The flesh shrinks back from the cross and is at enmity with it. Jesus said: "If anyone wants to be a follower of mine, let him renounce himself and take up his cross and follow me. For anyone who wants to save his life will lose it, but anyone who loses his life for my sake, and the sake of the gospel, will save it" (Mk 8:34).

This is a critical issue. There are many who have been touched by the Holy Spirit, having an initial taste of the new Pentecost, who begin to pull back as soon as the shadow of the cross appears. They want Pentecost without the "cost"! The genuine Christian journey involves being crucified with Jesus on the cross. It means a stripping away of the old self and an emergence of the new self in Christ. Our journey into Christ means submitting to this painful process. Paul likens this "stripping" to the painful operation of circumcision, which had to be undergone by all males under the old Law. He says that the baptised Christian, male and female, undergoes a circumcision of the heart, which is even more painful than any physical operation (Col 2:11-12). Paul speaks about it as accomplished in baptism, but this reality is far from fully appropriated in our hearts.

C.S. Lewis illustrates the resistance toward transformation by using an analogy of obstinate tin soldiers.[15] Imagine that as a child you could really bring your tin soldiers to life! What a joy that would be for you. It would involve turning the tin into human flesh and blood. But, maybe the tin soldiers would not like it. After all it is a painful process having to shed one's "tinnyness" and take on human form. As the transformation begins all the soldiers can see is that the tin is being spoilt! They think you are killing them. Maybe they can see the good ideal of being transformed into a human being, but the pain involved in the change is too great! They kick and scream, and put up a great deal of resistance, even though it is all for their own good to be brought to a higher level of existence.

Maybe we are like those tin soldiers, as God, in his love, seeks to change us into his likeness. The natural life in us, wounded from original sin, is self-centred. It wants to be petted and admired, and to take advantage of others and exploit them. It is afraid of the light and life of the spiritual world. As C.S. Lewis says: "It knows that if the spiritual life gets hold of it, all its self-centredness and self-will are going to be killed, and it is ready to fight tooth and nail to avoid that".[16]

Self-denial and Fasting

In the early stages of the spiritual journey we have to grow in personal self-discipline, and make the hard decisions that lead towards self-mastery. The whole Christian life involves denying our self-will and self-interest in favour of loving God and others. Broadly speaking this is what is meant by the "ascetical" life. It is a way of life which is ordered and disciplined in such a way that our hearts are educated towards God and trained in his ways.

Voluntary acts of self-denial help us towards self-mastery and being able to move in the Spirit rather than in the flesh. Acts of self-denial are only fruitful to the extent that they are genuinely motivated by the love of God. They are healthy if they are a response to the personal experience of God's goodness and express a desire for deeper life with God. They are unhealthy if undertaken to impress or to please others. Often people who are new to the things of the Spirit will rush into ascetical practices with wrong motivation. Maybe they want to measure up to what they perceive to be God's expectations on them, or the demands of significant others. Maybe they are just trying to reach a standard of "perfection" which they have built within their minds from reading the exploits of the saints. Maybe they are trying to win God's favour by their heroic actions.

When wrong motivation is at work, well-meaning people can become heavily burdened by their penances, bound up emotionally, and labouring under a flawed concept of God. Often these wrong motivations are unconscious and hidden. People can appear to be performing in a very pious manner; but, in fact, the motivation can be quite prideful, self-serving and confused. Paul says: "If I give away all that I possess, piece by piece, and if I even let them take my body to burn it, but am without love, it will do me no good whatever" (1Cor 13:3).

Sometimes people who are new in the spiritual journey can fall into a type of negative spirituality, which expresses itself in heavy bodily mortification and denial of the good things of life. Based in a wrong concept of God, they view the body as evil and needing to be beaten into submission. They regard pleasure as wrong; the more painful something is the more grace obtained. Human relationships and sexuality are highly suspect and dangerous. Created realities are a hindrance towards sanctification. They develop a negative attitude towards food, alcohol, money, books, art, literature, dancing etc.

The problem here is a faulty vision of human beings and their relationships in the world, and a failure to appreciate the goodness of God. It is usually rooted in a poor self-image and even a kind of self-hate. These people need to gain a new vision of self, others, the creation, and God. They need to learn to celebrate the goodness of God and his many gifts to us, and appreciate the intrinsic worth of every human being created in God's image and likeness. People break out of this outlook when they allow God's love to touch their hearts. He confirms them in their self-worth. This opens up new eyes to see self, others and the world.

The only way to holiness is by the love of God. Everything else is simply a means to that end. We must discipline our desires, and live appropriately according to the law of Christ, being moderate in eating, drinking, sleeping, dancing, sexual relationships, friendships, pleasure-seeking etc. Apart from ordinary moderation and discipline required by the commandments, there is no value in itself of denying ourselves these things.

There is nothing intrinsically good in wearing a hair shirt or sleeping on a bed of nails. Unless an act of self-denial has a clear and good reason behind it, and is a means to a higher end, it is folly to engage in it. It is always wise to submit what we are doing in this regard to a spiritual director for guidance, since there are many pitfalls for the beginner in the ascetical life. Having said this, it is good to emphasis that self-mortification is not an optional extra in the spiritual journey. It should be entered into with caution, heeding the warnings mentioned above, but it should not be avoided.

In this matter of self-mortification, it is highly advisable to keep an eye on the "fruits". The fruit of ascetical practice taken on with wrong motivation is anxiety, a sense of burden, lack of joy or a heavy heart. The fruit of ascetical practice taken on for the love of God is an increase of love, deeper peace of heart, and a light and joyful spirit. Acts of self-denial enable us to embrace the cross of Jesus. They help us identify with Jesus in his suffering. They train us in endurance and fortitude. They are a way of conversion of heart, of breaking with the old attitudes, the grooves that have been carved out in the mind, memory, and imagination through the old sinful way of life. They help us gain mastery over the fundamental drive to selfishness within us, and to build within us the fruit of self-control.

Fasting is a particular act of self-denial which can bear fruit in holiness. Jesus fasted in the desert for forty days as a preparation for his mission of preaching the gospel (Lk 4:14). He ascribed special power to fasting. On one occasion he stated that certain demons cannot be expelled except by prayer and fasting (Mk 9:29). Fasting expresses that "Man does not live on bread alone, but on every word that comes from the mouth of God" (Mt 4:4). The deepest hunger of the human heart is for God. Through fasting we realise that we are not self-sufficient; we depend totally on God, and the world cannot satisfy the deepest needs of the heart. Fasting helps us to be poor in spirit before God, with a deep awareness of our utter need for him, and with a deep longing for union with him.

Fasting is a way of self-emptying. Physically it involves the elimination of waste materials from the body. In the same way there is a cleansing of the spirit of accumulated rubbish, and we are made more pure of heart. Through fasting we become more in touch with the things of the Spirit. We gain "spiritual eyes" since we become more interiorly free of useless attachments. Fasting is a means of interior purification. It helps us to distinguish more clearly between what is essential and what is not. It brings an interior strength to a person's spirit and opens the heart towards the love of God and neighbour. The Desert Fathers always expected that their prayer and fasting would bear fruit in a greater capacity to forgive others and to humbly serve their needs.

Fasting expresses a deep hunger for God. When we fast we are prepared to experience this hunger in a physical way in our bodies, so that the whole of our being is longing for union with God. Fasting from the heart means growing in love for God who is coming, and to whom our heart calls out every day, longing for him "like the deer that yearns for running streams" (Ps 42:2). In fasting we become aware of our powerlessness, vulnerability, and nothingness. We experience the cry of our body and of our heart in seeking union with God, and we throw ourselves more upon his infinite goodness and mercy. It is a way of praying with our bodies, a way of making our bodies a living sacrifice of praise to God, and a way of praying always.

Dealing with Temptation

Temptation is inevitable in the Christian journey. A thousand temptations do not make a sin. If we take no pleasure in the temptations and stand against them, there is no sin. If we deliberately begin to entertain a temptation, and in some way take pleasure from it, then we have already begun to sin. Sometimes a temptation is so intense that we find ourselves involuntarily delighting in it. This is not a sin, as long as the will holds firm against the temptation. Sometimes temptations are violent, strong, and persistent. All we can do in the storm is keep our wills fixed in obedience to the Lord until the storm abates. If the will has held firm we have not sinned, regardless of the imagery and involuntary pleasure stirred by the temptation. If we do succumb and take some pleasure in the temptation, then our sin is to a greater or lesser degree depending on the length of time and degree of pleasure taken.

We can gain some insight into the anatomy of temptation from the account in Genesis of the temptation by Satan in the garden of Eden (Gen 3:1-9). Firstly, we note that the enemy poses the question in general terms to Eve. At this point he is not inviting Eve to do evil. He is simply enticing her into a conversation: "Did God really say you were not to eat from any of the trees in the garden?" This is a common ploy. We need to recognise the danger immediately and refuse to enter into the conversation and turn our thoughts and imagination to other things. This is the principle of "nipping the temptation in the bud", by not being drawn into thinking and question about the matter. Eve's mistake was that she allowed herself to be drawn into conversation with the serpent. She should have destroyed the temptation at the beginning, not weighing the reasons why she should or shouldn't eat the fruit.

Now that Eve is already entangled in Satan's web, he moves to direct attack. He tells a lie. "No! You will not die!" He undermines God's authority and credibility in her eyes, and suggests an enchanting possibility—that eating of the tree of the knowledge of good and evil will make them as God. Satan is the "father of lies" and the "prince of darkness". He deals in deception and confusion, causing a dark cloud to come over the mind. His offerings are always attractive, sometimes quite glamorous and alluring. Someone suggested it is like being offered a chocolate-coated cockroach. It is very alluring on the outside, but when you bite into it you discover the deception, and how really ugly it is.

If we are at this point in the unfolding of a temptation, we can still pull out. The only way is to end the conversation, otherwise it will inevitably result in a fall. If we toy with it, sin becomes more desirable and fascinating, and our resistance more and more weakened.

As the Genesis account describes, "The woman saw that the tree was good for food, pleasing to the eyes, and desirable". Here Eve is on the brink of falling into sin. With all the defences down, she was in so deep that she could not pull back. She now takes the step into sinful action. "So she took some of its fruit and ate it…" She sinned, and immediately drew her husband into the sin as well. Instantly they felt naked before God—too late they realised the deception, aware that they have lost their innocence before God. We can almost hear the sneering laughter of the tempter.

Yet the voice of conscience is at work immediately, convicting them of the sin. We are told they heard the sound of the Lord God searching for them in the garden, crying out, "Adam, where are you?" This same cry of the Lord has echoed down the centuries as he seeks out the lost. It is not only his coming to confront them with what they have done, but more so his coming to begin his loving plan of winning them back to him.

The Activity of the Enemy

The Lord allows whatever temptation comes our way. The enemy only has the sway in our lives that he is allowed by God. The enemy is like a ferocious dog on a long chain. It is God who keeps the length of the chain in check. The Lord allows the evil one to entice us into the perilous region marked out by the circumference of his chain. The wild dog can pretend to be asleep by his kennel, or he can even dress himself up to look like an attractive puppy. But it is only the foolish who fall for these tricks, and enter the area of danger, to their great peril.

It is ultimately a mystery why the Lord allows temptations. It seems this is one way he has of sharpening us in virtues. The more we learn to resist a particular vice, the more we grow in the opposite virtue. It is also a way the Lord has of strengthening us in our journey. There is a very consoling text which says, "You can trust God not to let you be tried beyond your strength, and with any trial he will give you a way out of it and the strength to bear it" (1Cor 10:13).

We need also to be aware that Satan is a defeated foe. Victory has been won by Jesus Christ over all the powers of darkness. Since Jesus was raised from the dead and exalted at the right hand of the Father, we are told, that "he has put all things under his feet" (Eph 1:22). Nevertheless, Satan is a formidable opponent. While we do not want to over-exaggerate Satan's power in the world, nor do we want to trivialise it. He is the enemy of our human nature, a "murderer from the start" (Jn 8:44). He has a profound hatred of God. Because he cannot attack God directly, he attacks God's creatures, attempting to draw us towards eternal death in hell.

Ignatius Loyola suggests three images for the activity of the evil one.[17] Firstly, he says the evil one is like a cowardly, vindictive person. If in an argument we stand up to a cowardly person, he or she will back down quickly. However, if we give ground in the argument, and allow the person to have sway, then the anger, vindictiveness, and rage of the coward surge up and have no bounds. In the same way, the enemy will flee, when we stand up to him. As it says in James, "Resist the devil and he will flee!" However, if we are afraid and lose courage during the temptation "no wild animal on earth can be more fierce than the enemy of our human nature".[18] The lesson is clear. As Scripture says: "Be calm but vigilant, because your enemy the devil is prowling round like a roaring lion, looking for someone to eat. Stand up to him, strong in faith…" (1Pet 5:8-9).

Secondly, Ignatius says that the enemy can be likened to a man who is a false lover. The false lover seeks to remain hidden and does not want to be discovered and exposed. When the false lover seduces with evil intentions, he wants his words to be kept secret. He is really upset if his suggestions are brought into the open and revealed by a daughter to her father, or a wife to her husband. When he is exposed, he will flee. In the same way, when the evil one tries to seduce us with his hidden temptations, he wants it to remain secret. If we bring it to the light with our confessor or spiritual director, he will be exposed and flee immediately. It is important to remember that no matter how embarrassing and perverse the thoughts presented to us, the best remedy is to bring them to the light as quickly as possible. This defuses the temptation, and we are free to let it go. Otherwise, it will fester in the darkness and gain a stronger hold within us.

Thirdly, Ignatius likens the conduct of the enemy to the tactics of a shrewd military commander. He will explore the walls of a fortress to see if he can find the weakest spot, the place of least resistance. He will then hammer away at this spot with all his forces until it caves in. In the same way, the enemy looks for our weakest spot, where our defenses are weakest, and concentrates his attack there, trying to take it by storm. It is crucial to have self-knowledge, to know where we are most vulnerable to temptation, and seek to strengthen this area.

Strategy for Preventing Temptation

Jesus told his disciples in the Garden of Gethsemane that they were to stay awake and to pray not to be put to the test (Mt 26:41). This is a succinct summary of the best strategy to avoid falling into temptation: watch and pray. Firstly, there is a need for *vigilance*. We should never become presumptuous. The enemy attacks when we least expect. At a time of consolation and peace we should still be alert. The enemy does not sleep. And, thanks be to God, nor does the Lord Jesus Christ, and all his angels and saints. In Ephesians we are encouraged to put on the armour of God "or you will not be able to put up any resistance when the worst happens or have enough resources to hold your ground" (Eph 6:13).

Paul speaks of different parts of the armour (Eph 6:14-17). We should have "truth buckled around the waist". This is the truth of who God is and who I am, which is humility. Humility is the one virtue the enemy cannot imitate. No wonder Michael, the Archangel, who leads the heavenly hosts in the spiritual battle, has a name which means "Who can compare with God?" The fundamental temptation of Lucifer was to want to usurp God, the sin of eternal pride. So, in the Book of Revelations all who prostrate before the beast cry out "Who can compare with the beast?", a parody of Michael's name. If we remain humble before God, Satan, who is consummate pride, cannot touch us.

Paul goes on to speak of "righteousness for a breastplate". This firstly refers to the gift of righteousness that comes through faith, making us in right relationship with God. Secondly, it refers to moral righteousness, right living according to God's commandments. This is our protection, when all areas of our life are submitted to God's law. Then, even the weakest and most vulnerable area has greatest protection. Paul also speaks of "wearing for shoes on your feet the eagerness to spread the gospel of peace". How important it is to avoid lethargy and sloth! The devil makes quick work of idle hands. Self-focus and introspection provide ready access for the evil one. The best form of defense against the enemy is offense i.e., to actively engage in proclaiming the gospel. Matthew's gospel assures us that the gates of hell will not be able to hold against the Church when she is fulfilling the great commission (Mt 16:18, cf 28:10).

Paul says we defend ourselves by "always carrying the shield of faith, so that you can use it to put out the fiery arrows of the evil one". Instead of being filled with anxiety and fear that would make us sink in the storm, like Peter on the sea of Galilee, we are called to maintain our focus on Jesus with a living faith in his power to save. The psalmist assures us that when you dwell in the shelter of the most high God then "you will not fear the terror of the night, nor the arrow that flies by day…" (Ps 91:1,5). No matter what temptations the enemy fires at us they will bounce off with no effect if the shield of faith is in place, and we have our eyes fixed on our Saviour.

Paul continues: "And then you must accept salvation from God to be your helmet". This is the call to guard the mind. The mind should be rooted in the truth of the salvation attained by the Crucified Jesus. When we have this helmet on we know that victory has been won by the cross of Jesus. It has been applied to our lives through baptism and renewed often in Eucharist. We have an active mind, filling our minds with everything that is good, true, beautiful, and holy (Phil 4:8). Finally, Paul says to have always ready the "sword of the Spirit", which is the word of God to use as a sword. This is a reference to the scriptural word, that we should have memorised and have ready to use against any attack from the evil one. Jesus did this when tempted in the desert. After Satan had misquoted scripture in order to confuse him, Jesus was able to draw from the Old Testament the texts that rebutted everything Satan had suggested.

The second area of our strategy against temptation is *prayer*. Paul exhorts, "Pray all the time, asking for what you need, praying in the Spirit on every possible occasion" (Eph 6:18). Jesus taught us to pray to the Father, "lead us not into temptation", that we be protected from the wiles of the enemy. Alphonsus Liguori regarded prayer of petition as a means that is "both necessary and certain to obtain salvation and all the graces that we need for it".[19] He points out that it is only by grace that we attain salvation, and that in God's ordinary providence we do not obtain grace unless we ask for it. He challenges us to realise that if we have fallen into sin in the past "the cause of it was that you neglected to beseech God and to seek from him the help needed to battle against the trials with which you were afflicted".[20] Jesus assures us "Ask and it will be given to you…" (Mt 7:7).

No matter how great the battle in our lives, if we beg the Lord he will always deliver us from the hands of the enemy. If we have a particularly weak area, then we should saturate it in prayer. In his mercy he will protect us in our brokenness, and what was previously a problem area will become in time a source of grace for many. It is especially annoying to the evil one if we give our temptations to the Lord as an offering, and hence turn them into a means of giving glory to God and a means of grace for us. This is the exact opposite outcome that the enemy is seeking, and he will not persist on that path for long.

In the spiritual battle we are not meant to be alone. We are meant to be part of a vigilant and praying *community*. This can be illustrated by returning briefly to the image of the Roman armour. The Emperor's soldiers carried long shields as high as themselves. These shields were designed to lock together as the army advanced against the enemy. Paul was writing to a community, not to a group of isolated individuals. We are intended to be "locked together" in committed relationships in Christ. This is our protection.

Jesus used another image to emphasise the importance of community. The wolf, he warns, comes to scatter the sheep, to divide and to conquer (Jn. 10:12). The Good Shepherd has laid down his life for his sheep "to gather together in unity the scattered children of God" (Jn 11:52). We must gather closely with the Good Shepherd and heed his voice, remaining within his flock, under his watchful care. The wolf will attack those who are straggling or have strayed from the flock. Our protection is in being together close to the Shepherd.

In Scripture it says, "A three-fold cord is not quickly broken" (Ecc 4:12). One strand of a cord is easily broken. Two strands may be snapped under pressure also. But three strands become difficult to break. Even more strands woven together make it impossible to break the cord. Community is like this. When we intertwine our lives with others in Christian community there is a built-in protection from the wiles of the evil one. As Jesus said: "For where two or three meet in my name, I shall be there with them" (Mt 18:20). A community gathered in his name, praying continuously for its members, and providing a context of support in the time of battle, provides optimal conditions for the individual to attain victory over temptations and walk confidently as a son or daughter of God.

Handling the Moment of Temptation

In the heat of a time of temptation there are some important points to remember:

- Do not enter into conversation with the temptation, discussing within yourself possibilities and the reasons why or why not you should do this. Remember the folly of Eve.
- Do not toy or flirt with the temptation. This is already opening the door to having your will conquered by the enemy.
- Do not try to tackle it head on and wrestle with it. i.e. by focusing on the temptation itself. You will more than likely find yourself embroiled. Rather than look the temptation in the face, flee to the Lord and gaze upon him.
- Rely upon the authority of Jesus to overcome it. You may choose to rebuke it (e.g., In the name of Jesus I rebuke Satan and all evil spirits). However, don't fall into the trap of becoming excessively aggressive. One rebuke is enough and then fly to Jesus.
- Most important of all is to fly to Jesus. Cling to his feet. Implore his help. Cry out in prayer for him to come and to assist you. Remember to call upon Our Lady of victories, who has crushed the head of the serpent. Her intercession and the protection of her prayers is powerful. Michael the Archangel is strong in the spiritual battle as well.
- Refuse to consent with your will, even though the temptation persists, seems overwhelming, and you are aware of in-

voluntary pleasure. This is not sin if your will remains in the Lord's will and does not yield.

- Move in the opposite spirit. Do the opposite to what is suggested. For example, you are tempted to slander. Then begin to speak well of the person. You are tempted to selfishness. Then make a generous act of self-sacrifice.

- Sometimes direct mental resistance to a temptation can inflame the temptation. The more you try to deal with the thoughts and images the more they seem to assert their power. This can be the case with suggestions of sexual impurity or when doubts of faith arise. In these cases, it can be best to simply distance yourself, and become absorbed in something totally different. It is best to distract yourself by relocating if possible and engaging in an activity, such as a hobby or a game, which will absorb the imagination and the memory.

- Remain calm. Do not get anxious. Anxiety is a great killer in the spiritual life. When the heart is troubled it loses the strength to maintain virtue and loses the means to resist temptation. This anxiety can be rooted in a pride which cannot accept the reality of the temptation. We ask ourselves "How can this be? I shouldn't be experiencing such a crass temptation at my stage in the spiritual journey!" We can have an unreal expectation of our own perfection and an inordinate desire for holiness. Remember that Jesus was tempted in every way we are (Heb. 4:15). When we think of all the ways human beings are tempted we cannot somehow exempt ourselves, as if we live on an angelic plane higher than that of the incarnate Son of God himself!

- Be open with your spiritual director. Lay open your heart to your director—all the suggestions, feelings, affections and movements of the heart. Remember the enemy delights in working in the dark. Bring everything to the light and you will walk free.

3
BECOMING FIRE
Freedom for Christ

"Christ Jesus… by God's doing has become… our virtue and our holiness." (1Cor 1:30)

Our conversion is never complete. In Chapter Two we were exploring the negative side of the process—the on-going fight against the powers of sin, the devil, the world and the flesh. The redeeming power of Jesus brings us freedom *from* these forces that threaten to dehumanise us. Now it is time to talk about the positive side of the conversion process, which brings us freedom *for* deeper union with Christ. God's aim is to shape us by the work of the Spirit into the image of Jesus, his Son. He does this by developing in us *virtues*.

Growing in Virtues

Virtue is a steadfastness and ease in doing good, springing from the heart of a person under the action of the Holy Spirit. Growth in virtue is not attained by a naturalistic, humanistic program to try and build up a person's character. It is brought about by the action of the Holy Spirit, who is the change-agent. We cooperate with his initiative and action. We grow in virtue to the extent that we live in Christ. Jesus said: "I am the vine; you are the branches. If you abide in me and I in you, you shall bear fruit in plenty. For cut off from me you can do nothing" (Jn 15:5). Virtues are the fruit of the indwelling of the Holy Spirit, the abiding of Christ's life within the person. Cut off from this indwelling of Christ we can do nothing towards genuine growth in virtue.

Grace perfects nature. We have natural powers of intellect, will, memory and imagination, which have been wounded and impaired by original sin. Now, by the healing and elevating grace of Christ they can be restored to right functioning, and we are able to act in a God-like manner. This cannot happen by the mere exertion of human effort, or the steeling of the will to do better than before. It is gift from God, his supernatural action working in and through our natural powers to bring forth good fruit. As Paul says: "For anyone who is in Christ there is a new creation; the old creation has gone, and now the new one is here. It is all God's work." (2Cor 5:17). God is about a work of "image-restoration". We were created in his image and likeness. Yet we have fallen, and now lack the capacity to function as we were intended for our true happiness. In his mercy he has redeemed us in Christ, who dwells within us by the Holy Spirit. The Spirit brings regeneration. We are being restored to our original dignity and beauty. The flowering of the virtues is the fruit of this restoration work.

Virtues are deep interior attitudes of the heart. They are habits of the heart. The heart, in biblical thinking, is the core of the person, the centre from which all attitudes, thoughts, desires and feelings flow. The Lord is about transformation of the heart. To the extent that the heart truly surrenders to the Lord, to that extent can the recreating Spirit enter into the depths of the person and change us from the inside to the outside. Jesus said that a "sound tree cannot bear bad fruit, nor a rotten tree bear good fruit" (Mt 7:18). If the heart is becoming pure, it will be single-minded for the Lord, and all the faculties and interior energies will be focused on Jesus and his kingdom. In this way, good fruit will emerge, even to the surprise of the person concerned.

The focus, then, should not be on some program of growth, as such, but on the Lord himself, who is the author of all growth. The more we simply surrender our hearts to him in love, the more he can fashion in us his attitudes, his mind, his outlook, his actions. Paul expresses this beautifully when he says, "but you, God has made members of Christ Jesus and by God's doing he (Christ) has become our wisdom, and our virtue, and our holiness, and our freedom" (1Cor 1:30). And elsewhere Paul underlines the point by saying, "We are God's work of art, created in Christ Jesus to live the good life as from the beginning he had meant us to live it" (Eph 2:10).

The Lord Jesus changes us into his likeness in many ways. A most privileged way is receiving him in Holy Communion. The ordinary food we eat is assimilated into our bodies for energy. But the Eucharistic food, which is the bread of life, Christ Jesus himself, acts in the opposite way. Instead of us assimilating Christ into our system, we are assimilated into him. His purpose in coming is to change us into himself. If we surrender to him, he will form in us his attitudes, values and ways of thinking, even though we are largely unaware of it at that time.

A beautiful and powerful extension of this transforming process is in Eucharistic adoration outside of the Mass. When we place ourselves in love before Jesus in the Blessed Sacrament, especially as the exposed host, we are giving him the space to touch deeply into our hearts and to change us. To be with the Beloved in love is to become like the Beloved. He puts his fire of love within us and energises us with his Spirit. We are drawn into him and we are made into other Christs for the sake of a hungry world.

Having emphasised that growth in virtue is God's action within us, it is necessary to also stress that we are not meant to be totally passive in the process. We honour the primacy of God's activity by praying often for growth in virtue, and by surrendering our hearts to him. However, we have to work hard at developing these good habits. Habitual orientations of the heart are formed by developing good habits of the mind and the imagination, and deliberately changing behavioural patterns, which do not measure up to God's commandments. For example, we should pray for chastity, but if we choose to enter occasions of sin, or if we refuse to discipline our eyes, then the habit can never really develop. We may pray for growth in charity and do long vigils to try and attain it. However, unless we begin to control our tongues from gossip and slander the habit of loving speech cannot develop.

Sometimes people will sit around in their armchair and pray to be able to develop a servant heart. What they really need to do is to actively get engaged in some service of others, and in the process, God will develop the gift more genuinely within them. External actions shape interior attitudes. If you want to grow in a particular way, then begin to act in that way. For example, you want to grow in a compassionate heart for the poor? Certainly, pray for the grace and draw close to Jesus in the Blessed Sacrament from which your power will come. But then actually go and embrace the poor in some activity which will help develop the heart in this way. Francis of Assisi was only converted to the poor through choosing not to flee from the leper who he encountered unexpectedly on the road. Even though he found the leper to be repulsive, he actually chose to embrace him. Afterwards he spent months living in the nearby leper colony allowing his heart to be formed in the way of Jesus.

When we begin to pray for a particular virtue, by the providence of our good God, opportunities arise that will aid us in this growth. For example, you pray for greater patience, and, sure enough, there appears in your circle of acquaintances a person whom you just can't stand! Here is your opportunity for growth! Or you pray for greater humility, and, quite unexpectedly someone accuses you of something outrageous, or you are totally humiliated in an unfair way. These are God's tricks of providence to help us get where we want go! The way you handle these opportunities determines whether they become means for growth, or irritations leading to bitterness and disillusionment.

We develop a steadfastness and ease in doing good over time. With the Spirit's work within us, and our cooperation, we develop a consistency in our good habit patterns. In the early stages of our growth, as we are trying to curb bad habits, we can be very erratic and inconstant. However, over time the Lord gives us greater confidence in our ability to do his will. The dominant inclination of our will becomes to do what he wants, and we find a new ease in doing good. For example, beginners in the journey can find their minds very disordered through wrongful fantasies. It can seem like this could never change. But as they grow closer to Jesus, and allow the Spirit to penetrate more deeply, and as they work hard at disciplining the mind, especially nailing all unruly thoughts to the cross of Jesus, they find a growing victory in that area, and a new peace that surpasses understanding.

Sometimes beginners can become "problem-centred" in their spiritual journey. This is a trap because it focusses on the problem, rather than on the solution that can be found in Christ. People can even fall in love with their problem, and adopt the attitude that Christianity is a dismal struggle with little hope of victory. For example, someone with a habit of unwarranted outbursts of anger may be content with the rationalisation: "That's how I am; I'll never change; you just have to accept me as I am!" This is defeatism.

The grace of God is available for the person to grow into a gentleness and meekness of spirit. God accepts us in our intrinsic value and dignity as persons "as we are". However, it is a mistake to think that we have the right to justify sinful behaviour by claiming "you will just have to accept me as I am". What the person is really saying is "I don't want to change my sinful behaviour". That attitude is not acceptable to God, because he loves us so much. He is not willing to leave us floundering in the mess of our sin. He gives us the power to move out of it.

Sometimes people create a pit for themselves and sit in it full of self-pity and self-justification. In John's Gospel there is a story of a paralysed man who had been waiting by the pool of Bethesda for 38 years. The angel of the Lord came intermittently to disturb the waters of the pool. The first person to enter the water after the disturbance was healed. Now this man had been around the pool for 38 years. He had not yet devised a strategy for getting into the pool first. One would have to wonder whether he really *wanted* to be healed! Notice the question Jesus asked him, "Do you *want* to be well again?" In reply the man pours out a lamentable sob-story about not being able to get to the pool first. Jesus simply says: "Get up! Pick up your sleeping mat and walk!" (Jn 5:1-9).

For the Lord to heal us and to restore us he needs to know that we really want this transformation. Many people cling to their sicknesses of heart and to their bad habits, because these things have become part of their identity. They are frightened of shedding them and taking on their new dignity in Christ. The Lord does not force his hand upon us. He asks us the question, which he asked the paralysed man. "Do you *want* to be healed?"

For growth in virtue, we must make every effort we can, but all our best efforts will be to no avail without the mercy of God. Thérèse of Lisieux[21] encourages us to be in touch with our utter helplessness, to know our weakness and nothingness before God; how impossible it is to change ourselves. In this experience of our littleness we are able to say from the heart with conviction these three words that can change our life: "I CAN NOT!" Then, in union with Mary, we are able to say by grace, "YES, LORD, YOU CAN!" ("Let it be done to me according to your word"). If we have this kind of surrender of heart, then we will discover the power of God. Wishful thinking, resolutions, or stoic will power, will not produce change. Rather, when we accept our human impossibility, then we discover the God of all possibility, "for nothing is impossible to God" (Lk 1:37).

Jesus said: "Unless you change and become like little children you will never enter the kingdom of heaven" (Mt 18:4). We have to learn to expect everything from God, the Father, as a child expects with confidence. Thérèse[22] offers the image of a child at the foot of the stair-case. The stair-case represents the seemingly insurmountable ascent in holiness through acquiring the virtues. The child is unable even to raise herself onto the first step. This is how incapable we are of acquiring virtue, and to do anything by ourselves for our salvation and sanctification. Yet the child is determined to get to the top of the stairs and perseveres.

Thérèse says the practice of the virtues is like that. We must work with the same desire, determination and perseverance as this child, even though we experience our helplessness and apparent failure. Meanwhile, at the top of the staircase is the loving Father, waiting with a heart of mercy, delighting in the feeble efforts of his child. His heart is won and he runs down the staircase, swoops up his child into his arms, and carries her forever into his kingdom. Thérèse says wistfully if you stop lifting your foot in perseverance, he will leave you there a long time. The strength of the request and the quality of the love in our hearts is what counts. When we cry out "I can't do it!" we are not to cry with self-pity or despair, but with utter confidence in the great mercy of our Father, and his majestic power to be able to do anything to save us.

As we perceive virtues growing in our life and maybe receive feedback from others, we must be careful not to think that these virtues are of our own making. John of the Cross refers to the virtues and spiritual gifts as "flowers and emeralds".[23] The virtues are flowers because they are so delicate; one puff of the wrong kind of wind and they are gone. They are developed, he says, in the "cool morning" i.e., we work hard at virtues, especially in our youth. They are woven in the soul by God and by ourselves—bound together by "one hair of my head". What is this one hair? It is *perseverance*. The only part of the process that is truly ours is our "yes", our persevering in response. The rest belongs to God. It is all his work. All he asks of us is to desire, to yield, and not to give up. Thérèse of Lisieux echoes this notion when she warns that one proud thought, voluntarily entertained (for example, that I have acquired a certain virtue by my own strength), means running the risk of falling into the abyss.

Theological and Moral Virtues

Traditionally the Christian virtues have been divided into two main categories—theological virtues and moral virtues. The theological virtues are faith, hope and charity. They are called "theological" because they draw us into divine life with God. Faith takes us beyond the confines of human knowledge to the truths revealed by God. Hope takes us beyond the finite limitations of the journey of this world to be able to fix our gaze upon God as our ultimate end. Charity enables us to love God above all things and in and through all things. Each of these virtues deepens us directly in our relationship with God. Faith involves the commitment of the whole person in full submission of mind and will to God who reveals himself. Hope brings the assurance of salvation already attained through the indwelling gift of the Spirit, and it guarantees the fulness of salvation yet to come. Charity is the virtue that unites us most intimately with God (1Cor 13:13). It is a supernatural habit infused by God into the will, enabling us to love God for himself above all things, and also to love our neighbour as ourselves.

The moral virtues are infused supernatural habits also. They are prudence, justice, fortitude and temperance. Each one of these virtues develops as the grace of God modifies and orients in a new way one of the interior faculties of the person. Prudence is infused by God into the practical intellect to bring right judgement of our actions, so that they give glory to God and fulfil our ultimate end and purpose in life. Justice is infused by God into the will inclining our decisions toward right and proper ordering of relationships according to God's plan. Temperance is a supernatural habit that empowers us to moderate the drive to sensual pleasure. It controls the movements of what the tradition has called the "concupiscible appetite". Fortitude is the infused supernatural habit which strengthens the "irascible appetite" and the will. It empowers us to endure through trials, dangers, persecutions, and ordeals; and to persevere in the work of the kingdom of God, the preaching of the Good News, and doing good.

Rather than give a detailed presentation of all the virtues according to this classical framework, it will be sufficient here to focus on just three virtues which are keys to the spiritual life. Their presence is generally regarded by spiritual writers as the best way to ascertain genuine holiness. They are practical love of one's neighbour, humility, and obedience. When these are flowering in a person's life there is genuine love of God, and the other virtues will also be evident.

Practical Love

Thérèse of Lisieux, confined to a Carmelite convent, found within her young heart great desires for sanctity. She wanted to be a warrior for God, a confessor, and a martyr. While she felt the utter powerlessness and littleness of her condition, she still held these enormous desires in her heart. Surely, she reasoned, the good and merciful God would not inspire these desires and not give her a way of realising them! One day in the midst of this interior struggle she opened the Scriptures and came upon this text from St. Paul:

> Be ambitious for the higher gifts. And I am going to show you a way that is better than any of them. If I have all the eloquence of men or of angels, but speak without love, I am simply a gong booming or a cymbal clashing. If I have the gift of prophecy, understanding all the mysteries there are, and knowing everything, and if I have faith in all its fulness, to move mountains, but without love, then I am nothing at all. If I give away all that I possess, piece by piece, and if I even let them take my body to burn it, but am without love, it will do me no good whatever... (1Cor 12:31-13:3)

Thérèse was overcome with a new revelation from this text. She could see that there are different members of the body of Christ. All cannot be apostles, martyrs, doctors etc. Yet there is a more excellent way—the way of love. As she considered the body of Christ, the Church, she saw herself not with any particular ministry; rather she saw herself in _all_ of the ministries. The Church had a heart, and it is love alone in the heart of the Church that makes it act. Love comprises all vocations. She cried out "My vocation is love!"[24] She was now content to find her place in the heart of the Church and simply be love. She could see that "the smallest act of pure love will pierce through the heavens".

St. Teresa of Avila would say that the surest sign of genuine spiritual advancement is a deep love of our neighbour. She would maintain that extraordinary experiences in prayer are somewhat irrelevant as a criterion of holiness. She stands with the Scriptures when it states, "Anyone who says 'I love God' and hates his brother is a liar, since a man who does not love the brother that he can see cannot love God, whom he has never seen. So this is the commandment that he has given us, that anyone who loves God must also love his brother" (1Jn 4:20-21).

When Teresa is dealing with the state of union, which is a high degree of prayer, she says, "The Lord asks of us only two things: love of his Majesty and love of our neighbour. These are what we must work for. By observing them with perfection, we do his will and so will be united with him…".[25] She goes on to lament how far we are from fulfilling this double commandment, and how much we should by God's grace be able to do so. Then she gives the wisdom of the ages as she continues:

> The most certain sign, in my opinion, as to whether or not

we are observing these two laws is whether we observe well the love of neighbour. We cannot know whether or not we love God, although there are strong indications for recognising that we do love him; but we can know whether we love our neighbour. And be certain that the more advanced you will be in love for your neighbour the more advanced you will be in the love of God, for the love his Majesty has for us is so great that to repay us for our love of neighbour he will in a thousand ways increase the love we have for him.[26]

Teresa, speaking of practical love as the criterion of holiness, is not referring to good works regardless of their motive. It is a love from the heart, which is formed by grace. Paul says to the Romans, "Do not let your love be a pretense…" (Rom 12:9). That is, make sure your love is without hypocrisy. Peter also tells us, "Let your love for each other be real and from the heart" (1Pet 1:22). While charity is meant to be active in doing good works, these good works will not be a sign or means of holiness unless they come from a genuinely sincere heart.

To speak about love is not easy because there are many meanings of the word in the English language. When in the gospels we hear Jesus say, "love one another as I have loved you", the word in the Greek is *agape*. This is God's way of loving. For clarity we need to distinguish it from other meanings of love. For example, the popular songs are always urging us that "love is all you need", but they are speaking of "romantic love". This type of love is based in sexual attraction. It becomes distorted through lust. Sexual love is good, but it is not what Jesus was talking about.

Another way we speak about love is to refer to the "blood ties" of family and relatives. This type of filial love runs deep and is good. In some cultures, the obligations of family love are much greater than in others. Nevertheless, it is a God-given love that is regarded in the Scriptures as binding on all. Yet this is not what Jesus was referring to either. In fact, those with *agape* love may find that this love divides families. Jesus warned his followers that during persecutions even family members may turn against them with violence (Lk 21:16).

We also use the word love to denote "friendship", a relationship based on mutual attraction, with similar interests and goals. Again, this is not what *agape* means, since Jesus says, "Love your enemies... For if you love those who love you, what right have you to claim any credit? Even the tax-collectors do as much, do they not?" (Mt 5:46). Friendship is a beautiful God-given gift, but *agape* love transcends even this kind of human affection as well.

Agape love is the way God has loved us. He empowers us to do the same. It is not based on attraction towards others because of their intelligence, wit, good looks, or ideals. It is not a question of whether we like the other person, but rather a decision to seek the other's good for their own sake. God chose to love us when we were at enmity with him as a result of sin. This way of loving is not about bodily chemistry, or emotional intimacy. It is about a deep respect for the inherent dignity of each person who is created in the image and likeness of God, and unconditional acceptance of each person, and decision to do good for the other person for their own sake. It is not exclusive, possessive or manipulative. It is a love built into us by Christ himself who dwells in us by his Spirit.

Our hearts are changed so we adopt his attitudes towards others and we act towards others as he would. This sort of love is not self-serving in any way. Paul exhorted the Philippians to humble service of one another "so that nobody thinks of his own interests first but everybody thinks of other people's interests instead" (Phil 2:4). *Agape* love works for the best of the other by self- sacrifice. As John says of Jesus, "This has taught us love—that he gave up his life for us; and we, too, ought give up our lives for our brothers" (1Jn 3:16). We follow Jesus by embracing his cross daily, losing ourselves for the sake of others so that we may gain ourselves.

Agape love is not opposed to family love. In fact, an affectionate, faithful and unconditional love experienced in early family life provides fertile psychological soil for this virtue to develop in later years. Those from dysfunctional families often have scars that need healing before their capacity to love unconditionally can develop. Furthermore, *agape* love is the way that the natural family bonds can be expressed most freely and productively.

Ideally each Christian family, and indeed each Christian community, should be characterised by this way of disinterested love. Nor is *agape* love in opposition to romance. It is the way that romantic love becomes properly ordered, otherwise it becomes self-seeking, possessive and destructive. Friendship also cannot flower and reach its full potential without being permeated with *agape* love. Otherwise, it can collapse into an exclusive huddle and fall into emotional dependency. *Agape* love should permeate all the relationships of Christians. Jesus said: "By this love you have for one another, everyone will know that you are my disciples" (Jn 13:35).

Our capacity to love others as Jesus has loved us is connected to our capacity to have a healthy love of ourselves. If we hate ourselves, we will unconsciously hate others. If we are harsh on ourselves, we will be inclined to be harsh on others. On the other hand, if we are gentle on ourselves, we are more likely to be gentle towards others. If we are angry at ourselves, and full of self-condemnation, we will probably be angry towards others, and condemning their behaviour. If we are forgiving of ourselves and compassionate towards our imperfections, we will be more capable of forgiving others and being compassionate towards them. If we are impatient with ourselves, we may well be impatient with others. On the other hand, if we are patient with our own failings, we will be patient with others when they fail us.

Jesus commanded us to "love your neighbour **as yourself**". If we do not love ourselves then we cannot love our neighbour. When we give our lives to Christ, and invite him to form his life in us, we are to die to the old self. This does not mean a depletion of our self-image, or a loss of self-worth. By making a home for Christ within us we become more at home with ourselves. And being more at home with ourselves we are more free to be at home with others, and to welcome them into our "home" without fear. The more we personally experience the unconditional and intensely personal love of God the more we discover our lovableness. As St. Augustine put it tersely: "Because You have loved me, You have made me lovable".[27] And knowing we are loved and lovable, empowers us to love others in the same way.

We are called to love with the same love with which Christ has loved us. That means that our capacity to love genuinely depends on our heart union with Christ. In a very real sense, it is Christ who loves in and through us. To grow in love we must imitate Christ. We can meditate on the gospels and model ourselves on what he did, how he loved. This will inspire us in following him. But to imitate Christ is more than this. It is to be "clothed" in Christ, to be transformed into him.

Once Paul spoke about himself, "I have been crucified with Christ, and I live now not with my own life but with the life of

Christ who lives in me" (Gal 2:19). We can alter the words slightly to emphasise the point we are making about love, "I have been crucified with Christ, and I *love* now not with my own *love* but with the *love* of Christ who lives in me". The aim is that Christ be formed in us, so that his own way of loving become evident in our lives. The more we become in communion with Christ who dwells in us the more we begin to identify with him. As we embrace Jesus in loving surrender, we have his gentleness, his patience, his generosity, his compassion formed in us.

To grow in practical love is to lay down all bad judgements on others. Jesus said: "Do not judge and you will not be judged… why do you observe the splinter in your brother's eye and never notice the plank in your own?" (Mt 7:1-3). In James we are challenged "who are you to give a verdict on your neighbour?" (Jm 4:12). We do not know what is in the heart of the other person. Only God knows. We cannot see the full picture. If we presume to judge the other we seek to take role of God himself. Just because we cannot see any virtue in a person does not mean that God cannot see something that is invisible to us.

The more we are becoming like Christ the more we will be able to see the good in the other and rejoice in the virtue that we find there. Interestingly psychologists speak of the phenomenon of "projection", where we tend to "project" onto others our own unconscious struggles. Maybe when we judge another we are simply finding in them what we are too frightened to face in ourselves. This is the "log in your own eye" which Jesus speaks about. Being harsh on others often is a sign of interior struggles that we are not facing up to ourselves. The very thing we are quick to condemn in others can be the area of darkness that we are not willing to address within ourselves.

To grow in love of others is to learn to forgive. Resentment and bitterness are major obstacles to genuine spiritual growth. Jesus told the story of a servant who could not pay his master the equivalent of six million dollars which he owed (Mt 18:23-35). The servant was to be sold with his wife and children into slavery to pay the debt. At this the servant threw himself at the master's feet and begged for mercy. The master was so moved with pity that he cancelled the whole debt! Then as the servant was leaving, he met a fellow servant, who owed him a measly ten dollars. He began to throttle his fellow servant and had him thrown into prison until he could pay the debt. What ingratitude! Jesus is saying we can be like this.

Out of his infinite mercy God has cancelled the debt owing to sin, which we had no hope of paying. Jesus nailed that debt to the cross, through his suffering for our sake (Col 2:14). Yet how easily we can lack gratitude for such an enormous gift, and become like the unforgiving servant, demanding "pay-back" from people who have offended us in some way or another. If we seek revenge, demanding that people make up for our loss, and make good the debt to our hurt feelings, our fate will be the same as the ungrateful servant in the parable. He was "handed over to the torturers". Indeed, unforgiveness is a form of torture, which we inflict on ourselves. It twists and distorts the human spirit, and brings severe emotional bondage, which can even at times be evident in bodily sickness. The master in the story said to the servant: "Were you not bound, then, to have pity on your fellow servant, just as I had pity on you?" So the Lord would address us.

Inside ourselves we can be quite constricted because we, as it were, are holding a clenched fist up against another person. Often, we hold a fist up against someone from the distant past, whom we still haven't forgiven. Forgiveness is releasing the grip, deciding to let the matter go, and giving it all over to the Lord. We need to stop the "blame-game".

By our own making we are dwarfed as human beings if we continue to blame others for the unfortunate and painful episodes in our life-journey. Regardless of the feelings that we are still carrying within us, we can still decide by the grace of God to forgive. When Jesus was being nailed to the cross, in the midst of all the agony of Roman crucifixion, he chose not to use his divine power to smite the soldiers, but he forgave: "Father forgive them…" (Lk 23:34). These are liberating words for all of us. No matter what the injustice that has been dealt to us, no matter how profoundly we have been personally offended, we can choose to forgive.

A touching story is told by Corrie Ten Boom,[28] who, as I related earlier had watched her sister Betsie die as a result of maltreatment in Ravensbruck Nazi prison camp during the Second World War. After the war Corrie travelled the world sharing about her experiences and preaching forgiveness as a way to peace. One evening, after giving a message in a small church in Munich, she was approached by a woman whom she immediately recognised. She was one the SS guards in the camp responsible for the brutal treatment of her and her sister. As she approached, Corrie felt anger and hatred rise up within her with real vehemence. This shocked her because she had not been aware of these forces within her. The former prison guard spoke, "You mentioned Ravensbruck in your talk. I was a guard there". Corrie realised that she did not remember her. But she remembered this guard, and she was horrified to be talking with one of her captors. The woman went on to say, "I have become a Christian now. I know that God has forgiven me for the cruel things I did there, but I would like to hear it from your lips as well". She extended a hand towards Corrie, asking "Will you forgive me?" Corrie was frozen to the spot. Her hand would not move. In her desperation she prayed silently "Jesus, help me!" She woodenly thrust out her hand, with no feeling at all. And then she felt a warmth flood her, and by the grace of God she found herself saying, and meaning it, "I forgive you, with all my heart!"

That ex-prison officer had been given the most precious gift, which she did not deserve—the gift of forgiveness. She went away with her burden lifted. Corrie too had found a deeper freedom within herself through making a decision by the grace of God not to be governed by her feelings, but to forgive her sister from the heart.

Often people carry buried hurts and grievances from traumatic incidents in the past which have been repressed below consciousness because they are far too painful to handle. As the Spirit of God moves in our lives, he brings these painful memories to light. Usually, the key to healing is through forgiveness of the person or group who were responsible for the damage done. This process of inner healing can be deeply disturbing for the person concerned. Sometimes, people find it helpful to allow the Spirit to recreate the scene where the hurt occurred, and to invite Jesus, who is not bound by time, to enter the scene. This imaginative exercise can bring beautiful results as the person experiences Jesus ministering and embracing him or her, and empowering the person to bestow forgiveness on the perpetrator of the injustice.

When we are finding it difficult to forgive, it can be helpful to imagine ourselves at the foot of the cross with the person we need to forgive. Standing together with the offender at the foot of the cross, we realise that it is only because of the mercy of God that any of us can stand at all! As the psalmist says: "If you never overlooked our sins, Lord, could anyone survive? But you do forgive us: and for that we revere you" (Ps. 130:3-4). It is the blood of Jesus which makes us one and brings peace (Col 1:20). Standing at the foot of the cross we can allow the precious blood of Jesus, shed for each of us, to soften our hearts and empower us to forgive and to embrace the other from the heart.

Forgiveness is essential for the life of any community. As a car without oil will seize up and dysfunction, so a community without forgiveness will seize up and dysfunction. Forgiveness is the lubricant that keeps relationships functioning as they should be. Paul says: "Forgive each other as soon as a quarrel begins" (Col 3:13), and "never let the sun set on your anger or else you will give the devil a foothold" (Eph 4:27).

We are to strive to be reconciled with our brothers and sisters. This means humbly acknowledging our fault when we have offended another and seeking their forgiveness. Jesus says: "if you are bringing your offering to the altar and there remember that your brother has something against you, leave your offering there before the altar, go and be reconciled with your brother first, and then come back and present your offering" (Mt 5:23). It also means a readiness to have mercy on one another and readily bestow forgiveness when it is sought. The person seeking forgiveness should be quite honest and straightforward in confessing fault, and the person bestowing forgiveness should do so simply and explicitly with the words "I forgive you", or similar words, to leave the other in no doubt that forgiveness has been granted.

Another important principle in reconciliation is given by Jesus: "If your brother does something wrong, go and have it out with him alone, between your two selves" (Mt 18:15). In other words, do not gossip about it, or complain about it to others; this brings the other into disrepute. We need to go to the other, and without judgement or condemnation, raise the matter and begin to sort it out together. Usually, for resolution these conflicts require mutual admission of fault and mutual forgiveness. For any genuine growth in holiness, we should be committed to being reconciled with anyone with whom there has been damaging conflict. An unwillingness to be reconciled is a sign of a blockage in growth in holiness. Jesus says: "Happy are the peacemakers, they shall be called sons of God" (Mt 5:9).

One of the greatest challenges to love, as Jesus has loved, comes when we are confronted with false accusation that cannot easily be defended, or when we have a judgement held against us by another even though we have tried to be reconciled, or when we are belittled and humiliated by someone before the eyes of others and have no way to redress the situation, or when we are persecuted because of our faith. These kinds of situations call for heroic love that flows from the heart of Jesus crucified. When we find ourselves being crucified by others, it is extremely painful, but can become for us a time of great grace. Jesus' words are life: "You have learnt how it was said: You must love your neighbour and hate your enemy. But I say this to you: love your enemies and pray for those who persecute you…" (Mt 5:43-44).

John of the Cross, who was thrown into prison in Toledo by his own brothers, humiliated and beaten by them, was able to return to his cell and write a beautiful lyrical song of love for God. He was able to love his brothers as they beat him. So filled was he with the Spirit of Jesus, who forgave as he was being nailed to the cross. There is a little saying of John's in an obscure letter in which he wrote about the ills he was experiencing at the hands of others: "Think nothing else but that God ordains all, and where there is no love, put love, and you will draw out love".[29] Love will always have the victory even if we have to bear great sufferings in the meantime.

In cases when our good name is being falsely damaged, we have a right to defend ourselves. However, we need a detachment even here. Ignatius Loyola, when he was falsely accused of heresy, was not so much concerned for his own good name, but for the good name of the work of God which was under his care. He fought tooth and nail to bring the case to the highest authorities in Rome, in order to make sure that the work of God would not be impeded. But when it is an offence against our own reputation, we often have no repeal but must surrender to the experience of Jesus crucified. In this way what comes against us can be turned to good. Through the time of humiliation the love of God can be infused more deeply into our souls. The very situation becomes an invitation into the crucifixion of Jesus and so a grace-filled opportunity to become formed in his perfect way of love.

There is much more we could say about the virtue of practical love. There is the challenge to grow in patience, kindness, thoughtfulness, gentleness, generosity, large-heartedness, and so many other fruits of the Spirit (Gal 5:22). But before leaving this topic, we should make a special mention of controlling the tongue. As we are formed into the likeness of Jesus, we need to work hard at taming unruly speech. Paul urges his communities to guard what comes out of their mouths; only to say what is going to be edifying for others and will bring a blessing upon them (Eph 4:29). The person who is genuinely growing in holiness will always speak the word that builds others up, rather than one that tears down. The spoken word is extremely powerful for good or for evil. Edifying conversation is the glue that binds a community together. Destructive conversation is the poison that kills community life bringing dissension, discord and division.

James says: "the only man who could reach perfection would be someone who never said anything wrong—he would be able to control every part of himself" (Jm 3:2). Just as the bit in the horse's mouth keeps the whole animal under control, so does a bridled tongue keep the whole person in self-control. James continues, "Think how a small flame can set fire to a huge forest; the tongue is a flame like that. Among all the parts of the body, the tongue is a whole wicked world in itself; it infects the whole body; catching fire itself from hell… We use it to bless the Lord and Father, but we also use it to curse men who are made in God's image…" (Jm 3:5-12).

People growing in the Spirit will be gaining control of the tongue. They will be eliminating slander, gossip, and negative humour from their conversation. Slander is speaking disparagingly about someone, even though we may be telling the truth. It is speaking against another by revealing things about the person that the listener does not have to know. It is a form of verbal aggression, by which we assassinate another's good name by speaking about their perceived wrong-doing, failures or incompetence. It is even more serious when a false accusation is made. St. Francis de Sales says:

> The detractor, by one blow of his tongue, commonly commits three murders; he kills his own soul, and the soul of him who listens, and takes away the civil life of the person he defames; for as St. Bernard says, 'Both he who detracts, and he who listens to the detractor, they have each the devil about them; the one has him in his tongue, and the other in his ear'.[30]

Francis has a perceptive comment on the way we can try to put a gloss on our detraction by protesting our deep respect for the person we are speaking about, but we tell our audience "the truth must be told". Francis says that just as an archer draws the arrow as near to himself as he can, so he can shoot it with greater force, "so these detractors seem to draw the detraction towards themselves, only to discharge it harder, that it may pierce into the hearts of their hearers the deeper".[31]

Gossip is not such an open form of aggression. It is more subtle, but very deadly. It does not produce outright charges of wrongdoing or incompetence, but spins a web of innuendo and provides information about others on hearsay. The Greek word for gossip, which is listed by Paul amongst the serious vices, has the connotation of "whispering" (2Cor 12:20). It arises from the perverse desire in our hearts to know some juicy information about the affairs of others, and its very mode of transmission ensures a gross distortion of facts is inevitable. The psalmist prays to the Lord, "set a guard at my mouth, a watcher at the gate of my lips!" (Ps 141:3).

Negative humour is a way of slapping someone with a smile. We make jokes of another's mistakes, weaknesses and eccentricities, or poke fun at some embarrassing feature of a person's life. It is often intended as a sign of affection. Sometimes it is used in an indirect way to correct a person. It does not display the loving heart of God. It is dishonouring of the person. Even though it can be an attempt at endearment, it backfires, and creates a climate of negativity and cynicism in which persons do not have room for personal growth. When we are moving in the Spirit of God, we will smile without slapping. When we are genuinely loving we will have a spirit of affirmation, and our words will be positive and upbuilding for others. The reason so many find it difficult to affirm others is their own poor self-image, and perhaps a struggle with envy. It should be a growing characteristic of our lives that we rejoice in the gifts and achievements of others and with a large heart celebrate them in an affirming manner.

Humility

St. Teresa of Avila wrote, "One day I was wondering why God so loves the humble, when it suddenly and unexpectedly struck me that this must be because he is the supreme Truth and humility is truth".[32] Humility is discovered through revelation from God of who he is and who we are before him. As Francis of Assisi used to say, "What a man is before God, that he is and no more". As we grow in the Spirit, we grow more in touch with our creatureliness and our utter dependency on God for everything. The word humility is derived from the Latin word "humus", which means earth or ground, from which the word "humanity" comes, and also, less directly, the word "humour". To be humble is to be well and truly earthed and to be able to laugh at yourself. Humble people cannot take themselves too seriously because they know their own nothingness before God. Paul says in Romans, "I want to urge each one among you not to exaggerate his real importance. Each of you must judge himself soberly…" (Rom 12:3). As we reflect in the Spirit upon our state before God, we realise that everything we have is sheer gift from him. We have nothing to boast about at all. The royal way to humility is through cultivating a deep gratitude to God for everything.

Once I was sitting in the hermitage on the side of Mt. Subasio outside of Assisi, where Francis used to pray. A cat jumped onto my lap. As I sat stroking the contented furry animal, I was having a sort of "Franciscan" experience, I suppose. At that moment, quite unexpectedly the Lord gave me a revelation. Here was this cat, happily purring on my lap, giving glory to God by its very existence, even though it was unaware of doing so. And here was I, a rational creature, with the inestimable dignity of being made in the image and likeness of God himself, and yet so often full of worries about achievement, concern about how I look in the eyes of others, jostling for positions of honour, and manoeuvring to ensure my "greatness". True peace is found in being happy with who I am; to have no pretenses, but simply to give glory to God through being his creature.

Truth is lived neither by self-aggrandisement nor by belittling oneself. Rather we are true to ourselves and to God when we choose to give glory to God by our existence. Then we have a happiness that the cat knows nothing about. We have been created to give glory to God here on earth and to be with him forever in heaven. The blessedness of heaven is already available to the humble; those who choose to accept the truth of their creatureliness, embrace their nothingness before God, and act according to their purpose for being here on earth, which is to give glory to God in all things.

God is attracted to the person of a humble and contrite heart (Ps 51:17). Through Isaiah the Lord says: "With heaven my throne and earth my footstool, what house could you build me, what place could you make for my rest? All of this was made by my hand, and all of this is mine—it is the Lord who speaks—but my eyes are drawn to the man of humbled and contrite heart, who trembles at my word" (Is 66:1-2).

The home where the Lord loves to dwell on earth is in the heart that is genuinely humble. The humble person is the last one to know he or she has this quality. One day Brother Masseo asked Francis of Assisi why the whole world was running after him. Francis replied that it was because God had found no one "less worthy" than himself. "Do you want to know", he asked with great fervour of spirit, "why all the world runs after me? It's because the eyes of the most high God haven't found anyone more vile among sinners, anyone less worthy or more sinful than I am".[33] Teresa declare, "You will know how advanced you are, my daughters, by whether each thinks that she is the most sinful of all; and not by the fact that she receives more favours in prayer and raptures and visions and other graces".[34]

Jesus said after the parable about people jostling for places of honour at the table, "Everyone who exalts himself will be humbled, and the one who humbles himself will be exalted" (Lk 14:11). We need to be clear what is meant by humbling oneself. It does not mean having a low opinion of oneself, thinking you are inferior to others, and feeling bad about yourself. That is an emotional problem called low self-esteem or a poor self-image. It often disguises itself as the spiritual virtue of humility, but nothing could be further from the truth.

C.S. Lewis makes this point in a humorous way in a passage from *The Screwtape Letters*. Screwtape is a senior demon in hell, writing to his nephew, Wormwood, a junior tempter in need of instruction. The man who Wormwood is commissioned to tempt is called satirically the "patient", who is under his "care":

> You must therefore conceal from the patient the true end of humility. Let him think of it, not as self-forgetfulness, but as a certain kind of opinion (namely, a low opinion) of his talents and character. Fix in his mind the idea that hu-

mility consists in trying to believe those talents to be less valuable than he believes them to be... The great thing is to make him value an opinion for some quality other than truth... By this method thousands of humans have been brought to think that humility means pretty women trying to believe they are ugly and clever men trying to believe they are fools. And since what they are trying to believe may, in some cases, be manifest nonsense, they cannot succeed in believing it, and we have the chance of keeping their minds endlessly revolving on themselves in an effort to achieve the impossible.[35]

False humility damages the soul. It is based on a lie. When Paul says, "Each of you must judge himself soberly", he means that we have a *truthful* opinion of ourselves, not a *low* opinion. This means we are able to celebrate our intrinsic goodness in the eyes of God who created us, and use our gifts happily for his glory. On the other hand, in the light of truth, we are able to see how perverse the heart is as a result of sin, and how desperately we need the on-going redeeming work of Christ through his Spirit within us. Humble people know their identity in Christ. They can stand up straight in him as sons and daughters of God. They know their giftedness and are not timid or shy about letting their light shine in the sight of others by using these gifts for the kingdom. There is nothing self-focused about humility. C.S. Lewis observes that the minds of humble people are not "endlessly revolving on themselves in an effort to achieve the impossible". They are not even trying to be humble in a self-conscious way. He reflects on what a truly humble person would look like:

> Do not imagine that if you met a really humble man he will be what most people call 'humble' nowadays. He will not be a sort of greasy, swarmy person, who is always tell-

ing you that, of course, he is nobody. Probably all you will think about him is that he seemed a cheerful intelligent chap who took a real interest in what you said to him. If you do dislike him, it will be because you feel a little envious of anyone who seems to enjoy life so easily. He will not be thinking about humility: he will not be thinking about himself at all.[36]

Humility as Service

Human beings have worshipped many gods over the centuries. We can think of all the ancient Roman and Greek gods, and all the gods of the many Eastern religions, and, indeed the gods of the peoples surrounding the Israelites in biblical times. Whatever qualities these gods of human construction were deemed to have, there was one characteristic that none of them had—and that is humility. Only the one, true God, revealed in Jesus Christ displays genuine humility. He chose to be born in a stable made for animals, not for humans. He went further by humbling himself unto death on a cross as a common criminal. He emptied himself even more so by giving himself to us under the appearance of bread and wine in the Eucharist.

The humility of God is for our imitation. Paul says: "In your minds you must be the same as Christ Jesus… he did not cling to his equality with God, but emptied himself…" (Phil 2:5-6). To the degree that we genuinely enter into the mystery of God, and share in his nature, to that degree do we share in this self-emptying humility. Paul says: "always consider the other person to be better than yourself" (Phil 2:3).

This is not a call to belittle ourselves, making ourselves as doormats for others to walk upon. Rather, it is a challenge to adopt the attitude of service which is characteristic of the heart of God revealed in Jesus. The attitude of a servant is to join with Jesus, who at the Last Supper took up towel and water (the task of the slave of the household) and washed the grubby feet of his disciples. Others should be my "betters", not because of any mistaken sense of my inferiority before them; but because I choose to give them the honour, respect and service, which is like that given by slaves in ancient times to their masters (their "betters"). It is a call to service. This is the trademark of humility.

In the wonderful song of praise of God for all creation, called *The Canticle of the Sun*, Francis of Assisi extols God's creature water as "precious, pure, chaste and humble".[37] It is easy enough to know what he means by water as a symbol of what is precious, especially in a land of deserts such as Australia. It is also easy to see what he means by water being a symbol of purity and chastity, when it is crystal clear, sparkling and refreshing. But why does he call it humble? Because water seeks the lowest place! It will always flow towards that place which is below. This is what it means to be humble; to seek the lowly place of the servant in any situation.

Jesus had a constant battle to convey this message to his disciples. One day they had been arguing with one another as they were walking behind him. They thought he could not hear them. When they reached the house to which they were going, he asked them, "What were you arguing about on the road?" They were embarrassed and said nothing, because they had been arguing which of them would be the greatest! So, Jesus said to them, "If anyone wants to be first, he must make himself last of all and servant of all" (Mk 9:35). A little later in the journey, Jesus was approached by James and John for a favour. When he asked them, "What is it you want me to do for you?", they said to him, "Allow us to sit one at your right hand and the other at your left in your glory". They wanted the glory seats in the kingdom! Jesus replied with a question "Can you drink the cup that I must drink?" He meant the cup of suffering, a share in his passion and death.

This is the only glory available to a true follower of Jesus—the glory in the cross of Christ. Interestingly, the other disciples became quite indignant about all this—maybe James and John were edging in ahead of them in the "glory stakes". Jesus called them together again and patiently instructed them, "Anyone who wants to become great among you must be your servant, and anyone who wants to be first among you must be slave to all. For the Son of Man himself did not come to be served, but to serve, to give his life as a ransom for many" (Mk 10:43-44).

We are to imitate the humility in the heart of God. God is not little. He is great and almighty. Nor does God feel little. He is true to himself. Rather, God *made himself little* in love.[38] The humility of the Incarnation was not a thought or sentiment. It was a deed. God *made* himself little for our sake. In our relationships with one another, if we have the mind of Christ, we too will make ourselves little for the sake of the other. That is, we will take up the disposition and behaviour of a servant, who is always intent upon fulfilling the needs of the other first before caring for oneself. All the same it is important to emphasise that to have godly humility does not mean having no ambition for holiness.

The devil seeks to delude us by making us think it would be hypocritical to aspire towards great things for God. We think it would be prideful to aspire towards sainthood. This is false humility. It is God's plan that we become saints. He puts that desire within us. Teresa says it is important to have a "holy daring". God is drawn to the person who desires much. Teresa says: "In this matter of desires, I have always had great ones…". God, she says, is "a friend of courageous souls". Oftentimes people choose mediocrity due to a mistaken sense of "humility". Underneath there is a timidity in doing great things for God. Genuine humility is not small-mindedness or meanness of heart. It brings a magnanimity—a large-heartedness. Jesus says: "If you want to be first…" and "If you want to be great…". He presumes that these desires are good. We are called to realise them not by dominating others, or by clambering over the top of others in order to attain our end, but by humble service of others in the spirit of Jesus himself.

Finally, we must point out that humility is the most elusive of all the virtues, even though it is the most fundamental. It is often fostered in us by experiences of setbacks, disappointments, difficulties, hardships, persecutions, and the like. Through suffering we are reduced more truly to total dependence on the Lord and stripped of all self-satisfaction and vainglory. The quest for humility is a life-long struggle. If we think we have attained it, then we are on the most dangerous ground of all. As Blaise Pascal wrote:

> Vanity is so anchored in man's heart that a soldier, a soldier's servant, a cook, a porter brags and wishes to have admirers. Even philosophers wish for them. And those who write against vainglory want it to have the glory of having written well, and those who read it desire the glory of having read it; and I who write this have perhaps this desire; and maybe those who read it will do the same.[39]

We probably never do anything with totally pure motivation. All we can do is continue to throw ourselves with confidence on the mercy of Jesus, begging that he change our wayward hearts and make us like himself.

Obedience

Obedience is a supernatural grace from God enabling the human will to embrace unreservedly God's will for our lives. St. Teresa says:

> The whole aim of those who undertake prayer—and do not forget this, for it is very important—must be to labour and resolve and dispose oneself with all the diligence he can to make one's will conform to the will of God; and as I shall say later, be very sure that in this consists all the greatest perfection which can be attained on the spiritual path.[40]

To grow in obedience in a healthy manner we must first love God. Otherwise, it can be merely doing one's duty out of servile fear. Genuine obedience is generated by the love which God awakens in us as he wins us to himself. The more we open up to the love of the Lord, the more we will desire to be obedient. On the other hand, the opposite is true also. God gives his Holy Spirit to those who obey him (Acts 5:32). Jesus makes it clear that his friends are those who do what he commands (Jn 15:14).

Obedience, then, is the way to God's heart. It is a response of love for him, and to the degree that we are obedient to him, to that degree will our love increase. Our capacity to obey God is rooted in the obedience of Jesus himself. By his obedience to the Father unto death, Jesus brought our salvation. In God's wonderful plan of redemption, Jesus made the act of obedience that we were unable to make. His whole life on earth was simply doing the Father's will. "My food is to do the will of the one who sent me" (Jn 4:34), and "I always do what pleases him" (Jn 8:29).

Even in the darkest hour of the passion, Jesus was able to make a perfect offering of himself in conformity with the Father's will.

In the Garden of Gethsemane, while sweating drops like blood, he cries out, "My Father, if it is possible let this cup pass me by. Nevertheless, let it be as you, not I, would have it." (Mt 26:39). This is the human "yes" to the Father's will that brought our salvation and opened heaven's door for us. On the cross in utter desolation of soul he did not fall into despair, but placed his trust in the Father's love, and died with the words of surrender on his lips, "Father, into your hands I commit my spirit" (Lk 23:46). We can now join our lives with Jesus. Because of his obedience we can obey. We can overcome our self-will, autonomy and self-sufficiency. We can surrender to God's will and do what he wants, no matter what the cost.

Obedience means doing the revealed will of God made known to us in the Scriptures, the tradition of the Church, and the Church's teaching. An obedient heart reverences the word of God and seeks to do it. The Greek word for obedience in the New Testament is *hupakouein*, which means to "listen under". This means a kind of docility whereby we are so persuaded by the truth of what we hear that we will subject ourselves to it and come under its authority. In Latin, the verb "to obey" is *ob-audire*, which means to hearken attentively, to listen very carefully. As we study the word of God it should not be our intention to dominate and control it by our clever analysis; rather, we should be ready to submit to it and obey it.

Obedience also means seeking God's will subjectively for direction in our life. We are meant to be obedient to his many calls, like the first apostles who, when they heard Jesus "at once they left their nets and followed him" (Mk 1:18). We are to be attentive to the quiet voice of the Shepherd within, who calls forth his sheep by name each day (Jn 10:1-3). By living with him we learn to know his voice and we do not respond to the voice of the stranger. When Abraham came back from Mount Moriah, God said to him, "I will shower blessings on you… All the nations of the earth shall bless themselves by your descendants, as a reward for your obedience" (Gen 22:18).

When we are deciding which way to turn in life, even if it is simply a matter of whether to take this trip, or to give that talk, or to take up a certain ministry, we should always consult the Lord first. Like Moses in the Old Testament, it is important to go before the Lord with the question and to seek his mind. We don't necessarily get a direct answer, but by doing this we consciously invite the Lord into the discernment process and submit the matter to him. Otherwise, it is possible to shut the Lord out of the consideration, and not give him a chance to intervene if he so desires.

When we consult him, we need to empty ourselves of our own will before him and wait on his leading. Having adopted this position before the Lord, we can then go through the normal discernment processes, trusting that he will make things clear for us, and that we will have the wisdom to do what he wants.

The Lord says in Isaiah: "I am the Lord, unrivalled, I have not spoken in secret in some corner of a darkened land. I have not said to Jacob's descendants 'seek me in chaos'. I, the Lord, speak with directness. I express myself with clarity" (Is 45:19). We may not receive substantial words or bright neon lights showing the way, but if we have a listening heart, and are faithful to the appropriate discernment process, we can be assured that the Lord will not leave us without clarity of direction.

In the Book of Samuel there is a profound contrast made between David and Saul. While Saul had been anointed by the Spirit as king of Israel, he disobeyed the Lord. As a result, he brought disaster upon himself. David, on the other hand, was a man "after the Lord's own heart". At every turn David sought the Lord's mind and obeyed him. When he had a notable lapse, lusting for Bathsheba, he was quick to repent when exposed by Nathan's prophecy. Saul, however, did not have an obedient heart. Unlike David he was presumptuous and arrogant before the Lord. When it had come to light that Saul had disobediently held back from God what was rightfully God's by trying to cover it up with offering sacrifices, Samuel, the prophet, declared:

> Is the pleasure of the Lord in holocausts and sacrifices,
> or in obedience to the voice of the Lord?
> Yes, obedience is better than sacrifice…
> Rebellion is a sin of sorcery,
> Presumption a crime of teraphim (idolatry).
> (1Sam 15:22-23)

The heart of the saints is the cry of obedience "God, here I am, I coming to obey your will!" (Heb 10:5; cf Ps 40:7-9).

Obedience also means conforming our wills to the permissive will of God. When things don't turn out as we had hoped, and circumstances turn against us, we have a new opportunity to make a deeper surrender to God's will. The death of a loved one, disappointment within family or community life, persecution, afflictions, sicknesses, all come to us as God-given opportunities to deepen in our love for him. John of Avila said: "One 'blessed be God' in the time of affliction is worth a thousand 'praise the Lords' in a time of prosperity".[41]

To be able to use our sufferings as a means towards growth by making a deeper surrender to the mysterious will of God is one of the greatest challenges of the spiritual journey. We are told that Jesus "learnt to obey through suffering" (Heb 5:7-9). Together with him in the loss, humiliation, and degradation of his passion we find a new capacity to love. Catherine of Siena says that under the "bitter rind" of our trials there is a "sweet fruit" to be found. Our pain of the moment hides an unspeakably sweet outcome if we endure through it all in love. The doctor, she says, gives bitter remedies to bring healing. The Lord allows loss in order to heal our wounds, especially the "stinking garment" of self-will. Our sufferings help us to face the strength of our own selfish will and yield with "yes" to God's will. As we surrender to his will, he covers us with his beautiful garment of light and joy.[42]

Obedience is the mark of the true disciple of Jesus. Francis of Assisi once proclaimed that "a person could give all that he has away, but if he still retained his self-will it would be an act of pride". We need to place our "self-will" on the altar with Jesus, whose will was broken before the Father for our sake, and is still the eternal victim on our behalf in every Eucharist. One of the servant songs of Isaiah says, "Each morning he wakes me to hear, to listen like a disciple. The Lord God has opened my ear" (Is 50:4). This is the attitude of the true disciple of Jesus; a readiness to hear and to do the will of God each day.

A love for Mary, and entrustment to her, brings us quickly into the obedient heart of Jesus. Mary is a model for us as a doer of God's will. She was the first disciple. Her yes to the Father was unconditional, when she replied to the angel that it be done to her according to the Father's will. When Mary and some of Jesus' cousins were seeking entry into the home where he was teaching, Jesus used the opportunity to explain that this attitude of obedience is stronger than blood ties. He stretched out his hand towards his disciples and said, "Here are my mother and my brothers. Anyone who does the will of my Father in heaven, he is my brother and sister and mother" (Mt 12:50). Elsewhere, when a woman in the crowd shouted, "Happy the womb that bore you and the breasts you sucked!", Jesus indicates the profound reason for Mary's greatness, "Still happier those who hear the word of God and keep it" (Lk 11:27-28). Her greatness is that she is a doer of God's word. As the Fathers of the Church used to say, Mary first "conceived the word in her heart and then conceived the Word in her womb".

The whole foundation of the spiritual life must be built on the principle of obedience to the word of God. Jesus said "It is not those who say to me, 'Lord! Lord!', who will enter the kingdom of heaven, but those who do the will of my Father in heaven" (Mt 7:21). He goes on to point out that people may have exciting charismatic gifts, such as prophecy, miracles and casting out of demons, but if they have not been obedient to the Father's will, he will not recognise them on the last day (Mt 7:22). Then he uses the image of a house built on sand for someone who lacks obedience. They will surely fall when the wind and rains come. On the other hand, the one who is obedient is like a house built on rock. No matter what storms arise in their lives they will stand because they are built on the rock.

Prayer of Petition

For progress in the virtues, indeed in the whole of the spiritual life, the prayer of petition is essential. Alphonsus Liguori says: "I see the absolute necessity of the prayer of petition… there is nothing which all the preachers, and all confessors, and all the spiritual books, should insist on with greater strength and greater fervour than this same prayer of petition".[43] Left to ourselves and our own resources, we are incapable of holiness (Jn 15:5). We can do nothing without the help of grace. And in his ordinary ways of providence, God does not give us this help unless we ask for it. Jesus said: "Ask and it will be given to you; search and you will find; knock, and the door will be opened to you" (Lk 11:9).

We must be aware of our total poverty before God. We are beggars before him. Only the Holy Spirit can give us what we need—charity, humility, obedience, and all the other gifts of the spiritual life. We cannot rely on human insight, counselling, persuasion, or good resolutions. We must beg to have the virtues, beg for victory over sin, the devil, and the flesh, beg for discernment, beg for perseverance. James says: "Why you don't have what you want is because you don't pray for it…" (Jm 4:3). In the time of temptation, for instance, we are prone to forget to cry out to the Lord for help and try to battle through by ourselves. What is characteristic of the saints is that in the time of doubt, confusion, or challenge, they turned again to the Lord who was their help. Jesus promises, "I tell you therefore everything you ask and pray for, believe that you have it already, and it will be yours" (Mk 11:24). And again, "If you ask for anything in my name, I will do it" (Jn 14:14). The promise of the Lord is clear. It is simply a matter of standing on this promise.[44]

Alphonsus appeals to the authority of Thomas Aquinas as he gives four conditions for the prayer of petition to be infallibly answered.[45] If any one of these is missing, we are not guaranteed a favourable result.

The first condition is that we ask for a gift for ourselves. This is not a plea for selfishness. Nor is it to deny the importance of praying for others, but simply to acknowledge that we cannot be sure of the disposition of others as much as we can for ourselves. Of course, to pray for others is very effective, if they choose not to put an obstacle in the way (Jm 5:16; Mt 5:44; 1Jn 5:16). And even when they do place obstacles in the way through hardness of heart or obstinacy, God can still move them by extraordinary graces. Our focus here, however, is upon care for our own soul. When we ask for ourselves, we can make sure that as best we can we have a right disposition.

The second condition is that we ask for graces that are necessary and useful for our salvation and sanctification e.g., pleading for the grace of deeper humility, or for victory over an area of sin, or for strength against a particular temptation. We cannot advance in virtue unless we ask for the gift. James says: "when you do pray and don't get it, it is because you have not prayed properly, you have prayed for something to indulge your own desires" (Jm 3:3).

This is not to say that we should avoid praying for temporal things. Our heavenly Father loves to provide for us in this way, even for the smallest and seemingly insignificant things. Yet, we cannot be sure that our prayer is in the will of God unless what we pray for is directly related to our salvation and sanctification.

The third condition is that we pray with humility and confidence. God resists the proud and listens to the cry of the poor. The psalmist prays with utmost confidence that God will not spurn a humble and contrite heart (Ps. 50:19). We must be free of all self-sufficiency and know the truth that our labour is in vain unless the Lord is building the house (Ps 127:1). We must be free of all presumption and be aware of our profound weakness. Paul warns us about deceiving ourselves with thoughts of self-importance (Gal 6:3). We must acknowledge our utter poverty and nothingness before God. We are also to be confident, believing in the promise of

Scripture. Jesus says: "If you remain in me and my words remain in you, you may ask what you will and you shall get it" (Jn 15:7). Our confidence is in the gracious mercy of God, who we trust will look upon our lowly state and raise us up.

The fourth condition is that we must pray with perseverance. Jesus' teaching on prayer in the Gospels emphasises that we should never give up. Unfortunately, this is precisely what we are prone to do when the answer to our prayer is delayed. Jesus told the parable of the neighbour who needed some bread late at night and banged on the door of his friend next door. His friend resisted getting up to unlock the door. Jesus comments, "I tell you if the man does not get up and give it to him for friendship's sake, persistence will be enough to make him get up and give his friend all he wants" (Lk 11:5-8). We are being told to become troublesome beggars before God, making a dreadful nuisance of ourselves, and never to cease asking until we receive it.

The other great parable in this regard is of the poor widow demanding her rights before the unscrupulous judge. The judge eventually gives in to her demands, because she "keeps pestering him" and "will persist in coming and worrying him to death". Jesus comments, "Now will not God see justice done to his chosen who cry to him day and night even when he delays to help them? I promise you he will see justice done to them and done speedily" (Lk 18:1-8). The message is simple. If you keep asking in humility and confidence, and never give up, you will eventually see it happen. To overcome sinful habits, to resist temptations, to break the power of the flesh, to develop particular virtues, to grow in prayer, or to do anything for our growth in holiness, we simply need to ask specifically for the gift, and stand on the promise of the Lord. It will eventually be given.

Why then does the Lord delay in giving what we ask for our sanctification? In an age when we are used to getting things instantly, from instant emails or texts to instant news and sporting results, we want everything immediately. If the Lord intends to give it to us in the end, why does he keep us waiting? Why do we have to keep asking? There are a number of possible reasons. Firstly, by keeping us waiting he tests how humble and confident we really are. The more we lower ourselves before the Lord in reverential fear of his majesty, the more he delights in *ultimately* raising us up. Secondly, it is his way of deepening our desire, increasing our longing for the gifts we are seeking. When we obtain things easily, we don't value them as much.

As an analogy, we can appreciate the difference in gratitude in the hearts of young people who have had everything in this world handed to them on a platter, and those who had to go without much, and have had to learn the value of hard work. Thirdly, it is a way of training us in love of the Lord. We become more aware of our utter dependence upon him. If we were certain of getting everything instantaneously, we would soon forget him, and become self-sufficient and presumptuous.

The prayer of petition keeps us in our true poverty of spirit before God, acutely aware of our creatureliness, and that he is the Lord of all. Perfection in prayer is not ultimately the gift of high mystical contemplation, as wonderful as this is, but it is to know how to ask and beg. The Desert Fathers often spent the whole day simply repeating the plea, "O God, come to our aid; O Lord, make haste to help us".

4
YIELDING TO THE FIRE
Conditions for Growth in Christ

"Father, into your hands I commit my spirit." (Lk 23:46)

In this section, we will look at three important attitudes that the Lord develops in the heart as we take up a journey with him. He puts in us a *desire* for holiness, which breeds a decisiveness of response and a determination to finish what has been begun. Secondly, he gifts us with a *detachment* from all created things, so that he can be our first love. In addition, he helps us to *trust in his providence* at all times and in all circumstances, no matter what happens along the way.

Desire to be Holy

St. Augustine considered that the whole Christian life is one uninterrupted desire for God. He teaches that our whole task on this pilgrim journey remains in the region of desire; indeed, the entire life of a devout Christian is simply a holy yearning for God.[46] We are to pray always. This simply means to be desiring union with God wherever we are and whatever we are doing. Augustine says "prayer sleeps when desire grows cold".[47] True prayer, he says is the desire for possession of God himself, and this involves subordination of all other desires to this. Prayer, he maintains, brings to the surface the basic orientation that is written into our human nature—a deep hunger for God. At the beginning of his *Confessions* Augustine cries out that because the Lord has made us for himself, our hearts are restless until they rest in him.[48]

This desire is a gift from God. We should ask for it often. "Lord, make me want to love you!" It is much more than a desire for personal human development. It is a God-directed desire for union with him. There needs to be a constant desire, a quiet burning fire within, which has been lit by the Lord. This desire is stoked and fanned into a flame by the word of God, Eucharist, healing and reconciliation, meditation on the passion of Jesus, praying for the infilling with the Holy Spirit, spiritual reading, and other means for spiritual growth. This desire is much more than wishful thinking or grandiose imaginings. It is much more than the noble sentiments stirred up by a retreat or conference. Rather than idealistic dreaming it is the real movement of God's Spirit in our ordinary life. This flame within is most effective when it avoids undue extremes of either over-enthusiasm or lethargy. It is most crucial that the flame does not go out. There is no respite in the serious spiritual journey. We are, as it were, rowing upstream in a constant fashion. However, if we rest on the oars the boat will drift backward, and if we rest too long, we may find ourselves careering over very hazardous rapids, or even taken over a perilous waterfall unexpectedly.

Desire for union with God breeds in us a determination. Teresa of Avila says about beginners:

> It is most important, all-important, indeed, that they should begin well by making an earnest and most determined resolve not to halt until they reach their goal, whatever may come, whatever may happen to them, however hard they may have to labour, whoever may complain of them, whether they reach their goal on the road or have no heart to confront the trials which they meet, whether the very world dissolves before them...[49]

We must keep our eyes fixed on the goal and never give up. This requires a singlemindedness of purpose, which is the meaning of "purity of heart". "Happy are the pure in heart, they shall see God" (Mt 5:8). The pure of heart are not double-minded or divided in their hearts. They are shooting straight for the target. The early Desert Fathers used the image of an archer aiming for the bullseye, on which was painted the prize to be won.[50] The archer needed to keep eyes fixed on the prize to be able to win. As St. Paul says: "I am racing for the finish for the prize to which God calls us upward to receive in Christ Jesus" (Phil 3:14).

In this race, we have to be careful not to be deflected. The enemy's ploy with those who are on a committed walk with the Lord is not so much to turn them around totally but to *deflect* them from the path sufficiently to render them ineffective for the kingdom. He does this by offering an alternative good that is quite alluring. However, it is not the way in which God intends to sanctify us. St. Bernard calls this the "noontide devil" since it appears like the noon as the "angel of light".[51] He describes it as "the scourge that lays waste at noon", referring to a text in Psalm 91 (verse 6). To succumb to its attraction is to finally end in the flesh what was begun in the Spirit. We must keep on the path that the Lord has marked out for us. If an ocean liner gets slightly off its bearings on one side of the ocean, it will eventually end up a long way off course by the time it has reached the other side of the world. We cannot afford even the slightest deflection from the goal.

When we set out on the journey, we need a decisiveness of spirit. The apostles left everything immediately and followed Jesus. To the man who said, "Sir, let me go and bury my father first" Jesus said, "Follow me, and leave the dead to bury their dead" (Mt 8:21-22). Not even the solemn duty of the ritual burying of his father should delay him. We are to be bold and daring in following Jesus. The Master said, "Since John the Baptist came, up to this present time, the kingdom of heaven has been subjected to violence and the violent are taking it by storm" (Mt 11:12). This is a call for aggression! We are to "grasp the nettle", to "seize the day"! To take hold of the kingdom with gusto!

When they were asking Jesus about how many would be saved, he said, "Try your best to enter by the narrow door..." (Lk 13:24). The original Greek text is stronger than this. It means "thrust yourself vigorously through the narrow door...". This is the decisiveness that we need. Let nothing get in the way of this one important goal, full possession of the Lord and his kingdom. Teresa of Avila says we are to have a "determined determination" not to give up once we have started. Sometimes people are good starters and can sprint for a while, but they do not last. The spiritual life is not a sprint, but a marathon race. The main thing is to be able to keep running. Nevertheless, the way you start in some way affects your race. As John Cassian observed of some of the monks in the desert: they were living out in their old age the lukewarmness acquired in their youth.[52]

Sometimes when people start the race they are running on the enthusiasm and zeal of others. This may be a useful way to get initial momentum but, if it remains like this, they will never finish. Walter Hilton tells of hounds hunting the hare.[53] He says some hounds run because of the excitement of the chase. They are running on the energy of others. They will eventually tire and straggle home without having reached the prize. However, those hounds which run because they smell the hare or have the hare fixed in their sights, will never tire until they have caught the hare and, hence, attained their goal.

We need to be careful that we are not running on the commitment of others but have truly placed our lives in a personal way under the lordship of Jesus. Even if everyone else should fall away, we would still keep running, because we love the Lord, and desire to possess and be possessed by him totally. Jesus said: "Once the hand is laid to the plough, no one who looks back is fit for the kingdom of God" (Lk 9:62). The image here is of the ploughman with his hand on the plough, which is drawn behind oxen. He keeps his eye fixed on a distant object, maybe a tree at the end of the paddock, so he can plough straight. If he looks back, he will swerve all over the place, and make strange-looking furrows indeed. Eventually, if he keeps looking back, he will not complete the task at all.

Our desire for God grows cold when we settle down to mediocrity, lukewarmness, and tepidity. On the outskirts of Canberra, there is a property named "This'll do". As I pass the gate with this sign, I am often reminded of the subtle temptation in the spiritual life to begin to put limits on the degree to which we will be stretched by God. We can lose the original fire, dig in at a certain point, and say, "This'll do! I shall go no further!" Teresa warns that we are prone to settling for a certain level of spiritual practice which is quite virtuous and commendable but lacks the heroic response. She says people like this "are eminently reasonable folk. Their love is not yet ardent enough to overwhelm their reason. How I wish our reason would make us dissatisfied with this habit of always serving God at a snail's pace! As long as we do that we shall never get to the end of the road".[54]

There is a type of "divine madness" that followers of Jesus need to have. This is the sort of love that filled Paul, who once exclaimed that life for him is Christ, but death would bring even greater gain

(Phil 1:21), and that all he wanted is "to know Jesus Christ and the power of his rising..." (Phil 3:10). The Lord can bring all sorts of testings to us; the loss of reputation in the eyes of others, or loss of possessions or relationships which were dear to us, but these are opportunities to stoke the fire even more through a deeper surrender to his will. Unfortunately, when these things happen, many shrink back and proclaim, "This'll do". For stalwart souls these happenings, in fact, become new sources of grace, as they grow more deeply in love and surrender to the Lord.

Determination can also wane when we are confronted with our own duplicity of heart, and experience our imperfections, failures, and sinfulness. This can make us so disappointed with ourselves that we want to throw in the towel with disgust. The problem here is over-attachment to our own growth in holiness. In a prideful way, we become overly distressed and anxious when we fall. St. Francis de Sales says: "Angers, spites and vexations against ourselves tend to pride, and flow from no other source than self-love, which is troubled and disquieted to see ourselves imperfect".[55]

If we become full of remorse, self-condemnation, self-pity, and anxiety, we fall into the hands of the evil one. The remedy for all this is simply to repent in a calm and steady manner. Thérèse of Lisieux concurs that to "brood over our imperfections paralyses the soul". She maintains that more harm is done through becoming down-hearted over falling, than by the fall itself. "The sorrow that casts us down", she says, "is the burden of our self-love". We need to be gentle and compassionate towards ourselves in the times of failure. Francis de Sales advises:

> When, then, your heart falls, raise it up gently; humbling yourself greatly before God, acknowledging your misery, but without being surprised at your fall... Detest,

nevertheless, with all your power the offence God has received from you, and return to the way of virtue which you had forsaken, with great courage, and confidence in his mercy.[56]

The life of the soul can be paralysed very quickly by anxiety. We can become so excessively anxious about a particular habit, because we are having difficulty overcoming it, that we fall into despondency, which is very dangerous. Francis de Sales warns:

> Anxiety is the greatest evil that can befall the soul, sin only excepted… when our heart is troubled and disturbed within itself, it loses the strength necessary to maintain the virtues it had acquired. At the same time, it loses the means to resist the temptations of the enemy, who then uses his utmost efforts to fish, as they say, in troubled waters.[57]

If we are struggling to have victory in a particular area of our life, it is best to keep calm and sober about it all. When a bird finds itself ensnared in a net it makes such a fuss, fluttering about and struggling to extricate itself, that it enmeshes itself more in the net. So also, when we are struggling with sinful habits, we must be gentle with ourselves. After a fall it is simply a matter of getting up again, and turning this sin into grace, by using it as an opportunity for a more determined focus on Jesus, and restored confidence in his redeeming power.

Detachment

We can make progress in the spiritual life only if we learn detachment of heart from all created things. Ignatius Loyola at the beginning of his *Spiritual Exercises* lays down *a foundational principle*.[58] We have been created out of love by God for a purpose—to praise, honour, and serve him here on earth and to be with him forever in heaven. All created things on this earth are a means for us to attain this end. We are to make use of these things in so far as they help us to attain this end. We must rid ourselves of them in as far as they are obstacles.

'Ignatius says that we must break with any inordinate attachment to created realities—whether they be things, persons, talents, relationships, dreams, or whatever. Genuine detachment of heart provides the space for us to be filled by God. We are to have a holy indifference; not to prefer health or sickness, riches or poverty, honour or dishonour, long life or short life. What matters is that everything works towards attaining our end. Our only desire and choice should be what is most conducive to the end for which we are created. When we are making a choice between two good possibilities, says Ignatius, we should always choose what is going to give greater glory to God.

John of the Cross has a similar teaching. He says that the aim of our life here on earth is union with God. Our unruly desires keep us bound to things of this earth and so we are not free for God. We need not only to break with sin, but also to become detached from all created goods, so we can be free to love God in a full and unhindered way. For John, as for Ignatius, it is not so much an emptying of the things in themselves, but an emptying of the desire or appetite for these things. We can have an inordinate desire for possessions, for particular relationships, for a special course, a career, or travel opportunities.

Speaking about people embarking on a committed life with the Lord, John says:

> It is a matter of deep sorrow that, while God has bestowed

on them the power to break other stronger cords of attachment of sin and vanities, they fail to attain so much good because they do not become detached from some childish thing which God has requested them to conquer for love of him.[59]

John goes on to use the well-known image of a bird held by a cord. He says it does not matter how slender the cord is. The bird still will not be able to fly. No matter how much virtue we have, says John, if there is one slender attachment that is holding the heart, we will be prevented from going to God.

If our hearts are held in bondage to something other than the Lord, the fulness of God's love cannot grow in them. As Alphonsus Liguori says: "if your soul is full of earth there is no room for the love of God".[60]

St. Paul shows his own heart on the matter when he says to the Philippians, "I believe nothing can happen that will outweigh the supreme advantage of knowing Christ Jesus my Lord" (Phil 3:8). When we think of all the exciting things that could happen in our lives this is an extraordinary statement. What if I was to win the lotto, or if that dream career path opened up for me, or if… we could dream about many things. But Paul goes on, "For him (Christ) I accept the loss of everything, and I look on everything as so much rubbish if only I can have Christ and be given a place in him" (Phil. 3:7-8).

This is the spirit of detachment. It is not a journey into the void, but into Christ. Paul had actually lost everything—loss of synagogue identity as a Pharisee, loss of respect from his Jewish family, loss of economic advantage with reduced opportunities as a tent-maker, loss of reputation amongst many former friends, loss of stability, with nowhere to call home, loss of health after being beaten, stoned and whipped many times, loss of physical freedom through imprisonment more than once, and ultimately he lost his head in martyrdom! Everything that I previously valued, says Paul, I now consider as "rubbish", which is probably better translated as "excrement", *so that I may have Christ!*

Paul saw himself as identifying with the self-emptying of Jesus which he had described earlier in Philippians. Paul had proclaimed that Jesus did not consider his equality with God a thing to be grasped (Phil 2:6). Here we see the close relationship between humility and detachment. The fundamental sin of humanity was a selfish grasping to be God by eating of the tree of the knowledge of good and evil. This grasping attitude is at the root of the consumer society and is totally opposite to the way of Christ. Paul radically identifies with Jesus. He refuses to grasp for reputation, honour, status, power, or possessions. Rather, he chooses to empty himself, ready to reproduce the pattern of the cross of Jesus in his own life. This is the way of detachment.

In Mark's gospel a rich young man ran up to Jesus and asked, "Good Master, what must I do to inherit eternal life?" This is an important question: "What must I do?" Maybe it is a question that each one should ask of Jesus often. Jesus answered by telling him to keep the commandments and listed them for him. The young man replied that he had been doing that for a long time. Now Jesus took him more seriously. He was after all a virtuous young man. Jesus gazed with love into his heart. It is important to notice this! Each one of us can allow Jesus to gaze steadily into our hearts with love. What will his gaze expose?

For the young man in the gospel, Jesus put his finger on the one thing that was holding him from a full-hearted response of love, "There is one thing you lack" said Jesus, "go sell all your possessions and give the money to the poor, and you will have treasure in heaven; then come, follow me." (Mk 10:17-22). The rich, young man went away sad, not wanting to let go of what was holding him back—his riches. It seems that some people, out of fear of being miserable through giving everything to Jesus, will hold tightly to pet projects, precious possessions, or highly desired relationships, even in the light of Jesus' love beckoning to let them go. In their attempt to avoid misery, they make themselves the most miserable of all. They are not free to love.

A priest who worked in Asia told me of a group of gypsy-like folk in India who make money by training monkeys to do circus tricks for gathered crowds in the town marketplaces. Apparently, they catch the monkeys by using heavy clay pots, which have a small opening just big enough for a monkey's hand to pass through. They fill the pots with nuts and other goodies attractive to monkeys. When the monkey puts his hand in the hole he grabs the nuts. Eager to withdraw his hand he finds he can't do so because his fist is too big. As long as he holds onto the nuts he is stuck! The poor monkey keeps holding on to the nuts! There's no way he is going to let go! But struggle as he may, he cannot be free! Maybe some of us are like this monkey at times. If only we would just "let go", we could be free!

Evelyn Underhill tells an enchanting story to illustrate this point:

> I read the other day the story of a Brownie who lived in a wood. He had a little wheelbarrow and passed his time in very moral and useful manner picking up slugs and snails. Yet there was something lacking in his life. The King of the World passed through that wood very early every morning, and made all things beautiful and new,

but the Brownie had never seen him. He longed to, but something prevented it. He had one cherished possession, a lovely little green blanket which had fallen out of the fairy queen's chariot and which he had not been able to help keeping for himself. It was very cold in the wood at night, but the blanket kept him so warm and cosy that he never woke up to see the King of the World. And one day there came to him a Shepherd who looked deep into the soul of the Brownie and said to him, 'Haven't you seen the King of the World?' And the Brownie said, 'No, I do so want to, but somehow I can't manage it'. The Shepherd replied: 'But I seem to see something in your soul that keeps you from the vision; something that looks like a blanket'. And at that a terrible fight began in the heart of the Brownie, a battle between wanting to go on being warm and a comfortable in his blanket and longing to see the King of the World. Perhaps the ultimate choice which lies before us may turn out to be the Brownie's choice between the Heavenly Vision and the blanket.[61]

God's love already within us motivates us to let go of everything that would prevent the growth of that love. In the gospels Jesus told the parable of the man who found a treasure in the field. It so filled him with delight, that he sold up everything he had to purchase the field (Mt 13:44). The treasure is God's love. Once we have found it, we are so filled with delight, that we willingly "sell out" in order to have it in its fulness. In the Prayer of the Church[62] there is a translation of a text from the Song of Songs which illustrates this, "Love is a fire no waters avail to quench, no floods to drown; for love, a man will give up all that he has in the world and think nothing of his loss" (Sgs 8:7).

For the lover there is little counting of the cost! When we become persuaded and overcome by the Beloved, we readily give up all for him. As the heart is possessed more by love it becomes less conscious of the lure of created things. The heart wants to speak about God, to hear nothing but what pertains to God, to love God above all things, and in and through all things. Francis de Sales says: "The pure love of God is like a living flame that consumes everything that is not God. It changes everything else into itself; so that all that was not love, now becomes love." The love of God motivates us to be detached; and the more we become detached the more we are filled with the love of God.

Ignatius helps us look at what degree of detachment we have, by a reflection on three types of people.[63] The first type talk a lot but do little. These people say they really want Christ fully in their lives. For this to happen they know they have to stop being dependent on all the things they possess. Yet, they keep putting it off until tomorrow to do something about it. They are the *"mañana"* people; "tomorrow, I will do it".

The second type of people have actually chosen to have Christ fully in their lives, but they do it on their own terms, and in their own way. They have a knack of not facing particular areas in their life where there is an inordinate attachment. They are prepared gladly to give 80 per cent, or even 90 per cent, but there is always a remainder, which they guard and keep under their own control. They tend to bargain with God, trying to buy him off. In some areas of their lives where the attachments are strongest, they subtly try to use God for their own ends, expecting him to dance to their tune, rather than genuinely surrendering fully to his will.

The third type of people have embraced Christ fully in their lives, on *his* terms, as he wills. They readily offer to him all that they have. They are happy for him to dispose of their possessions according to his will. These people are trying always to get rid of any attachments which would hinder their union with God. Every decision these people make is for the greater glory of God. Their desire, aim and choice is for whatever will give praise and honour to God. Ignatius offers a prayer, which expresses this attitude:

> *Take, Lord, receive, all my liberty, my memory,*
> *my understanding, my entire will, all I have and possess.*
> *You have given all to me, so now I return it. All is yours now.*
> *Dispose of it wholly according to your will.*
> *Give me only your love and your grace. That's enough for me.*

This third attitude is the most desirable. The heart has a "holy indifference". Whatever the Lord wants is what matters. We give to him our lives and all they contain, letting him dispose of it all as he wills. We give him our health, our length of life, our manner of death, our gifts and talents, our family and friends, and all that is nearest and dearest to us. Then we seek to be indifferent about the way he disposes of these gifts in our life. Everything is to be for his glory. That's what matters. Jesus said, "...none of you can be my disciple unless he gives up all his possessions" (Lk 14:33). The Lord does not mean that he will lead us into a life of deprivation, but that we are to entrust to him the distribution of the goods. After all it is all gift from him anyway. Yet there is much in us that resists belonging to God in this way. We want to in some way control him. His love at work within us is constantly beckoning us to let go of the hold we have on everything, and to trust in the hold he has on us.

The call for a detached heart is not only about our attitude toward material possessions. It means all our relationships as well. Jesus says: "If any man comes to me without hating his father, mother, wife, children, brothers, sisters, yes his own life too, he cannot be my disciple" (Lk 14:26). Here the word "hate" is not referring to an emotion of enmity; but means an attitude of total detachment. It does not mean that we stop loving our family, but that this love must be subordinate to our love for Jesus and for his kingdom. To be wholly for Jesus we cannot be overly attached to anything, not even to our good works which we might do in order to advance the kingdom.

Often, we find out how attached we are to something when we are threatened with losing it. We find out how attached we have been to some project when it fails, and our whole world caves in with it! St. Ignatius was once asked how he would feel if the Pope disbanded the Jesuits which he had founded. He answered that he would need 15 minutes with the Lord, then he would be fine. In other words, he would need the time simply to give back to the Lord what had been gift to him, and surrender more deeply to the Lord in love.

The Indian poet Tagore offers a beautiful little story to challenge us to give all to the King of Kings:

> I had gone begging from door to door in the village path, when your golden chariot appeared in the distance like a gorgeous dream and I wondered who was this King of all kings! My hopes were high and I thought that my evil days were at an end, and I stood waiting for alms to be given unasked and for wealth scattered on all sides in the dust.
>
> The chariot stopped where I stood. Your glance fell on me, and you came down with a smile and I felt that the luck of my life had come at last. Then, all of a sudden, you held out your right hand and said: What have you to give to me? Ah what a kingly jest was it to open your palm to a beggar to beg! I was confused and stood undecided,

and then from my wallet I took out the least little grain of corn and gave it to you.

But how great was my surprise when, at the days end, I emptied my bag on the floor to find a least little grain of gold among the poor heap. I bitterly wept and wished that I had had the heart to give you my all.[64]

Trust in the Providence of God

On her death-bed Catherine of Siena told her friends that her only task her whole life long had been to "hold on" and never let go of "unshakeable hope and trust in the providence of God".[65] Trust in God's providence is a child-like attitude, a confidence that we are constantly held in the loving gaze of the Father God, who has everything under control. It is grounded in a deep conviction that God's ways, even though mysterious, are ultimately for our good.

God is at all times in absolute control of the universe. Nothing is impossible to him, and he disposes his works according to his will. He is Lord of the universe. He shapes the hearts of human beings and governs their ways according to his designs. But he is not in any way an arbitrary dictator. God is a loving Father. His Lordship is exercised in a tender and loving relationship with every person. His activity is lovingly tailored to the needs and response of every single individual. As St. Teresa says: "What is there that you do, my Lord, which is not for the greater good of the soul which you know to be already yours, and which places itself in your power to follow you wherever you go, even to the death of the cross?".[66]

A deep trust in God as a Father who is "righteous in all he does" and "acts only out of love" (Ps 145:17) is foundational for the spiritual life. Jesus radicalised prayer by addressing God as *"Abba"*, an

Aramaic equivalent for "Daddy". It speaks of an intimate, close, loving relationship. The secret of the heart of Jesus is his absolute trust in his *Abba*. This is what carried him through the rejection, persecution and suffering at the hands of others. Deep within his human soul there was an assurance of the Father's love. This was also what enabled him to be responsibly "care-free" about what he would have that day to eat, or to drink, or where he was to sleep that night. The loving Father would provide these necessities of life. "Can any of you, for all his worrying, add a single cubit to his span of life? If the smallest things, therefore, are outside your control, why worry about the rest?" (Lk 12:25-26).

All is the Lord's providence. We must trust him in everything. I could become sick tomorrow. I could die tonight. There is no point in clinging to my life. "If anyone clings to his life he will lose it…".

When we come to know Jesus with the kind of knowledge born of love, we also come into his experience of the Father's heart. Jesus said, "To have seen me is to have seen the Father" (Jn 14:9), and no one knows who the Father is "except the Son and those to whom the Son chooses to reveal him" (Lk 10:22). This is why Jesus came, to bring us into a share in the life he has with the Father. St. Paul tells us, "The Spirit you have received is not a spirit of slaves bringing fear into your lives again; it is the Spirit of sons, and it makes us cry out, "*Abba*, Father!"—our share in the heart-experience of Jesus himself (Rom. 8:14).

When Jesus was baptised in the Jordan, he heard the words from heaven, "You are my Son, the Beloved, my favour rests on you" (Lk 3:22). To be baptised into Jesus means that we will hear these affirming words often in the depth of our being, speaking life and love into us: "You are my son, my daughter, my beloved, my favour rests on you". Knowing this truth in the depth of our being, gives us the deep security, self-worth, and sense of personal significance that each individual needs.

Many people today have difficulty experiencing the Father's heart for them. We tend to image God according to our own experience of parenting. If our earthly father was a tyrant around the home, then we are liable to image God, the Father, that way. If our earthly father was absent from the home, or inactive, or irresponsible, or critical, or unpredictable, or arbitrary in punishment, this will most likely impact negatively on our ability to experience God as *Abba*. The tragedy here is that people can spend their lives angry at God, and blaming him for unfortunate events and circumstances. They are unable to affirm the truth that God is good. They find it difficult to believe that God the Father really loves them, cares for them and provides for them in every way.

To be able to make the first steps on the journey they need some "cognitive therapy" in regard to their basic concept of God. It is a problem of perception. They need to soak themselves in the scriptural revelation, to become convinced of some basic truths about the qualities of God. He is a *faithful* God. Because we have experienced hurt, we can think God has failed us. He has not. Maybe others have, but the truth is in the Lord's words, "I have loved you with an everlasting love, so I am constant in my affection for you" (Jer 31:3). He is a *generous* God. Maybe we have experienced meanness from significant others, and so we are prone to expect this of God also. However, his word says: "Since God did not spare his own Son, but gave him up to benefit us all, we may be certain, after such a gift, that he will not refuse anything he can give" (Rom 8:32). He is an *affectionate* God. Many have a love-deficit in the heart through not receiving tender-hearted affection from parents in their early years. In Hosea, the Father says, "I was like someone who lifts an infant close against his cheek; stooping down to him I gave him his food" (Hos. 11:4).

The Father is always totally present to each one personally. God is always *present*. If we had first-hand experience of the "absent father" from the home, like so many in this society, then we need to hear the words "unload all your worries to him, since he is looking after you" (1Pet 5:7). He is *always* thinking of us.

God, the Father, accepts you totally, and has always accepted you for who you are from the first moment of your existence. Often parental love is conditional, depending on the child's performance. We can grow up in a world of "ifs"—I love you *if* you are good-looking, intelligent, wealthy. I love you *if* you have a good education, good job, good connections. I love you *if* you produce well, sell much and buy well. The "world" ranks people as more or less intelligent, attractive, successful. With the Father there is no "more or less". The "world" has an inner voice whispering "Go out; prove you are worth something". [67] So we try to impress others with our talents, achievements, status, wealth or whatever. The Father is simply saying, "Do not be afraid, for I have redeemed you; I have called you by your name, you are mine... you are precious in my eyes, because you are honoured and I love you" (Is 43:1,4). He is saying: "I love you, I love you... You are totally acceptable in yourself, just as you are".

To be able to flow with the providence of God we need to be able to accept that God's ways are not our ways. As Paul exclaimed: "how impossible to penetrate his motives or understand his methods!" (Rom 11:33). Through Isaiah we hear from God, "Yes, the heavens are as high above earth as my ways are above your ways, my thoughts above your thoughts" (Is 55:8-9).

At this present moment in our personal history, we are unable to fully comprehend the ways of God. We will only know the full meaning of what happens in our lives at the end in heaven. Then we will have the advantage of hind-sight and will be able to marvel at the wisdom of God. During our earthly pilgrimage we often have to make an act of trust in the Father, even though we cannot understand the way events are unfolding. We trust everything that happens is in a mysterious way an opportunity for grace to flow in our lives. Nothing happens by chance. Everything is in some way under the provident hand of our loving Father.

There is a story about an acrobat who was doing a tight-rope stunt between two very high buildings in New York. A crowd had gathered below. To their dismay the man was holding a young boy in his arms as he made some very dangerous manoeuvres. When they finally came down, the press was eager to interview the acrobat; but they were even more keen to speak to the little boy. "Weren't you afraid when you were up there?" they asked. The little boy replied "No, I wasn't afraid. I was in my daddy's arms!"

This parable gives us the secret to joyful living. By casting our cares upon the Lord, and resting securely in his arms, nothing can disturb us. Jesus assures us that those in relationship with him are in the hands of the Father and no one can snatch them away (Jn 10:29). We have nothing to fear. Deep within our being the Father who loves us passionately, and who is the Master of the whole universe, has us in his grip. He has every situation in his hands.

Suffering and Holiness

We are now in a position to talk about suffering as a means towards holiness. Paul says: "We know that by turning everything to their good God cooperates with all those who love him" (Rom

8:28). And St. Augustine assures us that Almighty God, because he is infinitely good, would not allow evil to exist "if he were not so all-powerful and good as to cause good to emerge from the evil itself".[68] Suffering does not have to be destructive of the human spirit. It can be the very means for deeper penetration into the ultimate meaning of life itself. For those who know Jesus, with a knowledge born of love, suffering becomes a privileged way of union with him. From the greatest moral evil ever committed, the rejection and murder of God's Son, God's grace abounded all the more, and brought the greatest of all goods, our redemption.

There is a beautiful story of God's providence in the book of Genesis. Joseph, who was favoured by God, is violently beaten by his brothers out of jealousy, and left for dead in a well. Through a chain of events far beyond anyone's expectations, Joseph eventually finds himself in Egypt as Pharaoh's chancellor, in charge of the distribution of grain during a huge drought. Jacob, Joseph's father, sends his brothers to Egypt in order to buy some grain. Unknown to them they are dealing with their brother, whom they had attempted to murder. It is a touching story as Joseph first conceals his identity. Finally, he reveals who he is to his brothers. Naturally they are fearful for their lives. But Joseph tells them not to be afraid, because "it was not you who sent me here but God... The evil you planned to do me has by God's design been turned to good, that he might bring about, as indeed he has, the deliverance of a numerous people" (Gen 45:8; 50:20).

Joseph's sufferings only made sense at the end of the story. While he was enduring his afflictions, which included being beaten, taken as a slave, being falsely accused, and being thrown into prison for a couple of years, he simply had to trust the Lord, knowing that there is always a bigger picture than our feeble human minds can fathom.

Catherine of Siena says that the Lord allows the "wearisome thorns" of life out of love for us, so we can painfully learn that nothing created can be a god for us.[69] Although everything else may fail us, we learn through our disappointments and frustrations, that the Lord will never fail us. He is our only satisfaction. Even in life's greatest tragedies he will bring good out of evil, life out of death. As Paul says: "These are the trials through which we triumph, by the power of him who loved us" (Rom 8:37).

Catherine heard the Lord reveal to her, "The soul comes to perfection by fighting these battles, because there she *experiences* my divine providence, whereas before this she only believed in it".[70] Through the unexpected shattering experiences that life can bring, she says, we will experience the truth of his goodness and love for us. Even the most painful disappointment, or the most heart-rending tragedy, can become a source of grace for us. At these times we are to make a deeper "yes" to the Lord, joining ourselves with him on the cross, sharing in the darkness of his suffering, and making his prayer our own: "Father, into your hands I commit my spirit".

Life has a way of wounding us. The experience of loss is extremely painful. We unexpectedly lose a loved one through an untimely death, or we lose a home through accidental fire, or we lose a spouse through separation or divorce, or we lose a business through economic downturn, or we lose a friend through false accusation. The human reality of loss brings a whole range of emotions—denial, anger, remorse, self-blame, blame of others, depression.

Through all this struggle the grace of God is at work. He does not allow these things to happen without giving us the interior resources to interpret them by faith, and to turn them into moments of grace. Ultimately, he leads us to a deeper acceptance of the mystery of his permissive will, and a deeper trust in him, who is "just in all his ways and loving in all his deeds" (Ps 145:17).

A video I once watched about Mother Teresa's work featured a convent of hers which was under threat from civil authorities. When asked how she felt about it she answered, "God is in charge. We must be prepared to take what he gives, and give what he takes". All is gift from God. He is the one who disposes his gifts as he wills, including the gift of life itself.

When Job experienced multiple calamities, losing all his possessions and family members, his response was, "Naked I came from my mother's womb, naked I shall return. The Lord gave, the Lord has taken back. Blessed be the name of the Lord! If we take happiness from God's hand, must we not take sorrow too?" (Job 1:21; 2:10).

Of course, we need to be careful not to use unhelpful platitudes when counselling people in the moment of their loss. We need to meet them in the reality of their grief. Nevertheless, the person of faith will always move through the pain into a deeper embrace of the cross of Jesus, and hence a deeper surrender to the Father's will. John of the Cross has a saying worth reflecting upon, "Remember always that everything that happens to you, whether prosperous or adverse, comes from God, so that you neither become puffed up in prosperity nor discouraged in adversity".[71]

Suffering will not be grace-filled unless we cooperate with God's providential love. He acts like a Father disciplining his children. In Hebrews we are taught that the Lord disciplines the ones that he loves and corrects all those he acknowledges as his children. The author assures us, "Suffering is part of your training; God is treating you as his sons. Has there ever been any son whose father did not train him?" (Heb 12:6-7).

Through suffering we are broken and made compassionate of heart, more able to be wounded healers for others. It is a form of pruning: "…every branch that does bear fruit he [the Father] prunes to make it bear even more" (Jn 15:2). As we surrender to the gentle, but firm hand of the Lord, we can become more supple to his touch, like pliable clay in the hands of the potter (Jer 18:1-4). The Lord uses suffering to train our hearts to be more dependent on him. He never makes a mistake in the way he relates to us, even though we may kick and scream and resist his ways. He is always caring for us, always totally concerned for our welfare. He is training us to become more surrendered to his will. As it says in Proverbs, "Like flowing water is the heart of the king in the hand of the Lord, who turns it where he pleases" (Prov 21:1). The Lord wants us to have a heart like that. Because our wills are so hard, obstinate, and resistant, and because we cling to many things, he knows that for our good we will need to pass through suffering of one kind or another for our purification and refinement.

The author of 1Peter says: "You may for a short time have to bear being plagued by all sorts of trials; so that, when Jesus Christ is revealed, your faith will have been tested and proved like gold…" (1Pet 1:6). Our faith is precious like gold. Its impurities will only be burned out through the purifying fire of God's love, which we encounter in suffering. Later the author says: "You must not think it unaccountable that you should be tested by fire… If you can have some share in the sufferings of Christ, be glad, because you will enjoy a much a greater gladness when his glory is revealed" (1Pet 4:12-13).

James counsels with the same message: "You will always have your trials, but, when they come, try to treat them as a happy privilege; you understand that your faith is only put to the test to make you patient…" (Jm 1:2). If we are children of God, says Paul, then we will share his sufferings so as to share his glory. But Paul says: "I think what we suffer in this life can never be compared to the glory as yet unrevealed, which is waiting for us" (Rom 8:18).

Paul endured immense hardships for the sake of Jesus' name, in fulfilling his commission to preach the Good News to the ends of the earth. He considered this a sign of credibility for someone who is genuinely God's servant: "we prove we are servants of God by great fortitude in times of suffering, in times of hardship and distress; when we are flogged, or sent to prison, or mobbed; labouring, sleepless, starving…" (2Cor 6:4).

While he was gifted with mystical experiences, (2Cor 12:1), he had been given a 'thorn in the flesh' to stop him from getting proud about them. Even though he pleaded with the Lord about this, he was told, "My grace is enough for you: my power is at its best in weakness" (2Cor 12:9). He goes on to say that he will boast only in his weaknesses, "so that the power of Christ may stay over me… For it is when I am weak that I am strong" (2Cor 12:10).

There is an important principle here. In and through our sufferings, when we unite them with the suffering of Jesus on the cross, we find a font of grace, and we can become a font of grace for others.

Pope John Paul II says that in Christ, "God has confirmed his desire to act especially through suffering, which is man's weakness and emptying of self, and he wishes to make his power known precisely in this weakness and emptying of self".[72] He adds: "The springs of divine power gush forth precisely in the midst of human weakness".[73]

This is the meaning of the cross of Jesus. At his weakest moment, in humiliation and defeat, he became the font of divine life for the world. All who willingly enter into this journey with him, by hanging on the cross with him, will become a font of his life to others. On the outskirts of Rome there is a place called *The Three Fountains*. Legend has it that this is the place where Paul was finally executed. His head was chopped off by a sword. Then the head bounced three times. From the spots where the head landed there sprung three fountains! Whether we believe the historical accuracy of the story, the legend conveys a profound truth. Through his weakness and self-emptying in suffering unto death in imitation of Jesus, Paul has become for generation after generation in the Church a font of living waters for our sanctification.

5

STOKING THE FIRE
The Context for Growth in Christ

"The one who received the seed in rich soil... is the one who yields a harvest." (Mt 13:23)

To walk with Jesus in a committed way requires a context that will support growth. To be a disciple means developing a whole new way of life. Jesus told the parable of the sower who was sowing the seed (Mk 4:1-20). As he threw the seed from his bag, some fell on the edge of the path; the birds came and ate it immediately. These are the people who hear the word, but they allow the evil one to rob them of it before it can take root. Other seed fell on rocky ground, where it found little soil. It sprang up straight away, but there was no depth of earth. It did not form roots. When the sun came up it was scorched and withered. These are the people who have an initial spurt of enthusiasm, but they fail to put down good roots in the spiritual life. When difficulties and trials come, they don't last, but fall away. Some seed fell amongst thorns. It started to grow, but the thorns choked it. There was no harvest. These are the people who start the journey well, but the worries of the world and the lure of riches get a stranglehold on them, and the spiritual life is squeezed out of them.

Some seed fell on good, rich soil. It grew tall and strong, and produced a good crop. These are the people who provide open hearts to the word of God, and organise their lives so as to yield a harvest. Beginners in the spiritual life need to have a vision for putting down deep roots so that their life will be abundantly fruitful for the kingdom of God. For this to happen they need to know how to provide "good soil" so that God's life can grow richly within them. To be able to really put down roots deeply in the Lord they will need the right heart attitudes, which were described in Chapter Four of this book. But they will also need to provide a context, or a way of life, within which the spiritual life can flourish.

There are a number of key ingredients for this "good soil", which gives a nourishing environment for growth. They are prayerful solitude, relationships in community, listening to the word of God, spiritual reading, participation in the Eucharist, the sacrament of Reconciliation, and the ministry of intercession, evangelisation and compassion. If they seek to have these elements in place within their lives, they give themselves the optimal conditions for growth. If a plant is to grow, its roots need to be put into soil that has the right nutrients for its nourishment. Similarly with the spiritual life, we need to be drawing from the sources that will ensure plentiful feeding; this will maximise conditions for growth.

To use another image, the Christian life could be likened to a wheel, which has a hub and a number of spokes between the hub and the rim. The hub is Jesus, on whom the whole life is centred and from whom all power comes. The spokes of the wheel are essential for its forward movement. They are the essential elements that have been mentioned above, namely solitude, community, the word of God, spiritual reading, Eucharist, Reconciliation and the ministry of intercession, evangelisation and compassion. In this section we will look at each one of these elements and how they fit into an ordered spiritual life. Before doing this, I want to make some preliminary comments on the need for a personal plan of life.

Plan of Life

Many people live spontaneously from moment to moment, carried along by the next whim or fancy. Some even espouse this as a virtue, saying they are moving under the influence of the Spirit, who is like the wind which blows where it wills. While this sentiment sounds very pious, this attitude usually contains a fair degree of self-delusion and does not provide the necessary stability and consistency for a steady growth in the Lord. It can indeed be a rather fleshy escape mechanism from the hard task of responding to God's love by seeking to do his will in all circumstances. On the other hand, some people are very organised about their lives, but their priorities are driven by the expectations of other's demands on them; whether it be the pressure of work, or of study, or of sporting practice, or of other obligations. Their life is a "roller-coaster" of events that seems to be out of their control. There never seems to be any time for personal spiritual nourishment.

In the increasing pressures of modern living, organisation of time becomes very important for the spiritual life. We will best be obedient to God's will by prayerfully drawing up a plan of life, which helps us make sure that the most important things have priority. We need to set our priorities by God's agenda. Otherwise, priorities are established in our life according to our own selfish agenda, or by someone else's agenda. A plan of life sets out the regular weekly schedule so that the most important priorities are included first. When we examine a typical week, it is possible that social media gains greater priority than prayer, that the gym is more important than family, that the football ranks higher than spiritual reading, and that work squeezes out everything else. Drawing up a schedule for the week is an attempt to make sure that high priority activities don't get ignored. It helps us use our time well, according to God's will for our lives; and it gives constancy and regularity to our lives.

It is particularly helpful to draw up a plan of life in consultation with a spiritual companion or director. The plan needs to be challenging, but not unreal in its demands. It needs to be fixed, but not rigid or inflexible. It needs to be adapted to our state of life, our health, our profession, and our temperament. Needless to say, quite a deal of wisdom and common sense is needed in this exercise. The word "balance" is important to remember. Much of the spiritual life is finding the right balance between what can seem competing claims on our time e.g., between prayer and work, between family and career, between work and play, between spiritual activities and physical activities. There is no ready-made formula, but we usually know when there is an imbalance, and need to put in some corrective. If we can't see it, our spiritual guide hopefully will. In all of this the fundamental ingredients dealt with in this chapter have high priority; we cannot afford to ignore them.

The Call to Solitude

Since Chapters Six and Seven of the book are devoted to various ways of praying, we will not need to define prayer at this point, nor will we give any hints about what is important in the time of prayer. It is sufficient here to simply stress the value of solitude for the development of the fire of God's love within us. Without solitude our lives are dissipated and dispersed by countless pressures and expectations, conventions and meetings, good works and endless recreation. Without solitude we lack any real centre as persons, and lose communion with God.

By solitude, I do not mean simply a time for ourselves, where we will not be bothered by others, and can have our own thoughts and do what we like. This attitude speaks of an escape from the world and being enclosed in oneself. Genuine solitude does not take us out of the world, but leads us more deeply into communion with others and involvement in the world for its salvation. It is not a self-serving exercise, but a God-seeking desire. Nor does solitude mean simply a time to recharge the batteries or to lick our wounds incurred in the rough and tumble of life. A time aside in the quiet may well function for this purpose, but it is not yet solitude unless it involves encounter with the Lord and on-going conversion of heart. Solitude will always bring us into dialogue with the Lord in the depths of our hearts, confront us with our weakness and sinfulness, and open us to rely more fully on the mercy of the Lord for our healing.

Solitude is primarily a way of the heart. It is the call of the heart to enter within oneself to that quiet place where we encounter the Beloved. Jesus said: "When you pray, go to your private room and, when you have shut the door, pray to your Father who is in that secret place..." (Mt 6:6). The spiritual tradition has interpreted these words as referring to a journey within. For the Desert Fathers it was not just a matter of going to their cell to pray, but to go within themselves to the interior "cell" where they would meet the Lord.

Francis of Assisi, knowing that his brothers were called to be itinerant evangelists, told them to take their cells with them, in their hearts, and never to leave this place of encounter with God. Catherine of Siena, when she was called into a busy, apostolic life had to forsake her early years of seclusion; but she sought always to stay within the "inner cell", the place where God dwells interiorly. She spoke of it as a "holy abyss" where we come to know both God and ourselves.[74] It is the place of interior communion with the Lord, within which we hear his gentle voice, and where we discover our true identity in him. In solitude we pay attention to the Lord; we listen to the quiet voice of the Shepherd gently leading us.

This solitude of the heart is the way of self-knowledge. For spiritual growth it is essential to be real about what is happening right now in our lives. In solitude we are confronted with the "many voices" that conflict with the voice of the Good Shepherd, and we find ourselves needing to choose more decisively for Jesus and his kingdom. In solitude the Spirit exposes the true state of the heart in all its deviousness. We become more aware of the inner compulsions to greed, lust, and power. We find ourselves in touch with our utter poverty, our nothingness before God. We are confronted with the "false self", which is shaped by the world. We are given the grace to own our brokenness and sinfulness and turn to the Lord with confidence and mercy.

Solitude as a way of the heart is fostered by occasional silent retreats and days of reflection. In a world of many words that have lost their meaning we need space for silence. In the silence we can quiet down sufficiently within ourselves to tune into the movement of God, and to become more aware of the demons that afflict us. Each day we should try to find some quiet time alone with the Lord. This can be difficult for some to achieve, but not impossible for most. If we are prepared to be "cut-throat" in turning off our phone or other devices, and going to that place in the house that is set aside as the "sacred place", we can develop a habit of having a regular "rendezvous" with Jesus. Once significant others in our life know the importance of this time for us, they will learn to respect it and not invade it.

In Chapter Six we will look more closely at the different modes of prayer—vocal prayer, meditation and contemplation—and how they develop. Without regular times of interior prayer, the fire within will die quickly.

Sometimes the busyness of work can persuade us that we have no time for quiet prayer, but only a few prayers on the run. This is a mistake. Jesus himself is our primary model. The gospels often depict him going off to a quiet place to pray. For example, after a long evening of healing ministry at Capernaum, Jesus must have been glad to get to sleep. But we are told by Mark, "In the morning, long before dawn, he got up and left the house, and went off to a lonely place and prayed there" (Mk 1:35). Luke tells us, "Large crowds would gather to hear him and to have their sickness cured, but he would always go off to some place where he could be alone and pray" (Lk 5:16). It was his customary practice. He would withdraw to be in communion with the Father, to listen to the Father's voice, and to draw strength for the road ahead.

Francis of Assisi, in his early days, was torn between two great desires—the passion for solitude and the passion to preach the gospel. To which should he give himself? Not trusting his own discernment, he asked one of his brothers and St. Clare to pray to the Lord for an answer to his dilemma. They returned to him with the understanding that the Lord wanted both, and that they were not in conflict. Francis always insisted that evangelists must first draw from hidden prayer what they want to communicate to others. Unless we ourselves are on fire with the Spirit, the words we speak will be cold and powerless to change hearts.[75]

Relationships in Community

While solitude is an essential ingredient in the spiritual life, we are to avoid solipsism. We are relational beings. No one is an island. We are interconnected. God chose to come to us as a human being in Jesus, and he continues to come to us in and through other human beings. His characteristic way of relating to us is by gathering us as a people. The spiritual life flourishes best in the context of a nurturing and challenging community of committed brothers and sisters in the Lord. It is no accident that wherever the Spirit is moving to renew the Church in these days he is birthing new communities. The Spirit calls us out of isolation into communion, and leads us out of autonomy into interdependence. After all, the Holy Spirit is the love between the Father and the Son, eternally given and eternally received in mutual self-giving. When the Spirit is at work he binds us together, making us one, in order to fulfill the heart-prayer of Jesus to the Father at the Last Supper: "Father may they be one in us as you are in me and I am in you…" (Jn 17:21).

Community life provides a context for nurturing the seed of God's word within us. We find the support of like-minded people who share the same beliefs and values of the kingdom, and are committed to living their lives for Jesus. It is, of course, possible for Christians to grow in the fire of God's love without belonging to one of the intentional renewal communities that have mushroomed within the Church in recent decades; however, it is not possible to grow without the Church itself. My point here is that the Church at the local level will always be expressed most richly in close, personal community life of one kind or another. I would maintain that we suffer from a deficient ecclesial experience if we are not part of some kind of identifiable community, whether it be a vibrant parish community, one of new communities associated with the new movements, one of the traditional communities of consecrated life, or one of the many other lay communities in the Church today. Community life provides maximal opportunities for growth.

This is increasingly the case in the secular environment in today's Western world. The common mind-set in the contemporary society is indifferent and apathetic towards the things of God; and in some cases blatantly hostile in opposition to the gospel of Jesus. In this milieu, our best chance for growth in the Lord is through belonging to a strong community of faith and love, which shares a common ideal of holiness through imitation of Jesus.

The Christian life was never meant to be lived as a *"lone-ranger"*. Since the Enlightenment we have been sold the lie in the Western world that true freedom is found through rugged individualism, rather than through interdependence. Most of us are tarnished with the false idea that the autonomous individual, who is answerable to no one, is the ideal human being. Yet, this doctrine is far from the notion of the Body of Christ, presented in Paul's letters. Paul would not have been able to conceive of a Christian who claimed to have a personal relationship with Jesus, but did not belong to Christ's Body. And his concept of Christ's Body was not primarily the universal Church (although this is certainly a dimension, especially in his later writings), but of a concrete, fairly intimate, community of brothers and sisters bonded together in love.

Through relationships in the faith community we hear the word proclaimed and receive the necessary instruction in the faith. We are given opportunities to use our gifts for the up-building of the body, and for its mission to spread the Good News of God's love. We are able to share our lives in a genuine way with others. This calls for the grace of vulnerability, by which we are prepared to lay open to significant others the struggles, difficulties, trials and joys of our life. This process has a way of keeping our spiritual life well and truly grounded.

In community life, we find the many interactions with others a *"school of love"*. As we discussed in Chapter Three, practical love is the primary fruit of a life in the Holy Spirit. In committed relationships with others this love is tested and refined. We inevitably experience tension, hurt and conflict in relationships. Handled well, these become means of grace, and opportunities for growth in holiness. The rubbing up against one another can be likened to the brittleness of sandpaper which is used to polish us in holiness. We learn how to forgive and how to resolve conflicts and move towards genuine reconciliation. We also learn how to be accountable to others, and to respect their intrinsic worth and dignity as persons. We learn to always think of the other person as better than ourselves by engaging in acts of humble service.

Probably even more challenging is learning to receive from others; to receive their affirmation and unconditional acceptance, and to allow them to wash our feet in service of our needs. In the climate of acceptance which we find in community we discover more clearly that our personal value is in who we are rather than in what we do, or what position we have, or in how much money we have. Community brings us into the experience of the warmth of the Father's love. The affection, tenderness, loyalty, correction, forgiveness, honouring and love of brothers and sisters mediate to us a deep sense of the Father's care and fidelity. This heals the wound of rejection, so often within people in today's society, restoring in us a healthy vision of self, others, and of the Lord himself.

Listening to the Word of God

Speaking about Scripture as the inspired word of God the Second Vatican Council said: "Such is the force and power of the Word of God that it can serve the Church as her support and vigour, and the children of the Church as strength for their faith, food for the soul, and a pure and lasting font of spiritual life".[76] This statement of the Church's magisterium echoes the words of Paul who says: "All scripture is inspired by God and can profitably be used for teaching, for refuting error, for guiding people's lives and teaching them to be holy. This is how the man who is dedicated to God becomes fully equipped and ready for any good work" (2Tim 3:16-17).

Anyone committed to following Jesus will be devoted to his word given in the Scriptures. They will learn to read God's word as a personal message to them.[77] While it is important to study the Scriptures for understanding, this should not become a barrier to listening to the word for oneself and being formed by it. It is not enough to study the Scriptures to gain the meaning intended by the author. We need to discover its meaning for us and how it applies in our lives. It is a personal communication to us from God himself. It is not the same as an impersonal letter from an advertising agency, or a general email sent by someone who is overseas to many friends back home. It is more personal than that. It is God's voice speaking to each of us individually, as a father writes to his son or daughter. Vatican II says: "In the sacred books, the Father who is in heaven comes lovingly to meet his children and talks with them".[78] When friends write to us, they don't just give information and facts, but they reveal themselves to us, because they love us and we love them. Scripture is God's message of self-revelatory love for us and an invitation for us to respond in love to him.

When we read Scripture prayerfully, we can find our hearts burning within us, like the disciples on the way to Emmaus (Lk 24:32). The action of the Holy Spirit brings the words alive to us, and they impact upon our minds and hearts, and shape our actions. Sometimes this will happen when we hear a reading proclaimed in the liturgy. Yet, some days the scriptural word will seem dead and lifeless. There will be no consolation or immediate revelation, even then the word is feeding us. Later, at a time we do not expect, a particular passage will "come alive" under the movement of the Spirit and be most applicable to our particular situation. Daily reading of the Scriptures is indispensable. It provides the saturation with the word that is necessary for it to spring forth at times of need and provide inspiration and strength.

Through daily reading of the Scriptures our minds and hearts are being formed in the mind of Christ. He promised, "If you make my word your home, you will indeed be my disciples, you will learn the truth and the truth will make you free" (Jn 8:31). Our minds need to be formed in the truth. We are still in some way shaped by the thinking of the "world". We can be like a sponge, soaking up all the thoughts, attitudes, values and ideals of the secular, materialistic, and hedonistic environment of modern society.

Paul says: "Do not model yourselves on the behaviour of the world around you, but let your behaviour change, modelled by your new mind" (Rom 12:2). He is speaking of the new mind formed in us by Christ and the work of his Spirit. Our minds can still be moving down the ruts of the old self, following patterns that are still in complicity with the sin of the world. Our minds need to be cleansed daily with the pure water of Scripture, to wash out all the deception and illusion. This is the only way we will be clear-minded and free of confusion. Rather than making the opinions of the talk-back radio kings the measure of one's life, or the latest popular cry in the press and the visual media outlets, we can be grounded in God's word, which is firm ground indeed.

The mind is the battleground. To take the word of God seriously means to have an active mind, rather than mindlessly absorbing the values and attitudes of the world. We should be vigilant and alert, guarding our minds; so that every thought becomes captive in obedience to Christ Jesus (2Cor 10:5). In the first letter of Peter there is a rousing call to free the mind of all encumbrances (1Pet 1:13). The image suggested by the original Greek text is to "gird up" the mind. This imagery comes from the time when men wore long robes as well as women. To be ready for an important journey, they needed to "gird up the loins", by tucking the long robes under the belt. Then they were free of all encumbrances and were able to move forward with speed.

The message intended is that we are to have active minds, vigilantly watching over the door of our hearts, and actively listening to God's word as our preferred nourishment. John Cassian offers another image for this vigilance over the heart. He says that the continual flow of thoughts running through the heart is like a mill-stone spinning around under the power of a waterfall.[79] As long as the water is running there is a lot of activity. Yet the miller can decide what is going to be ground by the stone. He can grind wheat, barley or darnel, and the stone will crush whatever he chooses. In other words, while we can't stop having a flow of thoughts in the mind, we can take charge over what comes into it. If we are constantly turning the word of God over in our hearts, they will be oriented towards God, and not governed by worldly thinking.

Daily listening to the scriptural word gives us a new energy and a new vision according to God's way of thinking. We allow his word to prune us and help us to grow (Jn 15:1). We make God's word the measure for our lives. It becomes the standard by which we judge our behaviour. Hebrews says: "The word of God is something alive and active; it cuts like any double-edged sword but more finely; it can slip through the place where the soul is divided from the spirit, or joints from the marrow; it can judge the secret emotions and thoughts" (Heb 4:12). The word will expose to us the interior ruses and deceptions of the evil one. It will call us to repentance for wrong thinking and faulty attitudes. And it will help us live in the light of God's truth. The word of God is likened by James to a "mirror" (Jm 2:23). Reflecting on this image Raniero Cantalamessa says: "The soul that gazes at itself in the mirror of the Word comes to know 'how it is'… and discovers how unlike the image of God and the image of Christ it is".[80] In the light of the word of God a real change of mind can happen, a conversion to the mind of Christ.

There are three movements to hearing God's word. Firstly, listening with the heart; secondly, interiorising this word in a reflective way; thirdly, doing the word. To this point we have been focusing mainly on the first moment—listening. But to really listen means to allow the word to become part of you. You become a scriptural person. You think according to the word of God. We are told of Mary, "she treasured all these things and pondered them in her heart" (Lk 2:19). The Desert Fathers had a practice of keeping a word within the heart for days, learning it "by heart". They had a saying that a monk should "daily till the soil of the heart with the gospel plough", and also that "the heart should be dyed the colour of the Scriptures". This is the practice of *lectio divina*, which will be described in more detail in Chapter Six, when we discuss contemplative prayer.

The Desert Fathers knew the intrinsic power of the word of God to change us. It brings us greater knowledge of self and of God. It teaches us who God is and who we are. Through the word we are convinced of the greatness, goodness, and mercy of God; and we have a mirror put before our souls, convincing us of the need for repentance, and God's power to change us.

To hear the word of God is also to do it. James says: "To listen to the word of God and not obey is like looking at your own features in a mirror and then, after a quick look, going off and immediately forgetting what you looked like" (Jm 1:23). The test that we have truly taken the word to heart and made it our own is that we are "actively putting it into practice". This is how we will be blessed (Jm 1:25). There is no place for procrastination or hesitation, but simply a call to immediate obedience in action. The word of God is transforming of lives. We must submit to the word and let it govern us.

Not only does the word of God shape our moral lives, it also gives us guidance and direction in significant decisions on life's journey. The story of St. Augustine's conversion is a case in point. Struggling to overcome his flesh, burdened with indecision, and deeply anguished in heart, Augustine heard what he took to be some children nearby singing the words "take and read". Interpreting this to mean he was to take up the Scriptures, he opened upon a word that cut him to the quick and provided the grace to embrace Christ fully for the first time.[81] Anthony of Egypt, in a similar way, heard a word of Scripture which changed his life. As a result of that word, he gave away everything he had, and embarked on an extraordinary journey in the desert. Francis of Assisi likewise heard a text from the Bible which so struck his heart that it catapulted him into a radical life of poverty as a missionary, preaching a message of repentance.

If we are growing in the Spirit, we can expect that, at times, certain words will be given to us that confirm us in God's will and his direction. These words become milestones for us to which we can refer at a later time. They should be recorded, since they are like markers that we can go back to at a time of subsequent lostness and confusion. They keep us oriented on the way. The prophet Jeremiah exhorted the Jews as they were going into exile in Babylon "to set up road markers, put up guideposts" (Jer 31:21) along the way, so that when the time came, they would more easily find their way home. The spiritual life is like a road marked out by the words we have received from God, leading us home.

Spiritual Reading

Growth in the spiritual life is fostered by good reading, videos, podcasts and music, and other online input, which feeds the mind and inspires the heart. Apart from the word of God itself, which is paramount, the committed follower of Jesus should be on the lookout for material that will feed the mind with the truths of God and help to stoke the fire of desire for God and zeal for the work of the kingdom.

The lives of the saints, and their spiritual writings, are highly recommended for this purpose. Some hagiography, however, should be avoided. Accounts of saints' lives that focus too much on extravagant claims, with an over-emphasis on the miraculous and extraordinary, can present a faulty vision of the Christian life.

Nevertheless, the heroic deeds of the saints, the way they lived the gospel radically in their times, is an excellent motivation for holiness. When we realise they were human beings just like us, with all the same temptations and imperfections, we find their response to God as a challenge and inspiration to make the same whole-hearted response to the gospel today.

A wise reading of the lives of the saints will always interpret them according to the culture and times in which they lived. This will avoid the mistake of trying to slavishly imitate a particular saint's exotic penances, or attempting to conduct missionary work in exactly the same manner. We are not given these testimonies for us to replicate what they did in their time, but to be inspired by their total response to the gospel, and to do likewise in our time and culture, in the way that the Spirit is showing us today. Hopefully, something of their "divine madness" will rub off on us, something of their boldness and zeal for the kingdom, something of their fortitude in suffering, something of their deep compassion for the downtrodden. We should pray that the fire of God's love which burned so powerfully within them would capture us as well, and help us to forget our petty, selfish concerns and become great in God.

The purpose of spiritual reading is not study, but to arouse the love of God and to awaken more deeply the longing for holiness. Consequently, the choice of material should not be too abstract or analytical. It is better to absorb a little in a reflective manner, rather than to consume much voraciously out of intellectual curiosity. In this age of cursory reading, internet browsing, and distracted online behaviour we find it difficult to quiet the spirit to be truly attentive to spiritual input. We need to cultivate the spiritual art of reading, watching, or listening in a truly reflective manner.

Books (and podcasts, videos, etc.) are good if they are experienced *now* as up-building and stimulating. The principle of selection is simply what speaks to you now. Some material will be attractive and useful at one time, but of little help at all later on. Other material may not be suitable at the early stages of the journey, but later on begin to speak quite powerfully. Even though some would believe the written word is going out of fashion, I would like to make a strong pitch for books. Some books can be read again and again, especially if they have touched deeply into our lives. It is good to be guided by one's spiritual director in the choice of material. Unlike some textbooks, which have to be read for study purposes, spiritual reading is not an exercise to be endured, but to be enjoyed.

It is best not to flit from one book to the next in a restless fashion, without really spending quality time with any book. Once you have found a treasure don't be afraid to spend as much time as you need in savouring your discovery, and drawing inspiration from it. Of course, if a book is proving to be quite sterile, you should have the freedom to leave it behind quickly in favour of something more nourishing. Spiritual reading will stimulate prayer. Indeed a good spiritual book can be used as a springboard into conversation with the Lord, and a deeper level of response to his love. It is not always the case, but spiritual reading can provide food for meditation, and can directly energise your conversation with the Lord.

Nourished by Eucharist

There is nothing that stokes the fire of love in our hearts more than the Eucharist. It is *the* sacrament of God's love. The Eucharist is fire! In Chapter One of this work, I made the case that meditation on the glorified wounds of Jesus will bring us into the fire of his love for us. I also pointed out that the fire of his love which he demonstrated so powerfully in his passion, has now been poured out into our hearts by the Holy Spirit. In the Eucharist we enter into the love given through the wounds of Jesus like nowhere else, and we experience the power of Pentecost like nowhere else. This infinite love of God in the heart of Jesus, which seeks union with each one of us, is present in a sacramentally guaranteed way in Eucharist. If we come with receptive hearts, we are drawn into the mystery of his love. He unites himself to us in a communion of love, and our hearts are inflamed with a love that is not of human making but is deeply human all the same.

In the celebration of the Eucharist, we are drawn into the perfect sacrifice of Jesus to the Father. We are penetrated with the love of God so we can allow ourselves to be broken with Jesus on the cross. At the Last Supper Jesus took the bread and *broke* it. The Eucharist in the early church was known first as the "breaking of the bread". This was not just an act of sharing by Jesus, but also an act of immolation. In breaking bread Jesus was expressing his willingness to be broken himself in his passion the following day. As the suffering servant "he was pierced through for our faults, crushed for our sins. On him lies a punishment that brings us peace; by his wounds we are healed" (Is 53:5).

A human being, who is the Son of God, "breaks" himself before God. This "breaking" is the surrender of his human will to the Father's will. He obeys unto death. This obedience makes us, who have been disobedient, right with God. Jesus says: "Do this in memory of me". By this he does not just mean "remember what I have done", but, more so, "do the essence of what I have done".[82] We are to "do" what Jesus did, in memory of him. We are to allow his grace within us to draw us into this mystery of his sacrifice, and to come ready to "break" ourselves before God; to lay before God all hardness of heart, rebellion and stubbornness. We are inspired into a deeper 'yes' to God in and through the perfect "yes" of Jesus. Our love for God and our willingness to make our lives a living sacrifice to God is expressed and deepened.

This "breaking", however, has another dimension. Jesus' sacrifice was "for us". At the Last Supper he broke the bread, and then "gave it" to his disciples. He said, "This is my body which will be given up *for you*". He is not only given over to the Father, but also given for every human being. The heart of Jesus burning with love for every person is made present in Eucharist. He is "given" for all. By God's grace, if we come with an open heart, we are drawn into the heart of Jesus. We are joined with his heart for the world. We become "broken", and "given" with him for others. As we enter into Eucharist with faith, we are caught up in the love of Jesus himself. This love cannot be contained. It is the love that embraced all men and women when he willingly stretched out his arms on the cross. Eucharist enflames our hearts with this love. We are made ready to be poured out for others in union with his heart, broken in love for the world.

Jesus said, "Take and eat...". This is why he comes in Eucharist; to be eaten. Eucharist is the bread of life come down from heaven for the life of the world. It is supreme nourishment for the human being. Jesus said: "As I, who am sent by the living Father, myself draw life from the Father, so whoever eats me will draw life from me" (Jn 6:57). The word used in this text for "to eat" is "*trogon*" in the Greek. The etymology includes the concept of an animal laying hold of what is its staple diet, what sustains it in life (e.g., horses eat hay, monkeys eat bananas). What is the staple diet for human beings? The Eucharist! This is nourishment for our life. Without it we die.

Communion brings profound intimacy and union with Jesus. There is no greater means towards intimate union with the Lord than this one. We should cherish the time immediately after holy communion, and allow the Lord to stir his love within us for him and for all men and women. The purpose of our eating is to be changed into Christ. St. Augustine paraphrases Jesus' words: "You shall not change me into your own substance. Instead, you shall be changed into me".[83] Normal food is assimilated by the body. It breaks up and is used by the body to nourish and sustain it. When we eat the bread of life an opposite process takes place. This is *living* bread. This bread gives life to those who receive it. It assimilates them and transforms them into itself. So, in a very real way, in Eucharist "we become what we eat". Eucharist is the most profound means of being changed into the likeness of Christ, whom we eat.

Taking Communion is not just a private affair between myself and the Lord. It expresses and effects deeper communion with one another in Christ. As St. Augustine said: "We eat the body of Christ to become the body of Christ".[84] The main purpose of the Eucharist is to effect unity. We are bonded more deeply in Christ and empowered to love one another as he has loved us. Paul says: "the bread that we break is a communion with the body of Christ. The fact that there is only one loaf means that, though there are many of us, we form a single body because we all have a share in this one loaf" (1Cor 10:16-17).

In the celebration of Eucharist, we should try to avoid all formalism, ritualism and over-familiarity. Eucharist will be a means to spiritual growth only to the extent that our subjective dispositions are pure.

We should enter the celebration in a recollected manner and should participate actively, consciously and as fully as possible. At the time of the consecration, we should foster within ourselves a sense of awe, reverence and surrender. Before Holy Communion we should do all we can to receive with faith, reverence, and humility. The sacrament does not bear fruit in us automatically. While all the graces are guaranteed to be present, we can only receive them to the extent that we are genuinely right of heart and have a sincerely open disposition. We should truly value the time of thanksgiving after Holy Communion, and not rush off into activity too quickly. After all, this is the most precious time of profound encounter with Jesus available during this earthly pilgrimage. We should not take it for granted, but savour the moment, spending time to soak up his presence within us in an intimate exchange of love.

Since the Middle Ages the Church has developed a deep devotion to Jesus present in the reserved Eucharist. Prior to that time the Eucharist was reserved primarily for the sake of bringing communion to the sick. The development of Eucharistic adoration outside of the Mass itself has become a precious means for growth in the spiritual life.

In the Eucharistic species the whole Christ is really, truly, and substantially present. The consecrated bread is not just a sign pointing to a hidden reality. Nor is the presence of Christ in the Eucharist simply a subjective belief of the faithful. The bread and wine are changed in substance. It is no longer bread and wine even though this appears to be the case from what the senses can experience, or from what scientific experiment could identify. It is the body, blood, soul and divinity of Jesus Christ, who died and rose for our sake, and is now graciously given for us in this humble manner. So, it is indeed fitting that we adore him. This adoration is a prolongation of the Mass. It enables us to continue drawing from the graces of the Mass in a profound way. It is praise, thanksgiving, worship, reparation for sin, and intercession—opening us more to the fruits of Calvary in our lives.

In Eucharistic adoration we bask in the sunshine of the Lord's love, allowing him to build a quiet burning love within us. We become more aware of Jesus' desire to win us for union with him, and his desire awakens a thirst in us for this union also. We look upon him whom we have pierced (Jn 19:34) and our hearts become pierced with love for him. We are wounded with love. We allow Jesus to place our hearts in the burning furnace of love in his own heart. Having been inflamed by this burning love, our hearts yearn more deeply for him and for reconciliation with others.

In Eucharistic adoration we have a heart-to-heart dialogue with Jesus. Deep is calling upon deep (cf Ps 42:1). We hear him address us as friends, and find a new intimacy, a deep bonding of hearts in inexpressible love. In Eucharistic adoration we also find the healing we need. The prayer before communion is still applicable, "only say the word and I shall be healed". We allow the power of Jesus' healing to flow into our hearts. We reach out to Jesus like the woman with the haemorrhage did (Mk 5:25-34). Over time we discover that the healing has taken place. If we suffer from a poor self-image, he affirms us in our worth and dignity. If there are sinful patterns or difficult temptations, he brings liberation and victory. If there is an addiction, he brings new power to change. If there is anxiety or despair, he brings new peace and new hope.

Eucharistic adoration is also a means of growing in sacrificial love, as we unite ourselves with the victim heart of Jesus, broken and given for the world. It also develops a surrendered heart, as we allow ourselves to be claimed more fully by his love and give all in return to him. It also builds in us a thirst for the salvation of others, as we are drawn into Christ's insatiable thirst for souls expressed in his cry "I thirst!' while hanging on the cross. We find ourselves being formed in the heart of the Good Shepherd for the lost (Mt 9:36). In Eucharistic adoration we fulfill Jesus' request of his disciples in the garden, "Watch and pray!" It is a powerful means of intercession and spiritual battle. It is a wonderful way, in the providence of God, to "bring fire to the earth".

The Sacrament of Reconciliation

The regular use of the Sacrament of Reconciliation is an indispensable means of spiritual growth. In this sacrament we encounter the reconciling love of God, ministered through the heart of Jesus, the good Shepherd. The sacrament also facilitates on-going conversion, and brings the healing touch of Jesus to our lives.

The post-Vatican II renewal of the Rite of Reconciliation reclaimed the communal dimension of the sacrament, restoring a sense of the corporate nature of sin and repentance. Consequently, in addition to integral confession, we now have readily available to us occasional celebrations of the second rite. After a liturgy of the word, which calls the community to repentance, and a common confession of fault, there is the opportunity for individual confession and absolution. This ritual has been effective in raising our awareness of being the body of Christ, and that all sin in some way affects the whole. We have regained something of the saying of St. Ambrose, "in the Church there are water and tears: the water of baptism and the tears of repentance".[85] Ambrose meant by this that the whole community weeps over the repentant sinner.

John Paul II stresses this communal dimension of the sacrament when he says, "The forgiven penitent is reconciled with himself in his inmost being, where he regains his innermost truth. He is reconciled with his brethren whom he has in some way offended and wounded. He is reconciled with the Church. He is reconciled with all creation."[86] This ecclesial dimension was already present in the celebration of the sacrament prior to the Vatican II renewal. The priest represents not only Christ but the Church in receiving the penitent and bestowing forgiveness. Now, however, this dimension has become expressed more loudly through the communal celebration.

The first form of the Rite of Reconciliation, which involves a private celebration with the priest and penitent alone, was not the normal practice of the Church in its earliest centuries. It became the regular practice in the 7th century. Since its inception it has been a powerful means of spiritual growth for the individual. Those who downgrade its importance in favour of the communal celebration are failing to realise its true value.

The fact that people are not seeking out this private form of reconciliation in the same numbers as before is not in any way an indication of its irrelevance. It is rather a sign that we as a Church need to be evangelised. The Good News of the saving love of Jesus needs to be preached with new fervour. When people begin to personally experience the love of God, and are brought into a conscious, personal relationship with Jesus as their Saviour and Lord, they readily seek out this sacrament for its on-going healing and restoration. With the help of a wise, prudent and compassionate confessor, they are able to advance quickly in a life with Christ.

The way of celebrating this first form of the rite has been renewed. The emphasis used to be on anonymity, and the ritual was performed in a fairly mechanical and impersonal manner. Now there is the possibility of having a personal conversation with the priest and receiving guidance in facing the root causes of the sins confessed.[87] In the context of a personal encounter in a relaxed, but not informal way, the penitents can talk about the deeper dilemmas of their lives, and be helped to make the decisions necessary for their growth in the Lord's ways. While it should not develop into a counselling session as such, it is possible for the priest to help penitents bring to the light the full extent of their burdens, and to give them over to Jesus to be healed by his holy wounds. Often the presenting sin confessed is only the tip of the iceberg. Underneath there is a whole complexity of woundedness that needs healing. Without labouring the issue, the priest can help penitents to simply turn their woundedness towards Jesus for his gentle healing touch. In this way the sacrament not only ministers the guaranteed forgiveness of the Lord, but also becomes a more effective means of empowering the penitent for change.

The Sacrament of Reconciliation is a wonderful instrument for us to be brought into the victory of Jesus over sin. Unfortunately, people have sometimes experienced it as a type of "sheep dip" on a Saturday afternoon, getting rid of unwanted contamination, which returns again during the following week. It is good to have a strong notion of how the sacrament forgives sins, "cleaning the slate" as it were. But we also need to understand how the sacrament aids on-going conversion. It helps us break with established sinful patterns. We are not doomed to be repeating the same sins for the rest of our lives.

The sacrament affirms us in the truth of our identity as a "new creation" in Christ. It is a celebration again of the power of our baptism. Paul says: "When he (Christ) died, he died once for all to sin, so his life now is life with God, and in that way, you too must consider yourselves to be dead to sin but alive for God in Christ Jesus" (Rom 6:10-11). The Sacrament of Reconciliation renews this baptismal grace of victory over sin. It applies to our lives the energy and power of the death and resurrection of Jesus. Its regular use is a most effective way of gaining the strength and confidence we need to grow in holiness.

A wise choice of a penance by the priest can help penitents to make the celebration of the sacrament an on-going power for change in their lives. We speak of having a "firm purpose of amendment". The Catholic Catechism says: "Absolution takes away sin, but it does not remedy all the disorders sin has caused. Raised up from sin the sinner must still recover his full spiritual health by doing something more to make amends for the sin...". [88] Good guidance from the priest as to a suitable penance can help penitents make the changes necessary to amend their lives and conform them more to the mind of Christ.

Above all, the sacrament is a celebration of God's mercy. There are two words for mercy in Hebrew.[89] The first is "*hesed*", which is the covenantal attitude of God. Even though Israel sinned again and again, God was slow to anger and rich in mercy (*hesed*) (Ps 103:8). He does not hold our sins against us. If the Lord weighed our guilt against us, we would not survive. But he has graciously brought us forgiveness, which we do not deserve (Ps 130:3-4). The other word is "*rehamim*". This word derives from the concept of a mother cherishing the child in her womb. It carries the emotional quality of mercy. "Is not Ephraim, then, so dear a son to me, a child so favoured, that after each threat of mine I must still remember him, still be deeply moved for him and let my tenderness (*rehamim*) yearn over him?" (Jer 31:20).

In Jesus' story of the prodigal son, (or forgiving father), both these meanings are present. When the son returned having brought disgrace on the household, having gravely insulted his father, by demanding his inheritance, and having squandered everything on loose living, the father is waiting. He catches sight of the boy in the distance and runs to him, throwing his arms around him, and kisses him tenderly. This is the *"rehamim"*! We notice there are no questions. The Father holds nothing against the son. In fact, nothing is held back in celebrating his return. He is given the ring on the finger—symbolising freedom of the house that belongs to a son; the best robe—that is kept only for the most favoured guest; sandals for his feet—symbolising the restoration of his dignity. This is the *"hesed"* of the heart of God. He does not hold our faults against us but casts our sins away as far as the east is from the west (Ps 103:12). The sacrament of Reconciliation enables us to encounter this wonderful mystery of God's mercy.

Through the regular celebration of the sacrament we learn to trust in the mercy of God given in the heart of Jesus. This is a foundational truth which is the bedrock of the spiritual life. While, as was presented earlier, the sacrament proclaims and effects the victory over sin in our lives, our fragile human condition means that we do fall again in one way or another. We are tempted to become discouraged, and self-condemning. We can carry the burden of irrational guilt, and anxiety about never being able to rise above the entrapment of sin. Catherine of Siena advises: "Hide yourself under the wings of God's mercy, for he is more inclined to pardon than you are to sin. Bathe yourself in the blood of Christ".[90]

For Catherine, the blood of Christ is the sign of God's infinite mercy for us. Like the prodigal son we can easily engage in negative self-talk when we have fallen. But Catherine reminds us that when humanity sinned, he did not command condemnation, but clothed us in mercy. He has paid the price for our sins in his blood, and he will not refuse his blood to anyone who asks. It is simply a matter of repenting with all our heart and turning back to the Father of all mercies.

Intercession, Evangelisation and Compassion

We are baptised into Christ. For this grace of our baptism to blossom we need to be growing in the heart of Jesus for the lost. There is no authentic spiritual journey which does not enlarge our hearts to be able to embrace all peoples with the love of Christ. No matter what our particular state of life or occupation our growth in Christ develops a profound zeal for souls. The more we grow in love of the Lord, the more our heart is turned outwards towards others, and especially towards those who are the most poor, because they do not yet know the love of God. As we enter into the heart of Jesus, who hung on the cross in burning love for all men and women, we adopt his attitude of mercy and compassion for all our brothers and sisters in the human race.

On the cross the heart of Jesus was pierced and opened for us. As we dwell upon Jesus crucified, we allow him to give us his own heart with which to love. We enter into his passionate love for the Father, and his passion for all men and women. We are pierced with the love that is in the heart of the Good Shepherd, and acquire a zeal for the salvation of all. Jesus on the cross cried out "I thirst", indicating not just a physical thirst, but also a deep longing in his heart for the salvation of every person. As we meditate upon his wounds, we find our hearts inflamed with this burning desire of Christ for men and women to come to him to find reconciliation and peace.

Eucharistic adoration especially unites us to Christ and to his prayer. Bursting with love for all as he hung on the cross, Jesus offered the perfect prayer on our behalf, making the love-offering that we could not make that was totally accepted by the Father in the resurrection. Now at the right hand of the Father, "his power to save is utterly certain, since he is living forever to intercede for all who come to God through him" (Heb 7:25). We intercede with and through Jesus; like Dominic, who prayed throughout the night, "O, Jesus… that sinners will repent…".[91] We can do nothing to change hearts. All we can do is pray. We beg with insistence for his kingdom to come. Catherine of Siena imaged herself at the foot of the cross of Jesus catching in a container the precious blood shed for the life of the world, and through intercession, pouring it out upon stony hearts. Hearts that are as "hard as diamond", she maintained, can only be cracked by the precious blood of Jesus.[92]

We live in the time of a "new Pentecost", which Pope John XXIII prayed for when he opened the Second Vatican Council. His prayer was heard. Throughout the Church there has been a new breath of the Spirit blowing. New movements and new communities are springing up to meet the challenges of preaching the gospel in our times. The more traditional communities are being revitalised in their original charisms and finding new vigour and excitement for the work of evangelisation. Dioceses and parishes are becoming mobilised with a renewed vision and energy for spreading the Good News.

At the beginning of the new millennium Pope John Paul II predicted a "new springtime" for Christianity, and maintained the first signs of this were already evident.[93] The grace of the "new evangelisation" is upon us. With prophetic vision, John Paul II declared: "I sense that the moment has come to commit all the Church's energies to a new evangelisation and to the mission *ad gentes*. No believer in Christ, no institution of the Church can avoid this supreme duty".[94]

This "new evangelisation" has the same content as before, namely the proclamation of the Good News of salvation found in Jesus Christ. But its "newness" comes from renewed fire in the hearts of those proclaiming, and new creative methods that are appropriate for our age. The Church has always been "born again" in each age through the power of the Holy Spirit. What is most distinctive about our present time is that the Spirit's work is not just with an elite band of priests and religious, but with all the baptised. The Holy Spirit is releasing a diversity of charisms amongst all the faithful so that the new evangelisation can be accomplished. What is also notable about the "new evangelisation" is that it does not just aim to gain more adherents for the Church to fill the pews on Sunday and organise the parish activities. It aims to lead people to a personal conversion to Jesus Christ as their Saviour and Lord, and then to support them in being able to grow as disciples of Jesus.

For this "new evangelisation" to be effective there will need to be a new flowering of holiness in the Church, a new fire of the Spirit in the hearts of many. There will need to be communities that witness the love of God incarnate in the way they relate to one another, welcome strangers, and reach out to the lost. As Pope Paul VI said: "Modern man listens more willingly to witnesses than to teachers, and if he does listen to teachers, it is because they are witnesses".[95] Our zeal for holiness is not meant to be only for ourselves. Ultimately it is meant to bear fruit for the salvation of others.

Evangelisation is not only witness of life. There is also a time to speak. All are called in some way to be proclaiming the Good News. As Paul VI said: "There is no true evangelisation if the name, the teaching, the life, the promises, the kingdom and the mystery of Jesus of Nazareth, the Son of God is not proclaimed".[96] The way this happens will vary greatly depending on our state of life and specific vocation. Yet for all, in one way or another, there will be many God-given opportunities to share the reasons for the hope that is within us (1Pet 3:15). The Spirit convicts us of the enormous privilege we have in sharing with others the precious gift of Christ.

We should not separate growth in prayer and the work of evangelisation, as if they are different vocations. It would be wrong to make a false dichotomy between the contemplative life and the active apostolate. While different callings have particular emphases, all in the body of Christ are called to both intensive prayer and to zealous evangelisation. To grow in one is to grow in the other. If we are growing in personal relationship with Christ through prayer, we will have his Shepherd's heart for the lost. We will experience within us the anguished heart of Jesus as he looked upon the crowds and "felt sorry for them because they were harassed and dejected, like sheep without a shepherd" (Mt 9:36).

A vocation to pray is a powerful way of reaching the lost. This is why Thérèse of Lisieux, a contemplative confined to a Carmelite monastery, has become the patroness of missionaries. Evangelisation is to do with the heart. Thérèse offered her life through all the little sacrifices of her daily existence, for missionaries. She joined her heart with the heart of Jesus on the cross, offering herself as an oblation for all men and women who do not yet know the love of God. It works the other way also.

As we step out in evangelisation to share our faith with others, we grow in faith ourselves. Faith is like a muscle. If it is bound up and not exercised, it slowly atrophies and dies. When we evangelise, we exercise our faith and it grows stronger. If we don't evangelise, then our faith becomes weak and loses its toughness. Paul tells us that one of our greatest protections against the tactics of the evil one is to be zealous to spread the Good News of peace (Eph. 6:13). And we are given a guarantee by Jesus himself that the gates of hell will crumble in the face of the Church's proclamation of the Good News (Mt 16:18).

Evangelisation is above all an act of deep compassion for others. It is acting in the name of the merciful love of the Redeemer. Unfortunately, some abortive attempts at proclaiming the gospel are anything but genuinely loving. These misguided attempts to proclaim the gospel obscure the face of Christ in today's world. However, when we come to others with the Good News, and meet them with the deep respect for their personhood, without any imposition, but simply offering the precious gift of the pearl of great price, this is a profound act of love and compassion. Consequently, by exercising this love we will grow in love also. Not only will we deepen in love for others, but we will find a deeper fervour in our personal relationship with Jesus and the Father as well.

This last principle holds good also when we engage in acts of mercy, such as feeding the hungry, visiting the sick, welcoming the stranger, clothing the naked, going to those in prison. Jesus says we will be judged on this account (Mt 25:31-46). We should not undertake these works looking for some "narcissistic kickback", or some "*kudos*" in the eyes of others. These are self-centred motives. Yet we are never totally pure in heart. It is best to go ahead anyway, trying to purify the heart as we go along. These acts of corporal mercy are great means of grace for us, even though we should be trying not to undertake them for this motive. The more we respond to the Lord's grace to be expanded in genuine love for the down-trodden the more we have space within us for the penetration of the Spirit of God. The more we actively love others the more God fills us with his love; just as the more we actively love God himself the more he will also fill us with his love. Indeed, these two movements are but two dimensions of one and the same love of God given us in Jesus Christ, and now dwelling within us by his Holy Spirit.

Mother Teresa has given powerful witness to the reality that we meet Jesus not only in prayer, word and sacraments, but also we meet him in "the distressing disguise of the poor". Pope Francis has also drawn our attention to the truth that it is not so much the down-trodden who need us; rather it is we who need them. He notes that often people will volunteer to work among those on the fringes of society, only to discover the real poverty lies in themselves, not in those for whom they came.

Our attempts to grow in imitation of Jesus should not be made in a closeted and rarefied atmosphere, immune from the uncomfortable challenge that is brought to us from the "little ones" of this world. They are part of God's plan for our sanctification. This is not to say that we must have an apostolate of this kind to attain sanctity. But it does mean our feet need to be firmly on the ground. Relationship with those whom the world finds unsavoury, or unmanageable, or contemptible, has a way of bringing healing to the heart and liberation to the spirit. We find our own pretences, prejudices and false sophistication shattered. We are able to embrace more really the poverty of our own humanity. Hence, we can be more open to the One who clothed himself in this frail humanity for our sake.

The human heart does not exist in a vacuum. It is constantly affected by good and bad influences from its environment, which shape it for better or for worse. It is also always struggling to shape its environment according to its own desires. This chapter of the book has been examining the environmental influences that a friend of God should desire to have. How will the heart choose to be formed? The heart which seeks the face of God will be a heart that listens in silence and solitude to the quiet voice of the Lord. It will be a heart that also seeks genuine communion with others, choosing not to take the journey alone, but with brothers and sisters in the Lord who will bring nurture and challenge when needed. It will be a hearing heart, that attends especially to the Scriptures, and wants to be formed by the word according to the mind of the Lord. It will be a heart that is fed often on literature, music, drama, and other cultural media, which lift the mind towards God. It shall be a heart that hungers for the Bread of Life and loves to be with Jesus in Eucharistic adoration. It will be a heart that is constantly broken open through repentance, and turns with confidence to the sacrament of God's mercy. It will be a heart, free from self-sufficiency and self-absorption, turned outwards towards the lost, alienated and marginalised. And it will be a heart that boldly shares with others the reason for the hope and joy that it knows within.

6

ABIDING IN THE FIRE
Towards Contemplation

"My heart has said of you, 'Seek his face'." (Ps 27:8)

Prayer is an experience of ultimate mystery. It cannot be easily analysed, defined, or pinned down in neat categories. In many ways it defies description. There is a strong tradition of Christian contemplation which asserts we know more truly what God is not than what he is.[97] For everything we can say about God, and how he relates to us, we need to immediately qualify it with a statement of our ignorance. As St. Paul exclaimed: "How rich are the depths of God—how deep his wisdom and knowledge—and how impossible to penetrate his motives or understand his ways" (Rom 8:33).

For this reason, prayer is a great risk. Hebrews warns us that it is a fearsome reality to come close to God, and to surrender to him (Heb 10:31). If we yield to God in prayer, we are no longer in control. We take the risk of responding to Love. There is no charter for the journey. No map to guide us to the treasure. There are numerous perils along the way. The Lord himself provides unexpected surprises, so that we learn not to domesticate him or turn his image into an idol. Yes, it is a risk, but well worth taking. The alternative is death. We are faced with a choice either to trust God, who is a "consuming fire" (Heb 12:29), or to trust ourselves, which is the way of destruction.

Gift of Desire

Prayer breaks forth as a gift of God from within. It is what we are created for. St. Augustine prayed that God has made us for himself, and our hearts find no peace until they rest in him.[98] The wonder of prayer can be likened to the first steps of an infant. The parents can coax the child and use all sorts of inducements to try and make the child walk. But one day the child simply finds the power from within, and to the delight of all, gets up and walks. The miracle of prayer happens like this. Yet, prayer is far more than a natural capacity. We cannot manufacture it ourselves. It springs forth within us as a miracle of grace.

All our efforts at making the space for God to work are important. We dispose ourselves and make ourselves available to him. We seek him earnestly and cry out to him from the heart. But these strivings are already the fruit of God's grace within us. They are signs of desire within us for him, a desire which he has planted within us.

Prayer is desire for God; and desire for God is prayer. St. Augustine says that Paul's injunction to "pray constantly" means we must desire eternal life always from the only One who can give it. So, we are to pray with uninterrupted desire in faith, hope and love. He says that the times we set aside to pray with words or meditation make us more aware of this desire for God alone and arouse the intensity of this desire even more.[99] So our times of prayer are intended to inflame the undercurrent of desire that is always being fed by the love of God. In fact, it is God's desire for us that is paramount. *His desire for us* causes the miracle of prayer to spring within us as desire for him. He awakens the desire, and he empowers the response to his love.

In John's gospel Jesus met the woman at the well (Jn 4:1-14). Jesus first proclaims, "I am thirsty". This is a symbol of the thirst in Christ for her heart and, indeed, for the hearts of all men and women. He cried out on the cross "I thirst!", expressing his longing through his loving suffering for union with every person. It is his thirst that awakened a response in the woman. After she registered surprise that he, a Jew, was speaking with a Samaritan, Jesus says, "If only you knew what God is offering, and who it is that is saying to you... he would have given you living water". When she expressed desire for this water, still not fully understanding, Jesus promises, "anyone who drinks the water that I shall give will never by thirsty again: the water that I shall give will turn into a spring inside him, welling up to eternal life". This is the gift of the Spirit who brings forth the life of prayer within. The Catholic Catechism, referring to St. Augustine, puts it succinctly: "Whether we realise it or not, prayer is the encounter of God's thirst with ours. God thirsts that we may thirst for him".[100]

Friendship with God

Prayer is an expression of friendship with God. Teresa of Avila says: "Contemplative prayer in my opinion is nothing else than a close sharing between friends; it means taking time frequently to be alone with him who we know loves us".[101] We are familiar with how ordinary relationships can become functional, lacking genuine intimacy. The marriage relationship, for example, which is intended for mutual self-disclosure, can become little more than co-existence, living together under the same roof with little genuine communication. Any marriage to survive needs times of heart-to-heart sharing in truth and love. So it is in our relationship with Jesus.

Relationships can become routine, task-oriented and lacking openness and vulnerability. Similarly, our friendship with the Lord can suffer due to excessive preoccupation with doing many things, even great things for the kingdom. Martha discovered this when Jesus gently, but firmly, reproached her, "Martha, Martha, you worry and fret about so many things, and yet few are needed, indeed only one. It is Mary who has chosen the better part" (Lk 10:41-42). Whether we are serving or praying we should be in communion with the Lord. Our times of prayer are invaluable moments of intimacy with Jesus whereby the relationship is deepened. Our times of service are meant to be an on-going expression of this intimate relationship.

While we enjoy a relationship of friendship with Jesus, it is not a relationship of equals. Jesus says: "I call you friends *if you do what I command you*" (Jn 15:14). The true friends of God are in humble obedience before him. Nevertheless, it is a genuine intimacy. It calls for self-disclosure from both God and ourselves. Jesus says: "I shall not call you servants anymore, because a servant does not know his master's business. I call you friends because I have made known to you everything I have learnt from my Father" (Jn 15:15). This friendship is sheer gift. We cannot earn it. He who is "nearest to the Father's heart" has decided in gratuitous love to reveal the secrets of the Father's heart to us (Jn 1:18). Even though he already knows the depths of our hearts, he waits upon us to be vulnerable with him, and to open the secrets of our hearts to him.

Prayer as Reality

When we come to prayer it is important to be ourselves before the Lord. We should pray from where we really are, rather than from some ideal of where we would like to be. Teresa of Avila teaches that, when we come to prayer, it is a matter of knowing who I am, and knowing who God is, and knowing how to speak to him.[102] Teresa means here that we be real with God about "where we are at". We need to be ourselves with all the pressures and circumstances of our lives here and now. Being in touch about what is happening in the present moment, and being vulnerable about it with the Lord, is the way we play our part in the self-disclosure demanded for intimacy with him. However, it is not an invitation to self-focus, or excessive introspection about problems. Rather, being in touch with the rawness of our struggle, we now turn to the Lord, praying to him from our situation. Being who we are at this present moment we allow the Spirit to reveal to us who Jesus is—the gentle Master, the Healer of souls, the Sovereign Lord, the Shepherd of hearts. The search for "who He is" is not so much a metaphysical or theological question, but who he is for us *now* in this situation. He is saving, redeeming, liberating God who is always present to us. When we pray, we simply advert more consciously to that presence, and this is what makes the difference.

Catherine of Siena heard the Lord reveal this truth in the following words: "Do you know daughter who you are and who I am? If you know these two things, you have beatitude in your grasp. You are she who is not, and I AM WHO IS".[103] The journey of prayer is an unfolding of this mystery. To know that we are creatures totally dependent upon the Creator for everything, and to know that we have been saved by the precious blood of Jesus and are a new creation in him. To know the affirmation of his love in the depth of our being. To know that we have absolutely nothing to bring to him but the decision of our will, and even this cannot be made without his grace. As Jesus said: "Cut off from me you can do nothing" (Jn 15:5). To know that even though we are a new creation we still have a deep state of sinfulness, the unredeemed part of us.

This inner poverty can be experienced as a global sense of being weak, wounded and shabby, a feeling of living in an interior slum.[104] It is being confronted with the truth that we are but undeserving beggars. This is the position of the tax-collector at the back of the Temple in the story told by Jesus. Unlike the Pharisee up the front, he had no achievements, no status, no claims on holiness. Yet his position was one of truth. There was no pretense, no cover-up, no denial, no social mask—just the simple truth, "O God, be merciful to me, a sinner" (Lk 18:13). This is the prayer which pierced the heart of the Lord.

To know the Lord as "I AM WHO IS" means depending totally on him as the source of all life and being. It is to know the gaze of his love upon our being at all times. It is to know that he is Lord of our chaos. When we call to him from the position of our chaos, he will speak his word of life into the chaos, as he did when he first called the world into existence. The same Spirit who hovered over the chaos at the dawn of creation acts within me now. This is the Spirit who raised the lifeless body of Jesus from the dead. He dwells within me, affirming me in who I am in God, and bringing forth the mystery of prayer which is beyond my capability. As Paul says: "The Spirit too comes to help us in our weakness. For when we cannot choose words in order to pray properly, the Spirit himself expresses our plea in a way that could never be put into words, and God who knows everything in our hearts knows perfectly well what he means, and that the pleas of the saints expressed by the Spirit are according to the mind of God" (Rom 8:26-27).

Modes of Prayer

There are three modes or expressions of prayer: vocal prayer, meditation and contemplation.

Vocal prayer is using words to pray; for example, saying the rosary or other devotional exercises. It includes prayers such as singing the psalms and hymns, and saying the prayers of the liturgy, as well as praising God aloud or calling upon him in a spontaneous way. Jesus himself prayed vocally to the Father, at times in praise and exultation, at other times in agony and desperation (Mt 11:25-26, Mk 14:36). When the disciples asked him to teach them how to pray, he gave them a vocal prayer—the Our Father. Sometimes people consider wrongly that vocal prayer is second rate and should be superseded once we experience contemplation. Teresa of Avila, and the whole Christian tradition, would maintain otherwise. Teresa counsels beginners to carry around an image of the Lord to help represent his presence to them, and periodically to speak with him. She says: "Since you speak with other persons, why must words fail you more when you speak with God?"[105] She is encouraging spontaneous conversation with the Lord, which is already the way into contemplation. In vocal prayer we use our bodies to express our love to the Lord. We are body-persons. We need to be able to verbalise our praises, to speak out our heart desires, to confess our sins, to be with Jesus who "offered up prayer and entreaty, aloud and in silent tears to the one who had the power to save him out of death" (Heb 5:7). Yet we are not to "babble like the pagans"; we are to pray from the heart (Mt 6:7).

Meditation is using our faculties of intellect, imagination and memory to reflect upon the mysteries of God revealed in Jesus Christ. It is not meant to be a barren intellectual exercise, nor an imaginative fantasy trip. Francis de Sales teaches that meditation should always lead us to make "affections", which he defines as "pious motions of the will"—such as greater love for God, zeal for souls, desire for holiness etc. "In these affections" he says, "our hearts should open themselves and expand as much as possible".[106] Teresa of Avila, likewise says, "It is not important to think much, but to love much. Do then what most arouses you to love".[107] Meditation flows into contemplation, which is the quiet, restful loving attentive gaze upon the Lord. It is equally knowing within the depths of the heart the loving gaze of the Lord upon us. It is the attitude expressed by the peasant, when the Curé of Ars asked him what he was doing as he spent hours before the Blessed Sacrament: "I look at Him and He looks at me".

While it is good to distinguish these three modes of prayer it would be a mistake to separate them. Any one prayer time could easily involve all three as we flow in and out of the different expressions. Vocal prayer can easily trip off a contemplative moment. Those who become deeply involved in recollecting on a mystery of the rosary, or are caught in a moment of loving encounter in Eucharist, experience this. Those who pray in charismatic tongues know also how this can be a sort of vocal contemplation, since it bypasses the use of the mental faculty, and can be a heart-to-heart prayer with the Lord.

Contemplation, likewise, can have moments when we burst forth in jubilation that cannot be contained; often in wordless utterances, expressing the joy of the Lord's love. Nor should meditation be seen in isolation as a practice by itself. The recent tradition has done meditation an injustice by calling it "mental prayer", since this has given the impression that it is all to do with the mind. While it is a reflective type of prayer, it is geared towards the type of "affections" encouraged by Francis de Sales. These affections activate the will in love and cause us to be more and more captive in our wills to the Beloved, which is the beginning of contemplation as such.

Prayer and Conversion of Life

There is a reciprocal and inseparable relationship between prayer and conversion of life. Unless we are growing in the virtues our prayer cannot be sustained. And without interior prayer, we do not have the strength to preserve the virtues. John Cassian uses the image of a stone archway with a keystone at the top of the arch to describe what we mean.[108] The life of virtue is represented by the two curved arches; the life of prayer by the keystone. Take away the keystone and the arches collapse. Take away the arches and there is nothing to support the keystone. It falls. Unless a life of prayer is undergirded by a sustained effort at growing in a disciplined way of life, it will not be supported. Like a keystone without arches, the prayer will fall away. Likewise, attempts to develop a Christian way of life without committed personal prayer will fail. These attempts will come to nothing because the vital "keystone" of prayer is not in place.

If we are growing in victory over sin and growing in love, humility, obedience and the other virtues, we will be well-disposed for contemplative prayer. To be able to receive the gift of contemplation, the heart needs to be purified, and our lives need to be conformed to the will of God. This is our best preparation for prayer. Cassian, using another image, says that our soul can be likened to a very light feather.[109] A slight puff of wind should be enough for it to rise up to the highest points in the sky. However, if it is dampened by any moisture at all then it will be weighed down and cannot rise above the earth. We cannot expect for prayer to happen within us unless we are assiduously working at overcoming sinful habits and worldly preoccupations, which weigh us down. If we are developing in way of a life according to the mind of God, then our hearts will be ready for prayer. The heart, he says, will then be "lifted up by the natural goodness of its purity, it will rise to new heights on the lightest breath of meditation…".

On the other hand, conversion of life is the fruit of prayer. We should aspire towards contemplation. It is a common fallacy to think that contemplation is only for specially favoured souls, who have particular mystical graces and are capable of heroic virtue. On the contrary, it is meant to be the normal flowering of the grace of baptism. As long as we are free of habitual mortal sin, and are seriously following Jesus, we can confidently dispose ourselves towards receiving the contemplative gift. Anyone in a living personal relationship with Jesus should wait expectantly for the advent of contemplation in their life. Contemplation is like drawing from a deep well in order to water the flowers in the garden.[110] The flowers are the virtues, that will grow more strongly in our lives the more we are abiding in the heart of Jesus. Contemplation is the heart on fire with love for the Beloved, and the more we become one with the Beloved, the more we become like him.

The gift of contemplation will not last if we are not using it to foster growth in holiness of life. In prayer we are exposed to the reality of God, and this is meant to bear fruit in our lives. Sometimes people can experience an intense infusion of the Holy Spirit at a particular moment in their life, which precipitates a deep experience of the Lord's love, almost instantaneously. Many in the charismatic renewal, for instance, have experienced this sort of outpouring in what is called the "baptism in the Holy Spirit". Such outpourings of the Spirit can open the individual immediately to what Teresa of Avila calls the "prayer of quiet", an effortless resting in the love of the Lord. Some make the mistake of thinking that the on-set of this prayer experience is an indication of an advanced state of holiness. It is never this easy. This inbreaking of the Spirit is given for the purpose of personal conversion. We cannot short-circuit growth in the Lord. If the Spirit chooses to anoint us sovereignly with particular graces, this is so that our lives will be changed more into the likeness of Jesus. Unfortunately, some who have been given the grace of the "baptism in the Spirit", or similar graces, have squandered this treasure by failing to work on overcoming ingrained sinful habits, and to grow in love, humility and obedience. Others, thankfully, have chosen to use the gift well and have grown markedly in both contemplation and a way of life conformed to the gospel. It is not possible to have one without the other.

Practical Ways towards Contemplation

No one can show us how to pray, except Jesus. With the apostles we can ask him, "Lord teach us to pray!" He cannot resist that plea. The Holy Spirit, who dwells with us, will direct us. There are, of course, valuable spiritual books, written by the great friends of God. These can inspire us and give us hints of how to avoid dangers and suggest methods to use. A good spiritual director can offer wisdom and light our way. Ultimately, however, it is a unique adventure for each person. No method can be absolutised. What we find useful in one season is expendable in the next. The rule is to "pray as you can". In one season it may be imaginative meditation, in another quiet repetition of the name of Jesus, in another a simple gaze upon the wounds of Jesus, in another a psalm prayed from the heart. Just as a craftsman has many tools in his kit to undertake the work, so the person of prayer will have a variety of implements from which to choose at any time.

Having said this, it will be useful to identify two main ways that friends of God have used the Scriptures as a means of entering into contemplation. The first is the method of Ignatius Loyola, used primarily in the second and third weeks of his Spiritual Exercises. The second is the ancient practice of the monastic tradition called the *lectio divina*, literally "divine reading", which is alive and well in most monasteries today, but is easily adaptable to ordinary life.

Before briefly describing each of these methods, it could be helpful to say something about the proximate preparation for prayer. I suggest a regular time each day if possible. It becomes your appointment with the Lord. If you were to have the opportunity to spend time in close conversation with the Pope tomorrow, you would be most unlikely to miss the appointment. How much more so with the Lord! Remember, the Lord is a thousand times more eager for this meeting than you are.

The time you set aside should be "prime time" in your day; not squeezed in between two very busy activities, or when you are worn out and sleepy. For most busy people the early hours of the morning are the best. It may mean rising half an hour earlier than before, but this is a small price to pay for such an enormous gain. It is also helpful to have a sacred place, which is your holy ground. Using symbols, such a crucifix, icons or other images can aid your focus. Some will need to find a way to quiet down the body and the mind, with helps such as relaxation techniques or soothing music. These aids can dispose us towards prayer, but they are not yet prayer. Your physical posture should be comfortable, but not too relaxed that you are inclined to sleep. The posture can change during prayer, depending on what is being expressed e.g., kneeling for supplication, prostration for adoration, sitting for meditation, standing for praise etc. Now let us examine the two methods.

Ignatian Approach

We are encouraged to use this approach as a way of encountering Jesus in the gospel stories. We come with confidence that Jesus will show us who he is. Ignatius directs us "to ask for an intimate knowledge of our Lord, who has become human for me, that I may love him more and follow him more closely".[111] We come with a desire for a personal revelation of Jesus to us. Through the gospels, we have privileged access to the historical Jesus. We are guaranteed, due to the inspiration of the Holy Spirit, that the gospels provide sure access to Jesus as he was, the Incarnate Son of God. Teresa of Avila says that no matter how far we go in the spiritual life we will never be able to let go of the gospels as our privileged source of knowing Jesus.[112] Meditation on the gospels grounds us in the humanity of Jesus. God has come to us in Jesus of Nazareth, and the only authentic way to go to God is through the humanity of Jesus.

Unfortunately, this approach has sometimes been used as an intellectual or imaginative exercise alone. We cannot love an abstraction. Ignatius was interested in having us encounter a person, Jesus, whom we come to know more closely and love more intensely. The imagination is used to create the scene of a particular gospel story as a vehicle to meet Jesus. We try to imagine the persons—what they look like, and how they are acting. We try to listen to what they are saying. We especially look at Jesus to hear what he is saying, and to behold what he is doing. We try to penetrate Jesus' attitudes, his thoughts, and his emotions. Why is he saying this? What are his motives? Why is he doing this? The aim is to enter into a heart-to-heart dialogue with Jesus.

The imaginative exercise is geared towards evoking an affective response—a movement of greater faith, or deeper love, or stronger conviction, or more expansive compassion, or gratitude, reverence or zeal. Most importantly we are to "look long" at Jesus. This is not an exercise of coming to know about Jesus, through thinking about him. Rather, it is a way of knowing Jesus through falling in love with him, and then from this knowledge deciding to love him completely and to follow him decisively. The aim is to "be with Jesus" as a companion, but also to "be with Jesus" from the inside of his human experience. Through silent loving gaze upon him, we enter into a heart-to-heart communion with him. The more we are "with Jesus" in loving adoration the more we "become like him". His attitudes become our attitudes; his values our values; his outlook our outlook; his vision our vision.

This way of meditation relies on the use of imagination. Some are deterred from using it because they say they have no imagination. In fact, everyone has an imagination. If we wince when someone tells us of a terrible car accident, we have an imagination. It is just that imagination functions differently in different people. Some are capable of recreating a scene in three-dimensional technicolour. This ability seems to be rare. In any case, an overly active imagination can be a problem, since it can pack the scene with so much detail that the central relationship with Jesus is lost. Others will experience the mystery more globally, but still be able to be interiorly present to the scene. The simple principle is to let God use what he has given you.

Another important point about this form of meditation is that it can engage our life experiences and invite the person of Jesus into our deepest struggles and joys. For example, meditating on the apostles being swamped in the boat while Jesus is asleep on a cushion in the stern, may surface within me the deep insecurities and anxieties of my life. The waves swamping the boat become the violent temptations I have been experiencing; I feel the weight of unfair accusations against me in the strong wind; I feel the strain of financial burdens as I fear the boat is sinking. I cry out "Can I survive? Where is the Lord in all this? He's asleep! Does he not care?" Then I behold him stand up in the boat and speak to the sea, "Quiet now! Be calm!" Now there is a new stillness within me. The Lord has spoken into the chaos of my life. I look long upon Jesus, my Lord, with awe and loving admiration. I find myself responding more deeply to the question that rises within me "Who is this? Even the wind and the sea obey him?" (Mk 4:35-41).

Lectio Divina

The *lectio divina* is the practice of listening to the word of God while reading the Scriptures. The aim is to cultivate the art of listening at ever deeper levels of inward attention. As we ponder the word or words of a text, we allow them to sink into our hearts and then the word carries us into an affective response to the Lord, and, quite possibly into a resting with the Lord in loving attention to him alone.

The way to begin with this is to set time aside in your favourite prayer place. Alone with the Lord in the quiet, you can now call to mind his presence. Then ask him to lead by his Spirit and yield the whole time to him unconditionally. Take up the Bible and open it to a text which you have already decided to use. Maybe it is one of the readings from the Mass of the day or from the Divine Office, or possibly a passage recommended by a book or suggested by a recent preaching or teaching you have heard. Read the passage slowly and carefully. As you do so, be attentive to whatever word, phrase, or verse strikes you.

When finished reading the passage, gently return to the part that impacted you in some way. Stay with it as long as you can. Chew over it like a cow chewing its cud. Treat it like a sweet, delicate morsel that you want to savour as much as possible. If it is not so much a consoling word as a message of challenge, then treat it with the respect that you give to necessary medicine that may not be pleasing but you know is definitely good for you. Absorb this text into your heart. You may even memorise it. This is not to be mechanical, but simply to repeat it slowly over and over again, and let it be something you come to know "from the heart".

Sometimes you will find that you can carry a memorised text in your heart for the whole day. That is far better than having a latest pop song ringing around in your mind all day. And it is a beautiful way to develop a heart that prays constantly. God's word has a power of its own to set your spirit towards him at all times.

Let whatever word you are dwelling upon become the basis for a conversation with the Lord. As you reflect on its implications for your own life, allow the Word of God to call forth from you a response to him. Don't make your prayer too complicated. Let it be simple, heartfelt, informal and unpretentious. Avoid clever thoughts and expressions. Sometimes, as in the case of the psalms, the words themselves can be your prayer, as you join with the cry of the psalmist to the Lord, whether it be joyful thanks, lamentation, adoration, repentance, or whatever. This approach can be a way that the heart becomes absorbed with the love of the Lord in contemplation. A single word may still be gently and effortlessly repeated within; but the word is now simply a crystallising of a deeper movement of the heart, which has been awakened by love, and is now delighting in the beauty of its Beloved.

Like the two disciples on the road to Emmaus our hearts can burn with love for God as Jesus opens the Scriptures to us (Lk 24:13-32). As the word penetrates and has its power within us, we are carried into communion with the Lord. We stay with him a while and he meets our deepest needs. It is best to use the least amount of the passage for the greatest length of time. One word or one verse can be enough for several prayer times. The word or verse quietly repeating itself within the heart becomes a springboard for the contemplative fire of love. It acts as a doorway into the inner chamber of the King. The heart opens with joy and gladness in his presence, full of praise for his immense love, and singing "how right it is to love you" (Sgs 1:4).

Growth in Prayer

There are some generally recognised stages of growth in prayer. Teresa of Avila has given what is probably the best description of the process.[113] I will not attempt here to present her teaching as such, but simply to give the reader an idea of some of the dynamics we can expect as our prayer life develops.

Normally, people begin with vocal prayer and are introduced soon enough to some form of meditation. As I mentioned earlier, meditation has the purpose of developing a heart-to-heart response to Jesus. This is the beginning of "affective prayer". Gradually, our prayer becomes more easily and quickly a committed response of the heart, and our love for Jesus is increasing. The normal progression then is to the next stage of prayer, which is called the "prayer of simplicity". Our prayer moves from being involved with an abundance of thoughts and images to maybe a single word, or a single image (such as the nail going through the hand of Jesus on the cross). This word or image is sufficient to carry one into a loving prayer of the heart. At this point it could be said that the person is experiencing "acquired contemplation". It is given this term since, while it is contemplation as defined earlier, the emphasis to this point has been largely on our quest for the Lord, our search for him, our hunger and desire for him, and our hard work seeking to find him.

Movement to the next phase brings a qualitative change in our prayer. It is a change that cannot be induced. We experience the onset of "infused contemplation". This is what Teresa calls the "prayer of quiet", when the will becomes captive in love and rests in God.[114] We experience now more clearly the supernatural action of God, rather than our own efforts. This is sheer gift from God and cannot be acquired no matter how hard we try. Consequently, upon its advent, the heart is deeply gratified and is full of intense love for the Beloved. Teresa notes that during the prayer of quiet, which initially may not last very long, there is absolutely nowhere else we would rather be. The will is absorbed with the Lord. However, the intellect and imagination can still be quite unruly. She counsels not to worry about this. She says: "The will shouldn't pay any more attention to the intellect than it would to a madman".[115]

The gift of infused contemplation can be likened to gaining sails for a ship that previously only had oars by which to make progress. Now the wind of the Spirit fills the sails and sends us forward effortlessly. A biblical image to illustrate the transition from meditation to contemplation can be found in the Song of Songs. The bride is seeking "him whom my heart loves" throughout the city. This is like the time of meditation, which is more a seeking than a finding. And then there is the moment when the bride finds "him whom my heart loves". She is now delighted. "I held him fast, nor would I let him go" (Sgs 3:4). This is the gift of infused contemplation.

Teresa offers a graphic image in *The Story of Her Life* to describe this transition.[116] Prayer, she says, is like going to a well in the garden to draw up water in order to help the flowers grow. The flowers are the virtues. At first it is laborious. A lot of energy goes into it for relatively little outcome. The bucket has to be put down by a rope and then hauled up manually. This is the toil of concentration as we fight distractions and aridities in our meditations. However, there comes a time, when God in his mercy provides a windlass with which to draw up the bucket. It now comes up much more easily and quickly. This, she says, is what it is like when we experience the "prayer of quiet". The fruits of this prayer are numerous. We have a deep assurance of our salvation; we are no longer fearful of trials, but have a new boldness and courage; we have an enlarged heart for God, and desire to do great things for him; it seems that there is nothing we would not be prepared to do for him; we see the misery of our earthly state and that everything is rubbish but to have Christ; and we are strengthened in all the virtues.

The next stage in prayer, says Teresa, is entry into union, where not only the will is captive to Love, but also now the intellect and the imagination are quietened. This she likens to God providing a stream in the garden to water the flowers. The later stages involve the spiritual betrothal and the spiritual marriage, which she likens to heavy rain upon the garden. It is good for the beginner to know about these advanced stages in prayer, but, practically speaking, it is best to focus upon the present challenges, and to ask the Lord for the grace of contemplation, always keeping oneself open to the fulness of what he can bestow in the future.

Difficulties in Prayer

The most common difficulty we have to handle is distractions. It is best not to try to hunt them down, but to let them go past, as it were. When we find we have become preoccupied with something foreign in prayer, it is simply a matter of gently turning the heart back to the Lord. There is no gain in becoming anxious or disturbed about the distractions. It is simply a matter of keeping a tranquil spirit and quietly correcting course again. Francis de Sales says: "Our biggest distraction, very often, is the care we take not to have any distractions!"[117] Nevertheless, when reflecting on the prayer time afterwards, it is valuable to take note of the distractions. They often indicate our inordinate attachments, and hence show us the need for deeper conversion of heart. On the other hand, we need to be careful not to make too much of them at all, since they are often bizarre and of no conscious origin. As we quieten in prayer, images of all kinds can surface from the semi-conscious and unconscious regions. We should treat them like most of our dreams, as having little or no significance for our spiritual journey.

Another difficulty in prayer arises from our broken human condition. We often suffer from emotional woundedness which restricts our freedom to enter into living relationship with the Lord. Because of this we can, as it were, keep the Lord at arms length, and maintain a regular and faithful prayer life that lacks any real dynamism. There are many kinds of emotional blockages e.g. a low self-image, which makes it difficult for us to believe that

God could really love us; or resentment, bitterness or unforgiveness towards someone, even toward God himself; or suppressed anger that is like a hidden volcano ready to erupt; or a prevailing depression that saps life of hope.

These difficulties usually call for some kind of pastoral counselling to help the inner healing to take place that is necessary. Nevertheless, their presence does not have to stop us praying. They will only block our prayer if we are not aware of them. The way through is, maybe with the help of another, to notice their existence, and to own their reality. Then in our prayer we can be very open with the Lord about the difficulty. Rather than hold it outside of our relationship with him, we can come to him as we really are, and pray from that place. We need to break out of the false idea that God is only interested in people who are whole and totally integrated persons. If that were the case, we would all be lost!

Another difficulty in prayer is a resistance to going any further or an avoidance of deeper intimacy with the Lord.[118] This is partly a spiritual problem, but also often has unconscious or semi-conscious emotional roots. Spiritually speaking it can be called "*acedia*", a sort of lethargy of spirit, a boredom, and inclination to seek something else perceived to be more "stimulating" or more "fulfilling". It manifests in falling asleep in prayer, doubting the reality and usefulness of the prayer, avoiding going to prayer, or finishing the prayer early in favour of some other preferred activity. From an emotional point of view, the resistance can indicate that we are putting limits on our vulnerability with the Lord and our readiness to be open to him in genuine intimacy. This pattern of avoidance often manifests precisely at the time when the Lord is coming closer.

As in any human relationship, intimacy places demand on our personal resources. Our guards go up. We have a strongly conservative streak in us that resists change. We sense that if the Lord is allowed to come too close this will mean a shake-up that we are not sure we want to undergo. We fear losing ourselves in the mystery of God, so we hold back from the invitation to trust and to surrender. Because this type of resistance is usually beneath our immediate awareness, we may need a spiritual director to help us identify it. Then it is a matter of owning the reality of the conflict within us and calling upon the Lord for help!

Another difficulty we have to come to grips with is dryness. Sometimes this aridity is a sign we have been complacent, lukewarm and lethargic in our spiritual life; or we have worldly attachments to which we are still clinging; or we lack child-likeness in seeking help from our spiritual director; or we have become vain and presumptuous about the consolations that the Lord has given us, or we have become more attached to consolations than to the Lord himself. Francis de Sales says that we should examine our heart on these matters, and if any of these attitudes are present, to repent of them and seek the Lord's forgiveness.[119]

However, if these factors are not clearly the cause of the aridity, then we can welcome it as a precious gift from the Lord. He uses aridity as a way of testing the heart and purifying it in a manner that would not be possible if he continued to give us consolations all the time. If we accept the aridity as the Lord's will and do not complain, it can be a way towards humility.

Teresa teaches that aridities come in doses decided by the Lord as a way of preparing the heart for contemplation, and also as a way of refining the heart once it begins to experience contemplative prayer. This is where her teaching on "determination" is important. In dryness we are tempted to give up because it is all too hard. She says to press on even more determinedly, relying not on consolations, *but on the God of consolation*. The great fruit from dryness is self-knowledge and humility. She says, out of dryness we can "draw humility—and not disquiet, which is what the devil aims after". Even though we may not be receiving any consolation at all, she says, we have the opportunity of growing in humility, which "will give a peace and conformity to God's will". She points out: "We are fonder of consolations than we are of the cross. Test us, Lord" she prays, "for You know the truth—so that we may know ourselves".[120] Dryness helps us to realise that everything is gift from God, and nothing is of our making. We discover our utter poverty before him, and he is able to purge us of interior attachment to anything but him alone.

Francis de Sales describes how the Lord refines our love for him through adversity. Experiences of aridity in prayer are a means the Lord uses to help us grow in disinterested love. Francis describes our first desires for God as stemming from "gratifying" love.[121] That is, we feel pleasure in God's goodness, and enjoy drinking deeply of his loving presence. Like a child at the mother's breast, we cannot get enough of what is on offer. The heart opens up in love for God because it is feeling gratification. This satisfaction it experiences creates a deeper hunger for the Lord. By "gratifying" love he is not necessarily meaning an elated feeling. It may be an empathy with the passion of Jesus, an experience of sorrow for sins, an intense experience of the in-filling of the Holy Spirit, or a zeal for following the Lord more closely. Nevertheless, there is an element of self-satisfaction in it. If our love for God stays at this level alone, we are not at all happy when desolation comes our way, and we tend to judge our prayer as inferior when it is dry and arid. We are still learning the meaning of sacrificial love.

God's purpose is to refine our love. While we retain this "gratifying" kind of love, we begin to want to love God for his own sake, and we want to return to God something for his goodness to us. However, there is nothing that we have to give God, except our wills. Hence, the emergence of "benevolent" love, which simply wants to praise the Lord for who he is, and to see him glorified always.[122] "Benevolent" love wants to do the Lord's will, simply to please him at all costs. Francis says that both these kinds of love are part of our journey to God. "Gratifying" love provides the passionate fire of the saints. But for this to happen it has to become purified and complemented by "benevolent" love. As we become more intent on simply pleasing God and doing anything we can for him, we seek "gratification" not for the delight it gives us, but for the delight it gives to God. The movement is toward disinterested love. And this is where aridity fits into our journey of prayer. Through occasionally having all the lights go out, and all the delights disappear, we are learning to love without any selfish intent, without any trace of narcissistic kick-back.

Francis de Sales tells a story of a fine musician, a marvellous lute player, who suddenly went stone deaf.[123] The lute-player kept his skill, which he had developed over years. He loved to play the lute for the King who was a child-hood friend of his. Even though the lute player could not gain any pleasure from hearing his music, he was still delighted to see the King's pleasure when he played. But one day the King commanded the lute-player to continue playing, because the music was pleasing to the King, but the King went out hunting! So now the lute-player was to play out of love for the King, and not even have the satisfaction of the King's presence and seeing the King's delight.

Aridity in prayer is like this. For the lute-player there was "nothing in it for him" anymore, except the knowledge that brought profound peace that he was doing what the King desired. As we develop more in this "benevolent" love, we do not judge our prayer time on the degree of pleasure we had, or the amount of enlightenment we were given, or the inspirations or images that came our way, or any other gift from God. We simply judge it by whether we were faithful and generous during the time of prayer. That is, no matter what transpired, we did not give up, but persevered in playing the song; and we were generous in doing so.

Francis observes that a person at prayer can seem so devoted and so on fire with the love of God. Their whole demeanour seems to indicate that they are truly absorbed in the Lord. However, as soon as the charm and gratifying feeling comes to an end, as soon as dryness appears, the person will very easily give up and only pray occasionally. Francis questions whether it was really God who the person was loving, or was it the *experience* of God? After all, God is still God! He suggests that such a person is in love with the consolations which God gives rather than the God of all consolation.[124]

Prayer as Self-Emptying Love

God has come to us in complete self-emptying love; the way we return to him is the same. To belong to Jesus means total self-emptying. We must come with nothing. Jesus said, "none of you can be my disciple unless he gives up all his possessions" (Lk 14:33). John of the Cross is quite relentless on this point. He says: "Spiritual nakedness, poverty of spirit and emptiness in faith are what is needed for union of the soul with God".[125] Jesus said: "Happy are the poor in spirit, theirs is the kingdom of heaven" (Mt 5:3). We must do all we can in active purification of the heart, as we discussed earlier in Chapter Two. This purification is not only of desire for external realities, such as fame, fortune, reputation, possessions, etc., but it is also a purification of interior possessions, a purification the spirit. As the journey proceeds, under the acute light of God, we become aware of our attachment to consolations, revelations and the pleasure of our prayer. We find ourselves greedy for spiritual goods, and vain about our progress in prayer. We find that our love for the Lord is grasping and possessive, and that our motives are often tinged with egocentric and hypocritical aspirations.

As we experience more intensely the love of God penetrating our hearts, we become more and more centred in "him whom my heart loves" (Sgs 3:1). We must let go of anything that is not God. Seeking *oneself* in God is contrary to love. As John puts it, "Seeking oneself in God is the same as looking for the caresses and consolations of God. *Seeking God in oneself* entails not only the desire of doing without these consolations for God's sake, but also the inclination to choose for love of Christ all that is most distasteful whether in God or in the world—and such is the love of God".[126]

What becomes painfully evident in the spiritual journey is that while there is a growing desire for union with God, there is at the same time a deepening sense of how crippled we are, and how totally incapable we are of reaching out with love towards God. No matter how much we seek to mortify ourselves we can never remove the obstacles to union by our own efforts. It is, of course, important that we work hard at it, but, ultimately we will experience failure to be able to do so. God has to do it himself. He begins to act to purify the heart in a manner totally beyond our capacity.

This is called "passive purification" of the senses and the spirit. It is totally God's work. We begin to undergo this purification in times of interior aridity and exterior adversity

Speaking about the beginner, Ross Collings says: "For the greater his zeal, the more deeply will he experience the inadequacy of that zeal to reach its own perfection directly; and the more profoundly he experiences the poverty of his own resources, the more he is truly prepared to receive the help of God "passively", which alone can bring him to his true goal".[127] This realisation of our utter incapability of reaching the goal, and yet the deep desire to do so, creates a sort of wound in the heart. It seems that God has wounded us with love, because he has created within us a longing which seems impossible to fulfil.

The Lord's main means to purify us through prayer and so prepare us for deeper union with him is interior aridity and exterior adversity. The journey into God involves a purifying fire of love. All our impurities are brought under the light of God. "God is light; in him there is no darkness" (1Jn 1:5). In his light we find all our hidden motives exposed as the Spirit of holiness penetrates us more fully. Through aridity our faith is purified and our love perfected. It burns out the roots of sin within us. It also makes us free to love God fully, by teaching us to cling to nothing else but to God alone. Now instead of us cleaning the window so God's pure and invisible light can shine through, God himself does the cleaning.

As he does so, the light, even though it is shining more brightly, becomes more undetectable. Consolations and revelations in prayer, sensible experiences of any kind are no longer cherished in any way. We simply let them go. If experiences of tangible blessings in prayer occur, we learn to receive them as God's gift for that moment. They are for the now only. They are not savoured afterwards or kept with lingering pleasure. Nor are they expected in the future or longed for in any way. We learn to avoid any temptation to try to induce them in order to repeat the delight. Exteriorly, the Lord will purify our love by allowing unexpected suffering to occur in our lives, or failure in our most cherished undertakings, or unfair accusations from others, or bitter disappointment from the infidelity of a friend, or some other affliction. His aim is to deepen us in our love for him.

The whole purpose of the Lord is to win us for himself totally and completely. When he wounds the soul with love with chastisements, aridities, afflictions and tribulations of all kinds, he is calling forth a deeper "yes" to him, to be made without any of the previous props and securities. In the midst of its suffering, the soul can choose to turn towards the Lord, to "look towards him and be radiant" (Ps 34), and to direct all its energies for love towards him in the darkness of naked faith. What is consistent, no matter what our experience in life and prayer, is the constant love of the Beloved. His aim is to heal us of our fickleness and inconstancy, so we can be free to love him in a generous and faithful way.

7

FANNING THE FIRE
A New Life in the Spirit

"Be happy at all times; pray constantly, and for all things give thanks to God." (1 Thess 5:17)

In this chapter we will explore ways that we grow in holiness by seeking to develop the gift of constant prayer. Aware that we are utterly poor and can do nothing without God, we learn to cry out in *supplication* for the help of the Holy Spirit at all times. Then aware of the Holy Spirit's activity in our lives we seek to be *docile to his inspirations* at all times. Filled with the Spirit we have a heart that is full of *gratitude and praise* for God at all times. Aware of the indwelling presence of the Spirit we develop an attitude of *attentive gaze upon the Lord* at all times. Aware that God is breathing his life and love into us through all the circumstances of our life we learn to *practice the presence of God* at all times. These are the themes that will occupy our attention. They help us to bridge the gap between contemplative prayer and life; we discover that prayer is life and life is prayer.

Supplication

We need to be thoroughly convinced that we are truly beggars before God. It is utterly impossible for us to pray. Yet he is the God of the impossible. We have no choice but to cry out to him in supplication. But it is not only for help in prayer. It is for everything.

Because all is gift from God. We cannot go anywhere towards God without his Holy Spirit. In our helpless poverty we learn to be with Mary in the Upper Room with the apostles imploring the Father in the name of Jesus to send the Holy Spirit. Seraphim of Sarov said that the whole goal of the Christian life is to be filled with the Holy Spirit.[128]

Even though the Spirit dwells within us through baptism and confirmation, we need to constantly call upon him to fill us more deeply. He is infinite and, at each moment, he can increase and deepen our capacity to receive him. The more we implore the Spirit to come to us, the more he hollows out depths in our hearts to receive him and increases in us an unending capacity to receive more of him.[129] We should get into the habit of invoking the Holy Spirit at the beginning of the day, and then often during the day. The gift of the Spirit is not given arbitrarily by God. To receive the gift we must believe in it, ask for it, seek and knock. Jesus says: "If you then, who are evil, know how to give your children what is good, how much more will the heavenly Father give the Holy Spirit to those who ask him" (Lk 11:13). Mary's prayer is powerful in touching the heart of God. She is given to permanent supplication on our behalf. We can especially join with her heart to invoke the Holy Spirit on our poor lives and on the whole Church.

John Cassian, voicing the tradition of the Desert Fathers, who were so aware of their frailty and poverty before God, counsels that a monk should repeat over and over again in the heart a simple formula, "O God come to my aid; O Lord, make haste to help me" (cf Ps 69:1). He says this carries with it the attitudes of inner poverty, watchfulness of heart, assurance in the help of the Lord, and confidence in God as our strength, especially in times of danger.[130] The quest is for uninterrupted prayer. Many have used the

Jesus prayer to seek to attain this. Again, this is a prayer of supplication arising out of our utter poverty, and our conviction that our salvation can only be attained through the gospel of Jesus Christ: "Jesus Christ, Son of the living God, have mercy on me, a sinner". It is to be repeated over and over within one's spirit.

The Russian pilgrim describes how repetition of this prayer brought the words quickly and effortlessly from his lips to his heart.[131] The prayer of supplication became part of him, even to the extent of continuing when he was not aware of it. In a similar way, it is powerful to be continually calling on the Holy Spirit. We invoke the fire of God out of a desire for more of his love and power. As he answers our prayer, we are filled with an even greater fire of desire for more of him.

Often Christians are not aware of the Holy Spirit's activity and are not expectant of his action in their lives. Even though they have been baptised and confirmed they do not personally experience in a conscious way the movement of the Spirit. John the Baptist said, referring to Jesus, that "he will baptise you with the Holy Spirit and fire"(Lk 3:17). The fire of the Spirit has come already at Pentecost. What was experienced in the early Church, and recorded in the Acts of the Apostles, is meant to be experienced today as well. Consequently, after a time of preparation, and a fresh conversion to Jesus as Saviour and Lord, many in the Church today are being led to ask for the Spirit to fill them with a new fire of his power and love. They are experiencing a new Pentecost in their personal lives. The activity of the Holy Spirit is being released in them in a new way. They become more aware of the sovereignty of the Spirit's action, and begin to experience more intensely his promptings. This new infusion of the Spirit is sometimes called "baptism in the Holy Spirit", using the scriptural terminology (Acts 1:5). This term simply means an immersion in the Holy Spirit in a deeper and fuller way. There is a new quality of indwelling of the Spirit and a new awareness and expectancy for the Spirit's activity in our lives.

This "baptism in the Spirit" is intended for all Christians, since it is an awakening and releasing of the graces of our sacramental baptism and confirmation.[132] However, it does not have to manifest itself in any particular way; nor does it have to happen in a single moment. We are meant to be constantly filled with the Spirit. We are to invoke the Spirit's fire of love at all times. No one can say, "I am filled with the Spirit", if by this they mean that there's no more to come. We are to constantly "fan into a flame" the gift of the Spirit that was given to us when hands were laid on us. Paul assures us this "was not a spirit of timidity, but the Spirit of power, and love, and self-control" (2Tim 1:6).

Docility to the Inspirations of the Spirit

Inspirations of the Spirit are interior movements initiated by the Holy Spirit to arouse us to greater holiness of life and to stir us towards apostolic activity. The Holy Spirit is constantly at work within us. Spiritual persons have a keen awareness and expectancy of the activity of the Holy Spirit in their lives. They are attentive to his promptings, always hearkening closely to his leadings, and seeking to be faithful to the grace he brings. The action of the Holy Spirit in the life of the believer has several characteristics, which give rise to different kinds of inspirations.

As the Spirit of truth, he opens the mind and heart to the reality and majesty of the Risen Lord, and brings the person into a loving, intimate union with Christ. So certain inspirations will open the mind to a deeper knowledge of who Jesus is. Maybe as we dwell on the crucified Christ, or open up a scriptural text, or participate in the Mass, or read a spiritual book, or listen to a homily, the Holy Spirit opens our eyes to the truth of the word and gives us heart conviction to actively respond to it.

The Spirit of truth also opens us to a knowledge of God as our "Abba, Father", and reveals to us that we are children of God. We will often hear the gentle voice of the Spirit within us in a manner like Ignatius of Antioch did as he was heading toward his martyrdom in Rome. He writes: "Earthly longings have been crucified; in me there is left no spark of desire for mundane things, but only a murmur of living waters that whispers within me 'Come to the Father'".[133]

The Holy Spirit is also the Spirit of love. He is the love between the Father and the Son from all eternity. As his activity within us becomes more prominent we will experience inspirations to love. There will be a whole range of promptings to love God above all things and through all things. The Spirit will lead us to a quiet intimacy with Jesus and with the Father. He will inspire us to make increasing acts of love for God during the day. This love will also be for others. He will be prompting us to say the kind word to others, to go the extra mile in serving someone, to visit the sick, to listen to someone we find annoying, to go to someone to ask for forgiveness, to help another who is in trouble, and so many other acts of sacrificial love which will bring us into the way of Jesus.

The Holy Spirit also comes to make us holy. He cannot abide with sin. Although he lovingly dwells within the sinner, he will act to convict us of sin. While he comes to comfort the afflicted, he comes also to afflict the comfortable! He acts within us to prompt us to genuine contrition and repentance of sins.

The Holy Spirit is also our guide and counsellor. He acts to show us the way ahead on the journey, unfolding to us the way God desires our lives to go. He is constantly giving us the wisdom to know the next step to take. He often gives specific inspirations that give us a new leading in our vocation or state of life, our family life or our employment, in our choice of ministry or our means of recreation.

The Holy Spirit also brings the fire of zeal for evangelisation. He desires that Jesus be glorified in every heart. He puts in our hearts a zeal for the kingdom that was in the heart of Jesus, and a boldness in proclaiming the Good News. Under the leading of the Holy Spirit, we are prompted to speak the word courageously, to pray over others for healing, and to spend ourselves in loving service of the poor and marginalised.

The Holy Spirit will always be providing "divine appointments" with people. Just when they need a word of comfort or a word of challenge to be spoken to them, or when they need a healing touch, or a testimony to the goodness of God or to the saving power of Jesus, the Lord arranges a situation when we can speak in his name. His timing is impeccable. Being open to these promptings enables us to flow in God's plan for the increase of his kingdom in hearts of others today.

These are only some of the ways the Holy Spirit acts in our lives. There are endless kinds of inspirations that flow from his indwelling presence. Paul says: "Everyone moved by the Spirit is a son of God" (Rom 8:14). The more we obey the leadings of the Spirit the more teachable we become, and the more richly the Holy Spirit dwells within us and possesses us (Act 5:32). When we resist the promptings of the Spirit, our hearts harden and become immovable, no longer sensitive to his action, preferring to live according to the flesh. Truly spiritual persons are faithful to these actual graces which are given to help us fulfill the responsibilities the present moment.

Often inspirations of the Spirit are directly given e.g., a revelatory word in prayer or a prompting to take a journey of mercy. At other times they are indirect, given through secondary causes e.g., listening to a homily, reading a book, observing the good example of another.

Whether they are indirect or direct the Holy Spirit is the principal author, and it is essential for our growth that we obey. Inspirations of the Spirit lead to growth in virtue in a similar way that temptations lead to sinful actions. If we say yes to inspirations, we will deepen in the particular virtue (just as when we say yes to temptation we deepen in vice). To resist inspirations of the Spirit is to frustrate the work of God within us and to prevent any real growth.

Thanksgiving, Praise and Adoration

As we are imbued with the Spirit of God, we cannot help giving him thanks. Gratitude rises in our hearts because we know the goodness of God's mercy and love. As the psalmist sings: "Bless the Lord, my soul, bless his holy name, all that is in me! Bless the Lord, my soul, and remember all his kindnesses" (Ps 103:1-2). Those who know that they are infinitely loved by God and have been redeemed by the precious blood of Jesus, have gratitude permanently in their hearts.

As Paul says to the Colossians: "Always be thankful… With gratitude in your hearts sing psalms and hymns and inspired songs to God, and never say or do anything except in the name of our Lord Jesus, giving thanks to God the Father through him" (Col 3:15-17).

Gratitude enlarges the heart. As we remember the good things God has done for us, we find a new song of praise rising within us. Grateful people know their own poverty. They know that all is gift. They have humble hearts, rejoicing continually in the good gifts of God. They joyfully sing with Mary: "My soul proclaims the greatness of the Lord, and my spirit exults in God my saviour" (Lk 1:46).

Gratitude necessarily leads to praise of God, which is exaltation of God's goodness for his own sake. To praise God is the highest function of the human being, the most fundamental activity of our existence. It is why we were created. Our eternal destiny is to be united with the angels and saints in heaven forever praising him (Rev 7:11-12). We don't praise God to obtain favours from him, but simply because he is worthy of praise (Ps 48:1). We no longer focus on ourselves and our needs, but live an other-centred life, focused on the goodness of God. We move humbly through life with a simple reverent awe before his splendour, majesty, and holiness.

Hearts that are becoming captivated by God will more and more find themselves praising him. They rejoice with the whole of creation and exalt the creator on behalf of all created things. They are always mindful of what he has done in rescuing us from the power of darkness through his death and resurrection. They join with the psalmist: "Acclaim God all the earth, play music to the glory of his name, glorify him with your praises… Come and see what marvels God has done… he turned the sea into dry land…" (Ps 66:1-3). The psalmist was rejoicing with the "festal shout" over the victory of God who parted the waters of the Red Sea and liberated the Israelites from Pharaoh's army. We Christians shout for joy even more so over the victory of God in our baptism, delivering us from the power of sin and Satan. Our festal shout proclaims, "Jesus is Lord!" (1Cor 12:3); we are meant to live always in awe of the power of God manifest in raising Jesus from the dead, a power which is now at work within us giving us lasting freedom.

The Church has a long history of exuberant expression of praise in the liturgy and in other communal gatherings for prayer. St. Augustine is one of the most eloquent witnesses of this. He speaks of the grace of jubilation in his congregations:

> He who jubilates utters not words, but a wordless sound of joy. The voice of his heart pours forth joy as intensely as possible, expressing its affection in the best way it can, without reflection on any particular thought. To manifest his joy, the man does not use words that can be pronounced or understood, but bursts forth into sounds of exaltation without words. It seems that he indeed rejoices with his voice, but with a joy so intense that he cannot express in words the subject of that joy.[134]

While this type of communal praise fosters the spiritual life of the individual, it should always be complemented by personal contemplation. In quiet prayer we experience a silent interior praise, which sometimes bursts forth spontaneously by the action of the Spirit. Many contemplatives down through the ages have experienced this jubilation of the heart. Cassian speaks on the one hand of the "prayer of fire", which is not vocal but is a "fiery outbreak, an indescribable exaltation, an insatiable thrust of the soul" towards God.[135]

This is a profoundly contemplative experience of praise. On the other hand, he describes times when the monks burst into *vocal* exaltation as a result of this fire within: "Often through some inexpressible delight and keenness of spirit the fruit of a salutary conviction arises so that it actually breaks forth into *shouts* owing to the greatness of its uncontrollable joy; and the delight of the heart and the greatness of the exaltation make themselves heard even in the cell of the neighbour".[136] So the monks experienced "jubilation" in an interior way, but also they gave vent to this by shouting the praises of God in exaltation. This contemplative "jubilation" of the early monks has been experienced by many friends of God down through the centuries.

The contemporary experience of gatherings for praise and worship outside the liturgy, or the introduction of charismatic praise into liturgy, is also confirmed by the spiritual tradition, as we have seen with Augustine at Hippo. Some of our contemporaries have made the mistake of looking for the totality of prayer experience in these praise gatherings. Others have gone to the other extreme and abandoned vocal communal praise altogether because they have discovered that of itself it cannot sustain the spiritual life.

In search of contemplation these people have forsaken a God-given gift of praise which was intended to aid this search. Mistakenly they have thought that their experience of charismatic praise was intended by God to be just for a time. Having discovered the gift of contemplation they have then decided that vocal communal praise is no longer useful and is maybe even a hindrance to their growth in the Lord. In fact, the communal expression of praise *fosters* interior, personal contemplation and praise; and, in turn, a spirit of interior contemplative praise overflows in communal worship. It is wrong to claim that charismatic praise is opposed to the contemplative experience. The two actually complement one another.

By developing the prayer of praise in the heart we can learn to pray always. The Holy Spirit who dwells within is able to express our prayer that we cannot put into words, and God who knows everything in our hearts knows what the Spirit means (Rom 8:26-27).

Many who open themselves to this gift of praise will find the Spirit will give them the gift of tongues. It is simply wordless sounds, uttered spontaneously, to the glory of God. It is not a mystical gift. It is more akin to yodeling or to singing a wordless tune in the shower. However, unlike these purely natural expressions, it is a gift of the Spirit. It is the Spirit praying through the believer, who cooperates by effortlessly bringing forth sounds that express things that are beyond conceptual language.

Tongues is not strictly a language but sounds like it. It enables the person to make a vocal prayer from the heart without worrying about formulating concepts or words. It can be started or finished at will, but often arises in the heart spontaneously under the inspiration of the Spirit. It serves to build up the spiritual life and can help fulfill Paul's counsel to be "praying in the Spirit on every possible occasion" (Eph 6:18).

We deepen in the Spirit as we learn to praise God in all circumstances. This means to say "yes" to the gift of life and providence in every situation. To resent an unfortunate turn of events, or to feel sorry for ourselves, or to blame others for our misery, is to refuse to accept our life as it is, and not to put our trust in God's provident love. On the other hand, if we say "yes" to God by opening ourselves in praise of him, we are set free from discouragement, and it makes it possible for the Spirit to bring good out of the situation. The promise of God is that all things work towards the good for those who love the Lord (Rom 8:28).

A dramatic example of this is found in Acts when Paul and Silas were imprisoned in Philippi. They were in dire circumstances. After having been whipped with "many lashes" they were thrown into the most secure part of the prison with their feet fastened in stocks. We are told: "Late that night Paul and Silas were praying and singing God's praises, while the other prisoners listened" (Acts 16:25). As a result, the prison doors suddenly flew open, and the chains fell from the prisoners!

This is a good model for us; rather than succumbing to self-pity or despondency, even though their situation seemed impossible, Paul and Silas continued to praise the Lord. As a result they were miraculously delivered. When we praise the Lord in adversity, we will always find a new liberation within ourselves, and a new capacity to deal with whatever challenges are before us.

The whole Christian life is meant to be an act of praise of God. Paul encourages us to keep the mercy of God in mind as we worship God in all we say and do "by offering your living bodies as a holy sacrifice, truly pleasing to God" (Rom 12:1). For Paul the "body" is the whole living person. He means that our whole lives, in all we think, say or do, are to be a sacrifice of praise to God. Then Paul spells out how this is to take place; through humility, patience, perseverance, hospitality, brotherly and sisterly affection, forgiveness, kindness to the poor; in short, the whole Christian life (Rom 12:3-21). Every aspect of our life is meant to be suffused with the praise of God. The measure of the value of our thoughts, words and actions is whether they truly give glory to God. We are to pray always, through offering everything we do to the glory of God.

An attitude of thanksgiving and praise leads to adoration. Our ultimate appreciation of God is expressed in adoration. We become lost in the wonder of who God is and what he has done for us. We surrender our whole selves in whole-hearted submission to his loving purposes. Adoration is the recognition that God has taken hold of us in love at the deepest level of our being. It is joyful surrender to this divine grasp. We allow ourselves to be claimed by him exclusively in love. We forget ourselves and attend only to the Lord and live in total submission to him. It is the truest expression of praise. We cry with Thomas, "My Lord and my God" (Jn 20:28), or with Francis of Assisi crying out all through the night, "My God, and my all!"[137]

Adoration is allowing the Lord to pour life and love into us. As we totally surrender to his love, and let his love have its way in us, we gradually *become* the fire of his love. This spirit of adoration is especially fostered deeply before the exposed Eucharist. Since the Middle Ages the Church has sung the Divine Praises during Eucharistic benediction. Praise of God finds its fullest expression in adoration. In Eucharistic adoration we are drawn into the once-for-all perfect sacrifice of praise of Jesus to the Father on behalf of all. We are overwhelmed by the fire of his love in his passion and death. We find ourselves willing to die with him a thousand deaths in order to be fully possessed by him and to be given completely in his service. We find ourselves repeating in the heart again and again "Jesus, I adore you". This gradually becomes the refrain of the heart at all times.

Living in the Gaze of God

It is a good practice to visualise God as always present to us. Some may find it helpful to picture the Father always holding them in his strong arms and keeping them secure in his love. One way to maintain this sense of his presence is to try to be aware of his loving gaze upon us at all times. We don't see him, but we know he is there through the eyes of faith. We become more keenly aware that every event in life is planned by the gentle hand of the Father, who is watching over us and will not allow a single hair to fall from our heads without his permission (Mt 10:30).

To foster this awareness it can help to have the simple words of Jesus in our hearts; repeating over and over the cry "Abba, Father", through the Spirit who dwells within us. As we constantly invoke God as "Daddy", our hearts are gradually changed into the heart of Jesus himself. We enter into the secret life of the Son and the Father. This invocation can become the background music of our lives and we find ourselves walking in the rhythm of the heart of Jesus himself.

Another helpful practice is to walk with the constant assurance of Christ's gaze upon us. We can visualise Jesus as our companion walking with us, or as the Risen Lord before us at all times. This can be helped by the presence of images in the home, such as crucifixes, icons of the Lord, and Our Lady and the saints. However, it is primarily an interior attitude, with the eyes of faith, whereby we are constantly recalling that the eyes of Jesus are upon us. Gospel texts, such as Jesus' merciful gaze upon Peter after his denial (Lk 22:61), or his gaze upon the repentant thief on the cross (Lk 23:42), or his gaze upon the adulterous woman (Jn 8:10), can help us grow in this awareness. It is especially in our experience of brokenness and sinfulness that we are aware of Jesus' gaze of mercy.

Maybe some will find the "Jesus prayer" useful—simply repeating over and over "Jesus, Son of the living God, have mercy on me, a sinner". If this seems too cumbersome, it is enough to simply have repeating in the heart the word "Jesus". Joseph was told by the angel that "you must name him Jesus, because he is the one who is to save his people from their sins" (Mt 1:21). The name of Jesus is powerful. To invoke his name is to open ourselves to his personal presence and power to save. It opens the heart to the constant presence of the merciful Jesus and brings us into awareness of his saving love.

The Practice of the Presence of God

Brother Lawrence, a 17th century discalced Carmelite, has left a compelling description of a way of living through consciously abiding in Christ. He says:

> It is only necessary to realise that God is intimately present within us, to turn at every moment to him and ask for his help, recognise his will in all things doubtful, and to do well all that which we clearly see he requires of us, offering what we do to him before we do it, and giving thanks for having done it afterwards. In this unbroken communion one is continually preoccupied with praising, worshipping and loving God for his infinite acts of loving kindness and perfection.[138]

The attitude to be cultivated is a simple, attentive, loving turning of the eyes to the Lord with the trust of a child and with gratitude for everything. Constantly recalling the Lord's presence, we "set an unbroken guard over ourselves, that we do nothing, say nothing, think nothing, which would displease him".[139]

The more we become aware of Christ's indwelling presence, the more we find ourselves in wordless conversation with him, even in the midst of many activities. We are more empowered to do everything for love of him, even the most menial chores. Brother Lawrence testifies that he had a natural aversion for kitchen duties, but he trained himself to do it all for the love of God and spent 15 years joyfully serving this way. He says: "Our sanctification does not depend upon some alteration in what we do, but in doing for God what we commonly do for ourselves".[140] As we allow Christ to dwell more richly within us, we are prepared to die to ourselves for love of him, so that he may live and love through us. "He must grow greater, I must grow smaller" (Jn 3:30). The aim is to do everything *with* Jesus and so to do everything *for* him.

The practice of the presence of God is not only awareness of his presence within us, but also his presence around us in all that is happening in our lives. Every moment mediates the presence of God in some way or another. Moment by moment God is breathing his life and love into us, and he encounters us through the many circumstances of our lives. Created realities and events can lead the mind to think of God. For example, a sunset can put a song of praise in the soul to the "divine painter"; a beautiful stream can evoke a desire within for the refreshment of the Spirit; an air-plane taking off can inspire wonder at God's gifts of ingenuity given to humanity; observing the bustling crowds of a big city can provoke an awareness of the thirst of Jesus for their salvation; a delicate flower can speak to us of the gentleness of God; looking into a child's eyes can be like looking into the eyes of God himself.

The Lord is present at all times and in every encounter we have. This is often called the "sacrament of the present moment". We can increase our expectation of meeting with him in every person, of discovering the movement of his Spirit in every gathering we attend. We discover him in the gift of friendship, in the beauty of art and music. We find him in books, poetry and drama. We find him in our joys and our sorrows, in our triumphs and our failures. We find him in the supermarket, the football crowd, the birthday party, and the barbecue lunch next door. We especially can find him present in what Mother Teresa called "the distressing disguise of the poor". A friend of God is especially drawn to the less sophisticated, those with little power or status, those who may be rejected or marginalised by society, those who may even be repulsive in appearance and lacking social graces. Jesus said: "As often as you did it to the least of these little ones you did it to me" (Mt 25:40). The person who loves God is able to find him in all things, in all places and in all people.

We can grow in the practice of the presence of God through offering frequent *aspirations* to him during the course of the day. We are able to make many acts of love from the heart. Francis de Sales says that for people who have a busy day it is important to make many aspirations to the Lord. "Aspire then frequently to God by short but ardent dartings of your heart; admire his beauty; invoke his aid; cast yourself in spirit at the foot of the cross; adore his goodness; address him frequently on your salvation; give your soul to him a thousand times a day; fix your interior eye upon his sweetness; stretch out your hand as a little child to its father, that he may conduct you; place him in your bosom like a delicious nosegay; plant him in your soul like a standard; and make a thousand sorts of different motions of your heart, to enkindle the love of God and excite within yourself a passionate and tender affection for your divine spouse".[141]

Francis goes on to say that these aspirations are so important that they can make up for any defect in other kinds of prayer. But without aspirations of this kind other forms of prayer become inadequate. Without aspirations, he says, "one hardly can lead the contemplative life and can but badly lead the active life".[142]

8
GUARDING THE FIRE
Developing a Discerning Heart

"Never try to suppress the Spirit… think before you do anything—hold on to what is good and avoid every form of evil." (1Thess 5:19-22)

In the previous chapter we saw how important it is to obey the inspirations of the Spirit in order to grow in the spiritual life. However, there is a difficulty in knowing whether the interior movements we experience are genuinely from the Holy Spirit or from our own psyche, or from the evil spirit. Because the origins of these movements are not immediately clear to us, and because we usually cannot have certainty they are from God, we need to be growing in a discerning heart. John Cassian encourages us to scrutinise our thoughts carefully; particularly to try and detect their origin. He says we are to become good "money changers".[143] Just as a money changer has a keen eye for the counterfeit coin so also do we need to be able to detect the subtle work of the evil one. The enemy disguises himself as an "angel of light", often urging activities that in themselves are good, but are not appropriate for us now. The trained money changer is able to tell what is "pure gold" and what has impurities in it. Good money changers also weigh carefully what is before them before acting. Likewise, we are to measure carefully what is presented to us in our hearts and to weigh it against scriptural revelation and the teaching of the Church.

Discernment then is the process by which we examine, in the light of our personal knowledge of Jesus, the interior movements of the heart. We do this in order to decide as far as possible which of these movements are inspired by God and lead towards God and more dedicated service of him, and which deflect us from this goal. Cassian tells us a story of a number of older men of the desert discussing the virtues with Anthony of Egypt. They were debating which virtue of all the virtues is needed most to keep a person free from the snares and deceptions of the devil, and to ensure perseverance on the true path to God. Each of them put forward a case for a particular virtue. One said surely it would be zealous fasting and vigils; another said detachment from all things of this earth; another profound silence and solitude; another practical charity. Anthony, however, retorted that while all these virtues are necessary, unless we have discernment, they will end up in disaster. Only discernment can protect us from falling into delusion. No matter how much faith and love, zeal for God and eagerness to do his will that we have, unless we have discernment it will become misguided, and we will fall into one excess or another. He says: "No virtue can come to full term or can endure without the grace of discernment... it is discernment which with firm step leads the enduring work to God and which holds utterly intact together all the virtues... For discernment is the mother, the guardian and the guide of all the virtues".[144] For this reason, this chapter, although the last in the book, is in many ways the most important.

To grow in the gift of discernment we need to have a personal, loving relationship with Jesus. Otherwise, we have no sense of his heart. Without this we find it extremely difficult to tell what is of God and what is not. The more we abide in Jesus, and become accustomed to his ways, the more the discerning heart grows. We also need to be humble and obedient of heart, readily teachable, and especially open to being wrong in what we first thought was happening. We also need to weigh everything to see that it is in conformity with the Scriptures, the Tradition and the teaching of the Church. And we need to receive guidance from a spiritual director, which we will look at in more detail later.

Some Rules for Discernment

Ignatius Loyola has given us some classic principles for discernment.[145] He came to formulate these guidelines through his experience at the time of his conversion. His conversion began when he was on his sick bed after the battle of Pamplona in 1521. His dreams of worldly glory had been shattered when a cannon ball had damaged his leg during the battle. While convalescing he started to read some pious books about heroic deeds on mediaeval saints. This would lead him into daydreaming about doing great deeds for the King of heaven, rather than for the earthly king he had been serving up until that time. He noticed that after having had such pious thoughts he would have peace of heart and a lightness of spirit. On the other hand, when he entertained thoughts of worldly ambition and self-made glory, he found disturbance and heaviness in his heart. This led him to realise the difference between what he called the good and evil "spirits"; those thoughts that brought peace and joy were from the good spirit; those thoughts that brought disturbance and sadness were from the evil spirit.[146]

Ignatius considers that all interior movements of the heart come from either the "good spirit" or the "evil spirit". The "good spirit" is the action of the Holy Spirit. He refers to the "evil spirit" as all movements that are contrary to the work of God in the heart of the person. Coming from his own culture he would have considered all these movements to be from the devil. While there is no doubt that Satan exists and that many of these negative movements do originate from his working, we probably need to nuance Ignatius' teaching a little. Having the advantage of modern psychology, we know that maybe many of the movements contrary to God originate in our inner psyche and are not directly attributable to Satan. In any case, the broad spiritual tradition has always acknowledged that the movements of the "flesh", the "world" and "sinfulness" originate within ourselves. Satan and his minions can stir up trouble through these channels and often do so, but it is not accurate to say that every negative movement arising within us has demonic origin. In other words, while we will use Ignatius' terminology of the "evil spirit", what we mean by this is all forces, which come directly or indirectly from demons, or from within ourselves, giving rise to interior movements in the heart which draw us away from God and the purposes of God.

The key to Ignatius' method of discernment is being able to detect "consolations" and "desolations". They are "felt states" of the soul. They cannot be identified with any particular thought or emotion. However, thoughts, emotions, desires and attitudes flow from these states of being. Ignatius says:

> I call it consolation when an interior movement is aroused in the soul, by which it is inflamed with love of its Creator and Lord, and as a consequence, can love no creature on the face of the earth for its own sake, but only in the Creator of them all. It is likewise consolation when one sheds tears that move to the love of God, whether it be because of sorrow for sins, or because of the sufferings of Christ our Lord, or for any other reason that is immediately directed to the praise and service of God. Fi-

nally, I call consolation every increase of faith, hope and love, and all interior joy that invites and attracts to what is heavenly and to the salvation of one's soul by filling it with peace and quiet in its Creator and Lord.[147]

So consolation can come from many different types of interior experience. But the most common factor in this felt state is peace in the Lord, and interior joy drawing us to Jesus, and a sense of increase in faith, hope and love. Desolation is a felt state of the heart which is the exact opposite. Ignatius defines it as:

> Darkness of soul, turmoil of spirit, inclination to what is low and earthly, restlessness rising from many disturbances and temptations which lead to want of faith, want of hope, want of love. The soul is wholly slothful, tepid, sad, and separated, as it were, from its Creator and Lord. For just as consolation is the opposite of desolation, so the thoughts that spring from consolation are the opposite of those that spring from desolation.[148]

Desolation can be a very confused and stormy experience, or just a sense of feeling "blah". What characterises it most of all is a lack of peace, a heaviness of spirit, and a distaste for the things of God. Ignatius says that desolation never comes from God, even though the Lord allows it to happen. Consolation, on the other hand, can either be genuinely from God, or from the evil spirit. Ignatius' first set of rules are intended for people who are in the early stages of breaking with sin, the devil, the world and the flesh, and are earnest in giving themselves to the Lord. Here the primary challenge is to learn to deal with desolation. The tactic of the evil spirit in these early stages of the journey is to bring discouragement. Ignatius says that, for those who are striving to break with their former life and embrace the new life in Jesus, "it is characteristic of the evil spirit to harass with anxiety, to afflict with sadness, to raise obstacles backed by fallacious reasonings that disturb the soul. Thus, he seeks to prevent the soul from advancing".[149]

This first set of rules seeks to give commonsense guidelines which help us to avoid giving up and throwing in the towel in the face of desolations. The ploy of the evil spirit is to tempt us to do just that.

The first important rule is that we never change a resolution or make a major decision when we are experiencing desolation. Since desolation always comes from the evil spirit, Ignatius says that this would be tantamount to making the devil your spiritual director! Commentators agree that if beginners could remember this rule they would be saved from much of the confusion that can come into their lives. Another important rule is to move in the opposite spirit to the desolation. Because we feel rotten we are likely to be governed by this and give up prayer, or at least cut it back. Ignatius counsels to increase our spiritual activity, and to do more prayer and penance rather than to slacken off. He says that while we may not clearly perceive it, the Lord always gives us the grace sufficient to resist the desolation. We should persevere in patience and be confident that consolation will return in time.

Ignatius offers three reasons why the Lord allows desolation to take place.[150] While the Lord is not the author of the desolation, in his provident care of us he permits it to happen, so that, with our cooperation, he can draw good fruit from it. The first reason is because we have become negligent, lethargic and indifferent in our spiritual life. The desolation comes as a salutary shock. It can be used to shake us out of our torpor and bring us to repentance and back to a whole-hearted commitment. In a time of desolation we need to check our hearts to see if this is the reason for our plight. If so, it is a matter of humbly repenting, and the desolation will lift. If, upon checking our hearts, this is not the case, then there are two other possible reasons for the desolation.

The Lord may want to test us by the purifying fire of suffering the loss of consolations and favours which we had begun to rely upon. The testing is like the way iron is made into steel. When iron is tested by intense heat the process fuses the carbon and the iron, making a new, purer and stronger substance, steel.[151] We can look upon the testing of desolation as the Lord using this to build steel in our soul, so we will have the fortitude to endure to the end. We are not to live by feelings but by faith. When the Lord allows the feelings to become distasteful and disturbing, we have to allow faith that is not dependent on feelings, to emerge more strongly within us.

The final reason why the Lord allows desolation is to humble us. He wants to teach us that consolation is pure gift from him. Early in the piece he spoils us with consolations, because he is winning us to himself. After a while, we tend to subtly think that we are doing it by ourselves. So the Lord "pulls the rug from under our feet", and we now feel our utter poverty, and how incapable we are of doing anything for our salvation. We experience more acutely all is gift from the Lord. We find ourselves necessarily having to cry out to him in earnest for help. We grow in humility.

The second set of rules deals with discerning between true and false consolations. There is only one type of consolation that is definitely from God and beyond question. This is what Ignatius calls "consolation without previous cause".[152] He means by this that the consolation comes totally "out of the blue", without any previous perception or knowledge. Most consolations do have a preceding cause. For example, we can trace the insight we had in prayer to a book we were reading the previous day, or we can be brought into a consoling moment of the Lord's embrace through meditation on a scripture text, or we can be filled with love for the Creator as we watch a beautiful sunset. Anything that has been prompted by our own acts of intellect or imagination or senses has a "preceding cause". This is God's normal way of communicating with us. So it is rare to have consolation *without* previous cause. Consequently, we need to pray for discernment of our consolations, since the vast majority of them do not necessarily have the stamp of God upon them. We need to check their credentials.

The evil spirit can assume the guise of the "angel of light". Ignatius says: "He begins by suggesting thoughts that are suited to a devout soul and ends by suggesting his own. For example, he will suggest holy and pious thoughts that are wholly in conformity with the sanctity of the soul. Afterwards, he will endeavour little by little to end by drawing the soul into his hidden snares and evil designs".[153]

As the "angel of light" the evil spirit can produce ecstasies and visions, can foster for his own ends noble and great works, and can stoke for his own designs great apostolic zeal. However, he can only mimic the consolations of God. He can never replicate them in their purity. For the discerning heart the "tail of the serpent" is always evident. The evil spirit's "fingerprints" will mar his cleverest forgeries. We need to be able to detect these forgeries, to be good "moneychangers". The Holy Spirit will always be inspiring us towards greater love of God, obedience to his will and humility. The evil spirit will have a different end. Ultimately, we can only tell the soundness of the tree from its fruits. We may have been thoroughly convinced that a particular course of action was inspired by God, but if it ends up in self-centred, ambitious posturing before others, we would have to question whether it was truly inspired by God at all.

A friendship that blossoms may seem to be given by God, since it has opened up a deeper sense of affection for God, but if it takes us away from our commitment in marriage or in the celibate state, we would have to ponder whether it was simply manipulated by the evil spirit for his own ends. An initial intense fervour for God and profound zeal for holiness can gradually over time be diverted into a false self-righteousness and "holier than thou" attitude, and an almost angry denunciation of others who are not so 'enlightened'. This sort of bad fruit is a clear indication of the evil spirit's presence, even though the person may still profess to be very zealous for the Lord and for his kingdom.

Because of the difficulty of detecting the movement of the evil spirit, it is very important to have a spiritual director with whom we can be transparent about what is happening and have an objective reference point for discerning direction. Ignatius says it is important to examine the beginning, the middle and the end of the course of our thoughts on a matter. We can best do this with the help of another who is wise in the ways of the Lord and knows the wiles of the evil one.

When reflecting on our prayer afterwards, and talking it over with our spiritual director, we could ask ourselves: How much was the prayer centred on myself and how much on the Lord? Even when our thoughts or images begin with the Lord, they can end up centering on ourselves; either focusing on problems in anxiety and self-pity, or centering on past or anticipated triumphs through the display of our gifts.

There are a thousand ways that the evil spirit attempts to lead us away from the Lord and back onto ourselves. The Holy Spirit's activity fosters humility, poverty of spirit, and self-emptying love; the evil spirit fosters vanity and self-centred attitudes. When our assessment after a prayer time shows us that we went astray into false consolation, we should avoid self-recrimination but simply laugh at ourselves and make a resolution to guard against it in the future. Our spiritual director can give valuable objective feedback, and maybe some advice about how to avoid these many "traps for young players".

Examen of Consciousness

Another legacy that Ignatius has given to the Church is the daily examen.[154] The examen is a means of developing a discerning heart. It helps us get in touch on a daily basis with the movements within us. Through this little exercise we grow in self-knowledge. It is different from an examination of conscience, which is concerned primarily with the good and bad actions I have done or not done. The examen is concerned with identifying how the Lord is moving us in our affective consciousness. It also helps us tap into the movement of the evil spirit, and other movements originating in our interior psyche.

The examen takes about 15 minutes and should be practiced each day at an appropriate time. When we stop from whatever is preoccupying us and quieten our spirit there are a number of steps to take.

a) *Prayer of Enlightenment*

> We ask God to shine his light on our heart so that when we look back over the day, we will be able to see God working in the things that have happened. We seek from the Lord the

grace to be sensitive to the interior movements of our heart, and to be able to grow in seeing ourselves as he sees us.

b) *Gratitude for the Gifts of the Day*

This is an opportunity to develop a grateful heart by growing in the awareness that everything that happens, both small and great, is gift from God. It fosters an attitude of genuine poverty of spirit. We simply thank the Lord from the heart for his gentle loving presence every moment of our day.

c) *Examen of the Movements of the Heart*

The question to ask ourselves here is: what has been happening to us and in us since the last examen? There are two parts to this. Firstly, we ask what the Lord has been doing in us. We look at what way the Lord has aroused our heart in love today. How has he been gently drawing us by his Spirit into fulness of life with him. We especially look at moods, feelings, urges. Where there have been movements such as lightness of heart, and interior peace, an expansiveness of spirit, a clarity of mind, and a desire for communion, we sense the presence of God's Spirit. We look at where there have been specific promptings or inspirations of the Spirit that possibly we have overlooked. While the examen of the interior affective states is important it is only in time that we gain a sharper awareness of their significance in the leading of the Spirit.

As we examine the movements of the heart and the actions that have flowed from them, we are not only aware of God's call, but also of our response. For example, we may detect a mood of self-pity, or an attitude of stubborn self-sufficiency, or an angry reaction, or a deep-seated anxiety. Detecting these movements from the darker side of the person should not mean that we condemn ourselves. It is simply a matter of bringing it all to the light, and trying to see things in our lives as they really are in the sight of God.

d) *Contrition for sinfulness*

Usually, we will be aware of some way we have failed to fully respond to the leading of the Spirit and not heeded the Lord's call of love. By opening our hearts to the light of Jesus we gain greater freedom. We simply acknowledge the sickness of our hearts, our helplessness to be able to change, and yet our faith in the victory of Jesus, our Saviour, who is at work within us to recreate us by the power of his Spirit.

e) *Hopeful resolution for the Future*

This is simply an affirmation of trust in the Lord that "those who hope in you are never shamed" (Ps 25:3). No matter what sinfulness and imperfections we see within ourselves, we make an act of trust in the mercy of God, and face the future with renewed vision. We avoid the temptation to just "get on with business as usual", without acknowledging that there is a deeper work to be done in the heart. Yet we don't allow the prospect of unfinished work to deter us. As Paul said, "With God on our side who can be against us?" (Rom 8:31). We simply set our sights on the goal and continue to run the race for the finish: "I forget the past and strain ahead for what is still to come" (Phil 3:13).

Particular Examen

When we are listening to the movements of the heart it can be useful to get in touch with the area in our life which at this stage in the journey is the growing point. There is usually one virtue or gift or special grace that the Lord is wanting to draw forth in us more than any other. He is the one who converts our hearts. The area he wants to work on may very well be quite painful for us to admit. We would prefer to hide from it. It may take some time for the beginner to discern what this area is. Once we have detected it, we can then each day spend a minute or two of the examen checking out how our response to God's grace in this area has been since the last examen. Once again it is not a matter of becoming guilt-ridden about the struggle, nor is it a matter of focusing too much attention on the sinfulness; rather it is a matter of daily attempting to put into practice the opposite virtue, trusting in the Lord's transforming power.

Making decisions

Life is full of decisions. In the ordinary events of life, we don't have to spend lots of time trying to discern whether this action is better than another. It is simply a matter of choosing the action that seems to be in conformity with God's will. It is counter-productive to become scrupulous and over anxious about whether we are doing God's "perfect will" or not. If we worry too much about this, we become paralysed and lose the opportunities before us for doing good. If we are regularly bouncing off a spiritual director what is happening in our lives, then this is sufficient to gain some objectivity and to correct our course if necessary.

Nevertheless, when it comes to significant decisions that change the course of our lives, we need a clear process of going about it. These choices are about deciding to take one of two or more good options. For example, whether to take an attractive overseas posting or to stay put for the sake of the stability of the family; whether to become a lay missionary for a number of years or to get on with a career; whether to enter celibate life in a particular congregation or to marry; whether to give a more substantial share of personal income to overseas missions or to use it for financial security at home.

Ignatius offers us three ways that decisions like these can be made. Firstly, and most rarely, we can receive a special revelation from the Lord. This is "when God our Lord so moves and attracts the will that a devout soul without hesitation, or the possibility of hesitation, follows what has been manifested to it".[155] God's will is so clear that the person can't doubt it. An example of this would be Matthew in the gospels, who immediately followed Jesus upon hearing the call, since he was so overwhelmingly convicted to do so.

The second way is to use ones' natural powers of reasoning and imagination.[156] Calling upon the help of the Lord, we list all the pros and cons for the proposed action, weigh them up carefully, and then choose what we think would be "more pleasing to his most holy will". The aim is to choose the option that has weightier motives, according to reason, rather than be governed by flesh desire. Ignatius also suggests three imaginative exercises. Firstly, I consider what I would advise someone else, faced with the same decision, who came to me for help. Secondly, I imagine myself on my deathbed and ask myself what I wish I would have chosen. Thirdly, I imagine myself standing before the judgement seat of God and ask what decision I would then want to have made. Then he says: "After such a choice or decision, the one who has made it must turn with great diligence to prayer in the presence of God our Lord, and offer him his choice that the Divine Majesty may deign to accept and confirm it if it is for his greater service and praise".[157]

The third way suggested by Ignatius is by getting in touch with consolation and desolation. This can be effectively joined with the "natural" way just described. It can be used to confirm in prayer a choice that has been made by assessing the pros and cons. However, Ignatius considers it can be used alone without the more "reasonable" approach of the second way. It involves a prayerful focus upon the person of Jesus. Then with eyes fixed upon the Lord we simply present to him each option. As we present a particular option, with eyes fixed on the Lord, we try to get in touch with whether it brings us consolation or desolation. At first we may have little sense of this, but over a few weeks of faithful prayer we may begin to either find it "sits right", and there is genuine peace in the soul about it, or there is no peace and a feeling that it is not right. When we first present something to the Lord in this way the initial reaction may be quite negative.

It is important not to leave it there. Rather, we should continue to offer it to him over time. Often the initial reaction is more a fleshy repulsion than the true indication of what the Spirit is saying. And the reverse is true also. Sometimes initially it seems very exciting and compelling, and we are full of enthusiasm for it. However, over the test of time we discover this was an initial natural attraction, but it was not right in the Lord's plan. The important attitude of heart to have throughout the exercise is loving surrender to the Lord, and desire to do whatever is truly for his glory.

When discerning significant inspirations of the Spirit, Francis de Sales gives us three criteria for their authenticity.[158] Firstly, he says, the Holy Spirit does not inspire us to do anything contrary to our state of life or particular vocation. An inspiration to change our state of life should only be acted upon if there is sufficiently grave reason. Normally, perseverance in one's vocation and state of life is the proof of an inspiration. Once we are set on a path of life, the Holy Spirit gives us perseverance in it. Secondly, he agrees with Ignatius that peace of soul is one of the best indicators of authenticity. There will be a calm assurance in the person. Even though the person may feel deeply challenged by the inspiration, there will be a quiet peace and tranquility within. If the person is troubled, anxious, restless, and causing disturbance to others, the inspiration is probably not genuine. Thirdly, we look for humility and obedience. Francis says: "A man who claims to be inspired, but refuses to obey his superiors or follow their advice is an imposter".[159] If the inspiration is to do ordinary things in an extraordinary way, or to do an extraordinary work in itself, there should be a readiness to submit the inspiration to a spiritual director and to appropriate authority.

Spiritual Direction

Francis de Sales says he could give no more important advice to a beginner than to find a spiritual guide.[160] Thomas à Kempis in the *Imitation of Christ* likewise insists on the need to be guided by another in our spiritual journey. He warns against following our own opinions and insights, and strongly advises the beginner to seek wise counsel in order to avoid deception and confusion.[161] Teresa of Avila, who had experienced great anguish at the hands of incompetent directors still maintained adamantly her need for them: "I understand that as long as God leads me by this path I must not trust myself in anything. So I have always consulted others even though I find it difficult".[162]

Very early in the spiritual journey we become aware that the Sunday homily, occasional adult catechesis, books and retreats are not enough to help answer the questions that arise, and to confirm what God is doing in us. We need personal guidance. How do we distinguish between a dryness in prayer that is due to selfish complacency and that which is actually a blessing from God? What sort of spiritual reading should we use? How do we discern our life's vocation? How do we gain a balanced rhythm of life which has sufficient prayer, recreation, work, and time for relationships suitable for our state of life? How do we know whether the direction in which we are heading is truly the leading of the Spirit? How do we know whether we are going forward or backwards? John of the Cross says: "A disciple without a master to lead the way is like a single burning coal; he grows colder rather than hotter".[163] The testimony of the saints reflects the wisdom of the Church, and echoes the scriptural principle, "If you see a man of understanding, visit him early, let your feet wear out his doorstep" (Ecc 6:36).

Spiritual direction is about guiding a person in the way of the Holy Spirit.[164] The Spirit is the principal director. Jesus made this clear with his promise, "But when the Spirit of Truth comes, he will guide you into the complete truth" (Jn 16:13). However, in God's plan, the spiritual director is present to help us to see more clearly what the Spirit is doing, to remove any obstacles to his activity, and to be able to respond to his leading. The director helps us to be more docile to the light and promptings of the Spirit, to identify blockages, and to help to overcome them.

To understand the purpose of spiritual direction we need to be clear about what it is not. Spiritual direction is not pastoral counselling, which is designed to help people deal with emotional problems and solve interpersonal difficulties. Spiritual direction focuses on a person's relationship with God. It seeks to aid the person in attending more closely to the activity of the Lord in one's life. Nor is spiritual direction a kind of psychotherapy, which embarks on an introspective analysis of past hurts, and sees the interaction between the therapist and the client as responsible for growth and healing.[165] Spiritual direction does not ignore the psychological dimension of human growth. Indeed, it can be useful for directors to be aware of psychological mechanisms that can impede holistic growth. And certainly, competent directors should be able to identify when a directee needs referral to a professional psychologist. However, psychological growth is not the primary focus of the good spiritual director.

The aim of spiritual direction is to aid the directee to love God with one's whole heart, soul and mind, and one's neighbor as oneself (Lk 10:27). Directors seek to guide the person in being a disciple of Jesus. They endeavour to draw upon the wisdom of the spiritual tradition of the Church, applying it to the unique circumstance of a disciple today. Spiritual direction aims to develop and deepen union with God. The director tries to help the directee come to deeper self-knowledge in the light of the Spirit, and to become more sensitive to the real presence of the Lord in all the activities of life. The director is constantly helping the person to look beyond present problems and to focus on the Lord. The primary goal is the growth of a lived relationship with God.

The director's role is not to tell the person what to do, but to help the person discern what God's will is, and how the Lord is revealing himself in any given situation. Good spiritual directors do not foster an unhealthy dependence in the relationship. They aim to help their directee come to full personal responsibility, and to grow to full maturity in Christ. They try to help the person be as real as possible in their relationship with God. This involves being attentive to spiritual or emotional blockages present in the directee's relationship with the Lord . The director gently leads the directee to a greater awareness of these blockages, which are often unconscious or semi-conscious, and helps the person to greater freedom.[166]

What are the qualities of a good director? John of the Cross urges a certain caution in choosing a spiritual director. He says that the director needs three qualities: learning, discretion and experience.[167] Teresa of Avila concurs with this. She adds that if we cannot find all three qualities in the one person, discretion (or prudence) and experience are the most important. By this she is not discrediting the importance of learning. But simply indicating that we can consult a learned person separately if we need to do so. The emphasis on the importance of learning may surprise some. What is meant is a good grounding in theology, scriptural studies, and the spiritual tradition of the Church. These days we could add as well some basic acquaintance with psychology, sufficient to recognise mental imbalance and emotional disorders that need referral.

This is a tall order. If we cannot find this knowledge in our spiritual adviser, we should take Teresa's example and consult learned people anyway. Teresa testifies she has "always been a friend of men of learning". Ignorance has never served the Church and does not help in the spiritual life. Teresa says: "I hold that the devil will not deceive with illusions the person of prayer who consults learned men, unless the person wants to be deceived, because the devils have a tremendous fear of that learning which is accompanied by humility and virtue...".[168] Knowledge saves from vain incredulity and sentimental piety. It also provides objective criteria for what we are experiencing. On the other hand, knowledge is dangerous if it is not in the service of love and held in humility.

By "discretion" (or prudence) the spiritual writers mean good discernment, a capacity to judge between the movement of the Spirit and the movement of the evil spirit, as well as to detect what is simply generated from our own psyche. It is the art of helping someone see more clearly what the Lord is doing, and how he or she is responding or not responding to this movement. It also means the gift of judging what is the best course of action to suggest in a particular situation. Often faced with the dilemmas of our lives , we need wisdom from another to be able to choose the right course. This prudence includes knowing when to speak and when to be silent. It means being a good listener, and able to respond to what is perceived to be happening with appropriate words and advice.

By "experience" the writers mean that a spiritual director needs to be a person seriously committed to the Lord, and seeking to live a gospel way of holiness. They mean a person of prayer, who is not necessarily experiencing advanced states of contemplation, but is genuinely undertaking the spiritual journey in a committed way. Nevertheless, the more profound the experience of prayer, the more equipped the director will be to lead others into a life with God. We might add here that a spiritual director should have a deep love for the Church and be faithful to the Church's teaching when guiding the individual. While the spiritual direction relationship is bound by the confidentiality of professional secrecy, it is still accountable to the Church. We should avoid spiritual directors who favour their own opinions over the Church's teaching on faith and morals.

When we enter into spiritual direction, we need to do so with a heart that is docile to the Holy Spirit working through the spiritual director. We need to be submissive of heart, eager to learn, and open to direction. This is not a "blind obedience"; rather it is a dialogue of discernment in which we trust that God will reveal to us what he is saying. We need to be open and vulnerable in disclosing to the director everything that is happening. The temptation is to hide behind platitudes and only speak about the good things. Everything should be brought to the light—temptations, successes and failures, good and evil desires, trials and joys. This enables the director to mirror back to us what is happening. We find the assurance of being confirmed in the work of God within us, and also become alerted to illusions, deceptions or hindrances to his presence and activity within us. If we want to grow we must be fully open and transparent, and seek help when we need it. We cannot go it alone. As John of the Cross points out, a blind person who falls "will not get up alone" and, in any case, alone in our blindness we "will take the wrong road".[169]

CONCLUSION

When in the 16th century Ignatius Loyola sent Francis Xavier to make a perilous journey to India in order to preach the Good News of Jesus, he told him to *"Go, set all afire!"* This was the Lord's commission, which is given to us today as well. We are sent to set all on fire with the love of God. Jesus' heart is bursting with love for every man and woman. He has come to "bring fire to the earth"! He longs that the fire of his love would be ablaze in every human heart. After returning to the Father, he sent the Spirit of fire upon his apostles to birth the Church. Mary was in their midst. As she prays at the heart of the Church she prays with the heart of her Son. She does not look upon the people for whom she prays as "reprobates", "pagans", "heretics", "atheists", "back-sliders" or "rebels". She simply prays for "those who do not yet know the love of God". To some extent at least that prayer includes all of us.

There has probably never been a time in the history of the human race when we have talked so much about "love". Unfortunately, however, the songs and popular images of love are so often about some cheap, sentimental, sugary love, which has no substance, and cannot satisfy the deep hunger in human hearts. We still remain so impoverished of genuine love. The last century has seen two World Wars, the horror of Hiroshima and Nagasaki, the totalitarian communist regimes in Russia and China, the Jewish Holocaust, the "killing fields" of Cambodia, Rwanda, Kosovo, and East Timor. In this century we continue to be a world at war—Syria, Yemen, Ethiopia, Iran, Democratic Republic of Congo, the Sahel, Haiti, and, of course, the tragedy in Ukraine.

In the Western world we have become accustomed to legalised abortion, famine, and starvation due to unequal distribution of the world's goods, and the displacement of ever-increasing numbers of homeless peoples. Marital break-down and dysfunctional families are commonplace. We live in fear of violence on the streets and of intruders at home. Most live with a "love-deficit". Deprived of unconditional love in their early years they crave for love, trying to fill the "hole in the heart" with what appears to satisfy, but they cannot find what their hearts long for most. This book proclaims that the human heart only rests in the experience of God's love. This is how we are designed, to be fulfilled by his unconditional love.

The message of the gospel has never been more relevant. It is a time for the intrinsic power of the Good News of God's love to be unleashed. This is a time of grace. The Lord is searching for men and women, who will be his hands and feet to bring the fire of his love to others. To be able to respond to his call we must first *receive the gift of his love*. To be able to proclaim the fire of God's love, we must first *become fire* ourselves. This book has been about how to become fire, how to allow the love of God so penetrate us that we can bring his love to others.

The fire of God's love purifies and cleanses our hearts. His love is a living flame within us, burning out all impurities and making us capable of loving others. His love is a light for the soul giving wisdom, knowledge, and power to share with others. His love is a consuming fire, making us his very own, claiming our lives for his purposes. This flame of love within us brings a zeal for his kingdom and a boldness in proclaiming the Good News. His love changes us by its own intrinsic power. His fire within us gradually transforms us into his very likeness. We are made into lovers, fashioned according to the heart of the Beloved. We find ourselves more detached from created things, more honest and humble before others, more inclined to adopt the attitude of a servant, and more obedient to the Lord. In falling in love with the Beloved we find ourselves also falling in love with those who are dearest to his heart—the lonely, confused, lost, estranged and marginalised of this world. His love melts the hardness, apathy, and indifference within our hearts towards others. We become free to love.

The fire of God's love takes hold of our hearts so that we willingly embrace his cross. In love with the Beloved, we are prepared to be crucified with him for the sake of the gospel. His love inspires us and empowers us to self-sacrifice, to give all for him and for the spreading of the kingdom of God. This love calls us to labour in prayer for others, and to work tirelessly to bring others into the kingdom before it is too late. This love gives us the heart of the Good Shepherd for the lost.

His flame of love within us invites us into heart-to-heart communion with him. There is nothing more sublime on this earth than union with Jesus. The fire of his love brings us into the mystery of contemplation, where we rest in him, feed upon him, know his tender gaze upon us and hunger more and more for this taste of heaven. His infinite love seeks union with us. He has held nothing back in giving himself totally for our sake. His "divine madness", shown by the folly of his cross, is infectious. His love wins us, conquers us, and frees us to love in return. His love impels us to share this mystery with others. He gives himself most richly to us in Holy Communion. The Eucharist is fire! We eat him to become like him. We become like him to be for the salvation of others.

In the gospel the wise virgins who brought oil for their lamps were ready when the bridegroom came. We also are to be ready. We are to make sure we have sufficient oil in order to fuel the lamps in our hearts, and so keep the fire of God's love burning within. The oil we bring is constant prayer, loving relationships in community, reading the word of God, feeding on the Eucharist, repentance and Reconciliation, self-denial, intercession, and the ministry of evangelisation and compassion. All this is the "good oil" for our lamps to be kept burning. Jesus told us to "watch and pray", to always be vigilant for the Lord's coming, and to be eager to meet him. When he comes at the unexpected hour, we trust that he will find us as good stewards, using the graces he has given us wisely. May he find us pure of heart, eager for holiness, and working our salvation in "fear and trembling". May he find us burning with love for him and reconciled with our brothers and sisters. May he also find us generously spreading the message of his love, which he has revealed to us, by the word of our testimony and the witness of our lives, which are *becoming fire.*

ENDNOTES

[1] Francis de Sales, *An Introduction to the Devout Life*, (London: Hodder and Staughton, 1998), p. 22.

[2] John of the Cross, *The Living Flame of Love*, Prologue 3-4, in *The Collected Works of St. John of the Cross,* trans. Kieran Kavanaugh and Otilio Rodriguez, (London: Thomas Nelson, 1966) p. 578.

[3] Francis de Sales, *The Love of God*, trans., abridg., (Bangalore: SFS Publications, 1981), Book 1, Ch. 7, p. 16.

[4] Ibid. p. 80.

[5] Ibid. p. 66.

[6] Alphonsus Liguori, *The Love of God in Practice,* (Ballarat: Majellan Publications, 1963), p. 76.

[7] Pope Paul V1, *Evangelii Nuntiandi,* Art.75, (Homebush: St. Paul Publications), p. 81.

[8] Catherine of Siena, *The Dialogue,* trans. Suzanne Noffke, O.P., (London: SPCK, 1980), p. 49, p. 325.

[9] Michel Dujarier. *A History of the Catechumenate.* (N.Y.: Sadlier, 1979) pp. 49-50

[10] St. Augustine, In ep. Jo. 1,6. Quoted in *Catechism of the Catholic Church*, Part 3, Par. 1863.

[11] The early monastic tradition preferred the term "thoughts of the heart". The tradition started first in the East. John Cassian, after visiting the Desert Fathers in Egypt, brought the tradition to the West in his *Conferences.* There have been a variety of listings. In the West the tradition settled for seven, whereas the East has eight. Various authors had different listings. What is given here is true to the East.

[12] John of the Cross, *The Ascent of Mount Carmel,* Book 2:14, 9, in *The Collected Works,* p. 145. We should note that John uses this image primarily to show how the more we are devoid of attachment to created realities (cleaning the window), the more empty we will be to be filled with God. As this purifying process takes place, the light of God himself becomes more mysteriously imperceptible to the soul.

[13] Corrie Ten Boom, *The Hiding Place*, (London: Hodder and Stoughton, 1971) p. 202.

[14] See 2 Samuel 12:1-4.

[15] C.S. Lewis, *Mere Christianity*, (London: Fontana, 1952), pp. 150-151.

[16] Ibid.

[17] Found in his Rules for Discernment of Spirits Nos.13-14, in *The Spiritual Exercises of St. Ignatius* trans. Louis J. Puhl (Chicago: Loyola University Press, 1951) pp. 145-146.

[18] Ibid., p. 146.
[19] Alphonsus Liguori, *The Prayer of Petition*, (Ballarat: Majellan Press), p. 7.
[20] Ibid., p. 8.
[21] Francois Jamart, *Complete Doctrine of Thérèse of Lisieux*, (N.Y.: Alba House, 1961) pp. 49-57.
[22] Marie-Eugene of the Child Jesus, *Under the Torrent of his Love*, (N.Y.: Alba House, 1995), pp. 131-132.
[23] John of the Cross, *The Spiritual Canticle*, Stanza 30, in *Collected works*, p. 527-529.
[24] Thérèse of Lisieux, *Story of a Soul: The Autobiography*, trans. John Clarke OCD (Washington DC: ICS Publications, 1996) pp. 192-194.
[25] Teresa of Avila, *Interior Castle*, V, 3, in *Collected Works* trans. Kieran Kavanaugh OCD and Otilio Rodriguez OCD (Washington D.C.: ICS Publications, 1976) , p. 351.
[26] Ibid.
[27] Peter Fransen, *The New Life of Grace*, (London: Geoffrey Chapman, 1969), p. 22.
[28] Corrie Ten Boom, *Tramp for the Lord*, (London: Hodder and Stoughton, 1974) pp. 56-57.
[29] John of the Cross, *Letter 24* in *Collected Works*, p. 703.
[30] Francis de Sales, *Introduction to the Devout Life*, p. 152.
[31] Ibid., p. 153,
[32] Teresa of Avila, *Interior Castle*, V1, 7, in *Collected Works*, p. 420.
[33] Francis of Assisi, *Little Flowers*, X, p. 188.
[34] Teresa of Avila, *The Way to Perfection*, 4, 4, in *Collected Works*, p. 54.
[35] C. S. Lewis, *The Screwtape Letters*, (N.Y.: MacMillan, 1961), pp. 63-64.
[36] C. S. Lewis, *Mere Christianity*, (London: Fontana,1952), p. 112.
[37] Francis of Assisi, *The Canticle of Brother Sun*, in *Francis and Clare: Complete Works* (London, SPCK, 1992), p. 39.
[38] Raniero Cantalamessa, *The Lordship of Jesus Christ*, (Darton, Longman and Todd, 1990), p. 213.
[39] Blaise Pascal, *Pensee*, n. 50 Br. in Cantalamessa, *Life in the Lordship of Christ*, p. 205.
[40] Teresa of Avila, *Interior Castle, 2*, 8 in *Collected Works*, p. 301.
[41] Quoted in Alphonsus Liguori, *The Love of God in Practice*, p. 193.
[42] See Mary Ann Fatula, *Catherine of Siena's Way*, (Collegeville: Liturgical Press, 1990), pp. 48-51.
[43] Alphonsus Liguori, *Prayer of Petition: The Great Means of Salvation*, (Ballarat: Majellan Press, undated), p. 7.

ENDNOTES 233

[44] See also Mt. 7:7, Mt. 7:11, Lk 11:10, Mt. 19:19, Jn 15:7, Jn 16:23.

[45] Alphonsus Liguori, *Prayer of Petition*, pp. 27-49.

[46] Quoted in Gervase Corcoran, *Prayer and St. Augustine*, (Dublin: Carmelite Centre of Spirituality, 1983) p. 28.

[47] St. Augustine, Sermo 80, 7, *The Works of St. Augustine* (N.Y.: New City Press, 1991), p. 355.

[48] St. Augustine, *Confessions*, Ch. 1: 3, (N.Y.: Penguin, 1961), p. 21.

[49] Teresa of Avila, *The Way of Perfection*, Ch. 21, 2 in *Collected Works*, p. 117.

[50] John Cassian, *Conferences*, I, 5 trans. Colm Luibheid (New Jersey: Paulist Press, 1985) p. 40.

[51] St. Bernard of Clairvaux, *On the Song of Songs*, Book 2, Sermon 33, 9 (Michigan: Cistercian Pub. Inc., 1983) p. 152.

[52] John Cassian, *Conferences*, 2, 13, p. 71.

[53] See, David Walker, *God is a Sea*, (Homebush: Society of St. Paul, 1977) p. 69.

[54] Teresa of Avila, *Interior Castle*, 111, 7 in *Collected Works*, Vol. 2, p. 312.

[55] Francis de Sales, *An Introduction to the Devout Life*, Part 3, 9, p. 145.

[56] Ibid., Part 3, 9, p. 146.

[57] Ibid., Part 4, 11, p. 186.

[58] Ignatius Loyola, *The Spiritual Exercises*, tras. Louis J. Puhl S.J., (Chicago: Loyola University Press, 1951), p. 12.

[59] John of the Cross, *The Ascent of Mount Carmel*, Book 1, Ch.11,4 in *Collected Works*, p. 97.

[60] Alphonsus Liguori, *The Love of God in Practice*, p. 189.

[61] See David Walker, *God is a Sea*, p. 77.

[62] *The Divine Office*, Vol. 3 (Sydney: E.J. Dwyer, 1974), p. 635.

[63] Ignatius Loyola, *Spiritual Exercises*, pp. 64-65.

[64] Tagore, quoted in Cuskelly, *Walking the Way of Jesus*, (Strathfield: St. Paul's, 1999) pp. 87-88.

[65] Mary Ann Fatula, *Catherine of Siena's Way*, p. 169.

[66] Teresa of Avila, *The Book of Her Life*, X1, 12 in *Collected Works* Vol.1, p. 83.

[67] See Henri Nouwen, *The Return of the Prodigal*, (London: Darton, Longman and Todd, 1994) pp. 40-42.

[68] St. Augustine, *Enchiridion*, 3:11, in *Catechism of the Catholic Church*, Part 1, 311.

[69] Catherine of Siena, *The Dialogue*, 141, (London: SPCK,1980), p. 290.

[70] Ibid., 144, pp. 301-302. The emphasis is my own.

[71] John of the Cross, *Maxims and Counsels* (Degrees of Perfection) 15 in *Collected Works*, p. 681.

[72] John Paul 11, *Salvifici Doloris*, 22.

[73] Ibid., 27.

[74] Mary Ann Fatula, *Catherine of Siena's Way*, p. 78.

[75] Hilarin Felder OFM.Cap., *The Ideals of St. Francis*, (Chicago: Franciscan Herald Press, 1982) p. 384.

[76] *Dei Verbum*, 21 in *Vatican Council II* ed. Austin Flannery O.P. p. 762.

[77] George Martin, *Reading Scripture as the Word of God*, (Ann Arbor: Servant Books, 1975), p. 55.

[78] *Dei Verbum*, 21, op. cit., p. 762.

[79] John Cassian, *Conferences*, 1, 18, p. 52.

[80] Raniero Cantalamessa, *The Mystery of God's Word*, (Collegeville: Liturgical Press, 1991), p. 71.

[81] St. Augustine, *The Confessions*, Book VIII, 12.

[82] Raniero Cantalamessa, *The Eucharist: Our Sanctification*, (Collegeville: Liturgical Press, 1993), p. 17.

[83] Ibid. p. 27.

[84] Joseph M. Powers, *Eucharistic Theology*, (N.Y.: The Seabury Press, 1967) p. 20.

[85] Ambrose, ep. 41m12 in *Catholic Catechism*, Part II, 1429, p. 359.

[86] John Paul 11, *Reconciliatio et Paenitentia*, 31,5 (Homebush: St. Pauls Publications, 1985) p. 126.

[87] See Michael Scanlan, T.O.R., *The Power in Penance*, (Notre Dame: Ave Maria Press, 1972), pp. 27-54.

[88] *Catechism of the Catholic Church*, Part II, 1459.

[89] *God the Father of Mercy*, prep. Theol-Hist. Commission for Great Jubilee, (N.Y.: Herder and Herder, 1998) p. 44.

[90] Mary Ann Fatula, *Catherine of Siena's Way*, p. 123.

[91] Simon Tugwell, *The Nine Ways of Prayer of Saint Dominic*, (Dublin: Dominican Publications, 1978) p. 26.

[92] Mary Ann Fatula, *Catherine of Siena's Way*, pp. 107-109.

[93] John Paul 11, *Redemptoris Missio*, Ch. 7, No. 86 (Homebush: St. Pauls Publications, 1991) p. 132.

[94] Ibid., No. 3.

[95] *Evangelii Nuntiandi,* Ch. 4, No. 41 (Homebush: St. Pauls Publications, 1982) p. 42.

[96] Ibid., Ch. 2, No. 22.

[97] Found in the writings of Gregory of Nyssa, Peudo-Dyonisius, the Rhineland Mystics, *The Cloud of Unknowing*, and John of the Cross. This is called the "apothatic" way, which emphasises the darkness of faith, and seeks to empty ourselves of all

created realities so we may have God alone. The other main line of prayer in the spiritual tradition is "kataphatic", which unlike the former, emphasises how words, thoughts and images mediate the presence of God to us. Representatives of this way would be Francis of Assisi, Catherine of Siena, Ignatius Loyola, Francis de Sales and Alphonsus Liguori. Both these traditions have great value, and no spiritual journey is totally without either perspective. The emphasis in this book is on the "kataphatic" way, since, in the judgement of the author, it is the best way to lead beginners into a thoroughly evangelical way of prayer and discipleship.

[98] Augustine, *The Confessions*, 1, 3, p. 21.

[99] Augustine, *Letter to Proba*, 130, 8-9, in *Letters of Saint Augustine*, ed. John Leinenweber (Liguori: Triumph Books, 1992), p. 172.

[100] *Catechism of the Catholic Church*, Part 4, Sect.1, 2560.

[101] Teresa of Avila, *The Book of Her Life*, Ch. 8, 5 in *Collected Works*, Vol. 1, p. 67.

[102] Teresa of Avila, *Interior Castle*, 1, Ch. 2, 8, in *Collected Works*, Vol. 2, p. 291.

[103] Cited in Mary Ann Fatula, *Catherine of Siena's Way*, p. 79.

[104] Maria Boulding, *The Coming of God*, (London: SPCK, 1982), p. 98.

[105] Teresa of Avila, *The Way of Perfection*, Ch. 26, 9 in *Collected Works*, Vol. 2, p. 136.

[106] Francis de Sales, *An Introduction to the Devout Life*, Part 2, 6, p. 71.

[107] Teresa of Avila, *Interior Castle*, IV, 1, 7, in *Collected Works*, Vol. 2, p. 319.

[108] John Cassian, *Conferences*, 9, 2, in *The Classics of Western Spirituality*, trans. Colm Luibheid, (New Jersey: Paulist Press, 1985), p. 101.

[109] Ibid., 9, 4. p. 103.

[110] Teresa of Avila, *The Book of Her Life*, Ch. 11, 6-8 in *Collected Works*, Vol.1 pp. 80-81.

[111] Ignatius Loyola, *Spiritual Exercises*, 104, p. 49.

[112] Teresa of Avila, *The Book of Her Life*, Ch. 22, 3-7 in *Collected Works*, Vol. 1, pp. 145-147.

[113] Teresa of Avila, *Interior Castle* and *The Way of Perfection*, in *Collected Works*, Vol. 2, passim.

[114] Teresa of Avila, *Interior Castle*, IV, 2 in *Collected Works*, Vol. 2, p. 323.

[115] Teresa of Avila, *The Way of Perfection*, Ch. 31, 8 in *Collected Works*, Vol. 2, p. 156.

[116] Teresa of Avila, *The Book of Her Life*, Ch. 11, 6-8 in *Collected Works*, Vol. 1, pp. 80-81.

[117] Francis de Sales, *The Love of God*, Book 9, Ch. 10, p. 301.

[118] William A. Barry and William J. Connolly, *The Practice of Spiritual Direction*, (N.Y.: Seabury, 1982) pp. 80-100.

[119] Francis de Sales, *An Introduction to the Devout Life*, pp. 195-197.

[120] Teresa of Avila, *Interior Castle*, III, 1, 9 in *Collected Works*, pp. 308-309.

[121] Francis de Sales, *The Love of God*, Book 5, Chs. 1-5.

[122] Ibid., Book 5, Chs. 6-12.

[123] Ibid., Book 9, Ch. 9, p. 299.

[124] Ibid., Book 9, Ch. 10, p. 302.

[125] John of the Cross, *The Ascent of Mount Carmel*, II, 24, 9 in *Collected Works*, p. 192.

[126] Ibid., II, 7, 5, p. 123.

[127] Ross Collings, *John of the Cross*, (Collegeville: The Liturgical Press, 1990), p. 86.

[128] Jean Lafrance, *Give Me a Living Word* (Manila: St. Pauls, 1995), p. 155.

[129] Ibid.

[130] John Cassian, *Conferences*, 10, 10, p. 132.

[131] Jean Lafrance, op. cit., p. 57.

[132] For an explanation of the sacramental dimension of baptism in the Spirit see: Killian McDonnell and George Montague, *Fanning the Flame*, (Collegeville: The Liturgical Press, 1991). For a more extensive study see the same authors, *Christian Initiation and Baptism in the Holy Spirit* (Collegeville: The Liturgical Press, 1991).

[133] Ignatius of Antioch, *Letter to the Romans*, 7, in *Early Christian Writings*, (N.Y.: Penguin, 1968), p. 106.

[134] Paul Hinnebush O.P., *Praise: A Way of Life* (Ann Arbor: Servant Books, 1976), p. 37.

[135] John Cassian, *Conferences*, 10, 11, p. 138.

[136] Eddie Ensley, *Sounds of Wonder* (N.Y.: Paulist Press,1977), p. 86.

[137] *The Little Flowers of St. Francis,* trans. Raphael Brown (N.Y.: Image Books, 1958), p. 43.

[138] Brother Lawrence, *The Practice of the Presence of God* (London: Hodder and Staughton,1981), pp. 28-29.

[139] Ibid., p. 61.

[140] Ibid., p. 29.

[141] Francis de Sales, *An Introduction to the Devout Life,* p. 82.

[142] Ibid., p. 83.

[143] John Cassian, *Conferences,* 1, 20, p. 54.

[144] Ibid., 2, 4, p. 64.

[145] In this section I have been helped in my interpretation of Ignatius by Thomas H. Green S.J., *Weeds Among the Wheat,* (Notre Dame: Ave Maria Press, 1984), pp. 91-141.

[146] Ignatius Loyola, *A Pilgrim's Journey: The Autobiography of Ignatius of Loyola,* trans. Joseph N. Tylenda, S.J., (Wilmington, Delaware: Michael Glazier, 1985), pp. 14-15.

[147] Ignatius Loyola, *Spiritual Exercises*, 316, 3, p. 142.
[148] Ibid., 317, 4. p. 142.
[149] Ibid., 315, 2. p. 141.
[150] Ibid., 322, 9. pp. 143-144.
[151] Thomas Green, *Weeds among the Wheat*, pp. 117-118.
[152] Ignatius Loyola, *Spiritual Exercises*, 330, 2. p. 147.
[153] Ibid., 332, 4. p. 148.
[154] George A. Aschenbrenner, S.J., "Consciousness Examen", *Review for Religious*, Vol. 31 (1972/1): pp. 14-21. This presentation follows the outline given in this article.
[155] Ignatius Loyola, *Spiritual Exercises*, p. 74.
[156] Ignatius puts this way third.
[157] Ibid., 183. p. 76
[158] Francis de Sales, *On the Love of God*, pp. 270-275.
[159] Ibid., p. 274.
[160] Francis de Sales, *An Introduction to the Devout Life*, Ch. 1, 4, p. 27.
[161] Thomas à Kempis, *Imitation of Christ*, 3,7 trans. Leo Shirley-Price, (N.Y.: Penguin Books, 1952), p. 102.
[162] Teresa of Avila, *Spiritual Testimonies*, 3, 13 in *Collected Works*, Vol. 1, p. 322
[163] John of the Cross, *Sayings of Light and Love*, No. 7 in *Collected Works*, p. 667.
[164] The vision for spiritual direction here is inspired by Thomas Dubay S.M., *Seeking Spiritual Direction: How to grow the Divine Life Within*, (Manila: St. Paul's Publications, 1995) pp. 11-86.
[165] Gerald G. May, M.D., *Care of Mind, Care of Spirit*, (San Francisco: Harper, 1982): pp. 7-20
[166] Particularly helpful for this is William A. Barry and William J. Connolly, *The Practice of Spiritual Direction* (N.Y.: Seabury Press, 1982), pp. 65-100.
[167] John of the Cross, *Living Flame of Love*, Stanz.3, no. 30 in *Collected Works*, p. 621
[168] Teresa of Avila, *The Book of Her Life*, Ch.13, 16 in *Collected Works* Vol. 1, p. 94
[169] John of the Cross, *Sayings of Light and Love*, no.11, in *Collected Works*, p. 667

APPENDIX I
PRAYERS OF POWER

Before the Crucifix

> We adore you, O Christ, and we bless you,
> Because by your holy Cross you have redeemed the world.
>
> *Francis of Assisi*

After Holy Communion (Anima Christi)

> Soul of Christ sanctify me
> Body of Christ save me
> Blood of Christ inebriate me
> Water from Christ's side wash me
> Passion of Christ strengthen me
> O good Jesus, hear me
> Within your wounds hide me
> Permit me not to be separated from you
> From the wicked foe defend me
> At the hour of my death call me
> And bid me come to you
> That with your saints I may praise you
> For ever and ever. Amen
>
> *Ignatius Loyola*

To the Heart of Jesus

> Lord Jesus, send the fire of your Spirit into our hearts.
> Inflame us with a deep hunger for prayer,
> An enduring desire to do the Father's will,

A burning zeal to spread the Good News of the kingdom
And a thirst for the salvation of all men and women.
Draw us into the fire of love in your heart
So that, embracing your Cross,
We may truly be missionaries of your love to all whom we meet.
Now and always. Amen.

Missionaries of God's Love Prayer

Prayer for Virtue

Most High and Glorious God,
Bring light to the darkness of my heart
Give me right faith, certain hope, true humility and perfect charity.
Lord , give me insight and wisdom
So I may always discern your holy and true will.

Francis of Assisi

Make me an Instrument of your Peace

Lord, make me an instrument of your peace.
Where there is hatred, let me sow love;
Where there is injury, pardon;
Where there is discord, union;
Where there is doubt , faith;
Where there is despair, hope;
Where there is darkness, light;
Where there is sadness, joy;
For your mercy and for your truth's sake.
Divine Master,
Grant that I may not so much seek

To be consoled, as to console;
To be understood , as to understand;
To be loved, as to love;
For it is in giving that we receive;
In forgiving that we are forgiven;
And in dying that we are born to eternal life.

Memorare

Remember, O most loving Virgin Mary,
That never was it known in any age
That anyone who fled to your protection
Implored your help,
Or sought your intercession,
Was abandoned.
Inspired with confidence, therefore,
I fly to you, O Virgin of Virgins, my Mother.
To you do I come; before you I stand, sinful and sorrowful
Do not, O Mother of the Word Incarnate, despise my prayers
But graciously hear and grant them. Amen.

Entrustment to Mary, our Mother

Immaculate heart of Mary, I entrust myself to you
Draw me into the heart of Jesus your Son
Share with me the mystery of his Cross
And the fire of his Spirit
Gentle mother, since Jesus gave me to you from the Cross
I am yours
Nurture me in his love and help me to pray
Guide me in his Spirit and teach me his ways

Pure and chaste virgin as I place my life in your hands
Bring me closer to Jesus your Son
Make me obedient to the Father and humble of heart
Have eyes of mercy on me in my weakness
Protect me from the evil one
And bring healing grace to my life
So with your spirit of gratitude and praise
I may have your heart for the mission
To spread the Good News of God's love
Now and always. Amen

Missionaries of God's Love Prayer

In the Spiritual Battle

St. Michael the Archangel, defend us in the hour of conflict
Be our protection against the wickedness and snares of the devil.
May God rebuke him we humbly pray
And do then, O prince of the heavenly hosts,
By the power of God, thrust Satan into hell,
And all the evil spirits that roam the world for the ruin of souls. Amen.

Invocation of the Holy Spirit

Come Holy Spirit, fill the hearts of your faithful,
Enkindle in them the fire of your love.
Send forth your Spirit and they shall be created
And you shall renew the face of the earth.

O God, who by the light of the Holy Spirit didst instruct the hearts of the faithful,

Grant that by the same Holy Spirit we may be truly wise and ever rejoice in his consolations. Through Christ our Lord. Amen

The Divine Praises

> BLESSED BE GOD!
> BLESSED BE HIS HOLY NAME!
> BLESSED BE JESUS CHRIST, TRUE GOD AND TRUE MAN!
> BLESSED BE THE NAME OF JESUS!
> BLESSED BE HIS MOST SACRED HEART!
> BLESSED BE HIS MOST PRECIOUS BLOOD!
> BLESSED BE JESUS IN THE MOST HOLY SACRAMENT OF THE ALTAR!
> BLESSED BE THE HOLY SPIRIT THE PARACLETE!
> BLESSED BE THE GREAT MOTHER OF GOD, MARY MOST HOLY!
> BLESSED BE HER HOLY AND IMMACULATE CONCEPTION!
> BLESSED BE HER GLORIOUS ASSUMPTION!
> BLESSED BE THE NAME OF MARY, VIRGIN AND MOTHER!
> BLESSED BE ST. JOSEPH, HER MOST CHASTE SPOUSE!
> BLESSED BE GOD, IN HIS ANGELS AND IN HIS SAINTS!

APPENDIX II

GIFTS AND FRUITS OF THE SPIRIT

Interior Gifts of the Spirit

PURPOSE: To enable the interior heart to obey more easily and promptly the voice and impulse of the Spirit. These gifts habitually dispose the person to the interior promptings of the Holy Spirit (Is 11:1-2)—under the direct action of the Holy Spirit these gifts are a means towards growth in sanctity.

Wisdom

A divine instinct by which one judges all things, seeing everything from God's point of view. Can lead to "divine madness" - doing things that are foolish in the eyes of the world, but wise in the eyes of God viz. the wisdom of the cross (1Cor 1:21).

Understanding

Illumination of the mind under the action of the Spirit, giving simple and clear apprehension of revealed truths. An intuitive penetration into the truths of the faith, expressed in Scripture, liturgy and doctrine (1Cor 2:13).

Knowledge

A divine instinct from the action of the Spirit enabling the person to judge rightly the connection between created things and their supernatural end. Realises the emptiness of created things and sees them as God made them (2Cor 4:18).

Counsel

Ability to discern the right direction to go and danger to avoid. The Holy Spirit inspires and directs the person to move in a particular direction, even if it is contrary to what human reason might dictate (Acts 16:6-10).

Fortitude

Enables the practice of heroic virtue, perseverance in the spiritual battle, suffering with patience and joy, and heroism in self-sacrifice (2Cor 6:6-10; 11:23-33).

Piety

The Holy Spirit enables a filial love of God as Father, and a sense of universal love of all as brothers and sisters. Brings forth respect and honour for parents and legitimate authority (Ex 20:12).

Fear of the Lord

Not only a servile fear (fear of hell), but also a filial fear - love and reverence for the Almighty God. Awareness of the holiness and awesome majesty of God (Is 6:1-7).

Charismatic Gifts of the Spirit

(1Cor 12:4-11; 12:27-28; Rom 12:3-8; Eph 4:11-13)

These lists are not meant to be exhaustive. Endorsed by Vatican II in *Lumen Gentium*, 12.

PURPOSE: Given for the upbuilding of the body of Christ and for the mission of evangelisation. These gifts flow from baptism and can be released in a greater or lesser degree in individuals. An individual can exercise a particular gift in such a way as it becomes a ministry for the whole body.

Jesus sent the apostles to "proclaim the kingdom of God and to heal" (Lk 9:1). This gives rise to two types of gifts—"word gifts" and "healing gifts". Some examples of these gifts, taken from 1Cor 12:4-11, are the following:

WORD GIFTS

Wisdom

Leading of the Spirit in a ministry situation whereby one knows what to do next, or what to say next. Helps in preaching, counselling, leading prayer etc.

Knowledge

A word, image, or vision given by the Holy Spirit in a ministry situation, which helps one to know how to pray, or how to help the person or group. It is especially useful in healing ministry.

Prophecy

Gift of receiving a message from the Lord for a particular congregation, and of proclaiming that message with authority. Purpose is encouragement, inspiration, correction, and guidance.

Tongues

A type of prophecy given in an unknown language. Purpose is to draw the attention of the listener. Useless without the gift of interpretation. To be distinguished from "prayer tongues", which is a gift of praise, and was explained in Chapter Seven.

Interpretation

A gift of understanding the message of a prophetic tongue delivered to a gathering. Makes it intelligible and upbuilding.

HEALING GIFTS

Faith

Expectant faith. The faith that moves mountains. Ability of standing on the promises of God, against all odds.

Healing

Gift of praying effectively for physical, emotional, or spiritual healing. The Lord uses the person as an instrument to bring his own healing.

Miracles

Gift of performing miracles; through the action of the Spirit, bringing about change that cannot be accounted for by natural causes.

Discerning evil spirits

Gift of being able to detect the presence of evil spirits oppressing a person or active in a particular situation.

Fruits of the Spirit

The presence of the charismatic gifts is not in itself evidence of personal holiness. Jesus said, "you will know them by their fruits". The fruits of the Spirit give a clearer indication of sanctity. They are the "sweetness" that can be tasted in meeting a person who is growing in the virtues. St. Paul listed them in this famous text: "What the Spirit brings is different: love, joy, peace, patience, kindness, goodness, trustfulness, gentleness and self-control" (Gal 5:22).

www.ingramcontent.com/pod-product-compliance
Lightning Source LLC
Chambersburg PA
CBHW071620170426
43195CB00038B/1586